PRAISE

"I have lived nearly my entire life in the shadow of this case and its injustice. Josh has been living inside the injustice of this case nearly his entire life. We are indebted to his passionate pursuit of truth and closure. It is right for him to seek his own justice, but it is honorable for him to also seek justice for our family." —**Valerie Ward Lawless**, Mischelle Lawless's sister

"Josh Kezer's story is yet another tragic account of our failed criminal justice system and further proof that anyone can be wrongfully convicted. Josh was the victim of fabricated testimony by individuals, but more importantly he was the victim of a system that allows such testimony to be used by the government to convict the innocent. There is much to learn from Josh's story and much to do to stop it from happening again." —**Justin Brooks**, Director, California Innocence Project, Director, Latin American Institute of Law and Justice, California Western School of Law, Author of *You Might Go to Prison, Even Though You're Innocent*

"*The Murder of Angela Mischelle Lawless* is a detailed account of the people, events, and murder trial that captivated a small town in Southeastern Missouri. As a volunteer in corrections in the chapel at the Missouri State Penitentiary and later Jefferson City Correctional Center, I became familiar with Joshua Kezer's case. Joshua was and remains a complex but compassionate person, always seeking the "why" of any situation. He continues his fight for justice. Our friendship has continued and deepened since Joshua's exoneration. His faith remains his greatest asset. Details not previously known are revealed and will leave the reader with a better understanding of the judicial system: the good, bad, and ugly. Heartbreaking and intriguing, it's a must-read and riveting account for crime story enthusiasts and the general reader alike." —**James Jackson**, former pastor at the Missouri State Penitentiary Chapel and volunteer at the Jefferson City Correctional Center

"As someone who has known about this case for more than fifteen years and spent the last five years deeply investigating it, I highly recommend this book by Stephen Snodgrass and Josh Kezer. Snodgrass and Kezer give behind-the-scenes insight into the grossly mishandled investigation of Mischelle Lawless's murder—insight and information that is not otherwise available to the public, including my podcast. I commend Snodgrass for his work in not just helping free an innocent man, but also for taking on the responsibility of telling this story. And of course, I commend Josh for being brave enough to involve himself in sharing excruciating details that are perpetually hurtful to talk about. Here's hoping that the book will not just be an "interesting read" about a serious miscarriage of justice and an "unsolved" murder, but that it will also play a role in pushing Mischelle Lawless's murder (and the flagrantly dishonest original investigation) into public consciousness." —**Bob Miller**, award-winning investigative journalist, and host of The Lawless Files podcast

THE MURDER OF
ANGELA MISCHELLE
LAWLESS

THE MURDER OF ANGELA MISCHELLE LAWLESS

An Honest Sheriff and the Exoneration of an Innocent Man

STEPHEN R. SNODGRASS
WITH
JOSHUA C. KEZER

ROWMAN & LITTLEFIELD
Lanham • Boulder • New York • London

Published by Rowman & Littlefield
An imprint of The Rowman & Littlefield Publishing Group, Inc.
4501 Forbes Boulevard, Suite 200, Lanham, Maryland 20706
www.rowman.com

86-90 Paul Street, London EC2A 4NE

British Library Cataloguing in Publication Information Available

Library of Congress Cataloging-in-Publication Data

Names: Snodgrass, Stephen R., author. | Kezer, Joshua C., author.
Title: The murder of Angela Mischelle Lawless : an honest sheriff and the
   exoneration of an innocent man / Stephen R. Snodgrass with Joshua C.
   Kezer.
Description: Lanham : Rowman & Littlefield, [2023] | Includes
   bibliographical references.
Identifiers: LCCN 2022039381 (print) | LCCN 2022039382 (ebook) |
   ISBN 9781538172063 (cloth ; alk. paper) | ISBN 9781538172070 (ebook)
Subjects: LCSH: Kezer, Joshua C. | Lawless, Angela Mischelle, -1992. |
   Murder--Missouri--Case studies. | Judicial error--Missouri--Case
   studies. | Criminal justice, Administration of--Corrupt
   practices--Missouri--Case studies.
Classification: LCC HV6533.M8 S63 2023 (print) | LCC HV6533.M8 (ebook) |
   DDC 364.152/309778--dc23/eng/20230109

LC record available at https://lccn.loc.gov/2022039381

LC ebook record available at https://lccn.loc.gov/2022039382

♾™ The paper used in this publication meets the minimum requirements of
American National Standard for Information Sciences—Permanence of Paper
for Printed Library Materials, ANSI/NISO Z39.48-1992.

"Trial by jury is a fundamental tenet of our criminal justice system. A populist notion in its very essence, the right to be judged by one's fellow citizens serves as an important check on the State's power to deprive its citizens of their liberty. A jury trial is intended by purpose and design to limit the power of prosecutors and judges to incarcerate. Just as important, however, is what the right to jury trial is not. A jury trial is not a shield for prosecutors to avoid difficult charging decisions, and deference to a jury verdict is not a substitute for meaningful judicial review. In the final analysis, our system of trial by jury is there to protect citizens from [their] own government, not to protect government from its own mistakes."

Judge Richard G. Callahan
Cole County (Missouri)
Circuit Court
February 17, 2009

CONTENTS

Part IV. Never Too Late

Part V. The Aftermath

ACKNOWLEDGMENTS

I would like to acknowledge the countless, often sleepless, hours Josh Kezer has invested into the completion of this book. It has not been easy for him to relive the trauma he went through, but in doing so, he has improved the quality of the book considerably. I would like to thank Josh for the information, photos, and personal stories he's provided, along with revealing his innermost thoughts. I am especially grateful to Josh for introducing me to Angela Mischelle Lawless's mother and sister, Esther and Valerie Lawless, to get their blessing for this book, and to Esther and Valerie for giving their blessing. I acknowledge that it's impossible to share a 30-year story in a single book, but I have made every effort to share as much as I could. Perhaps someday, Josh will get an opportunity to share his entire story, which is far more exhaustive, but until then, I hope this book serves Josh and Angela Mischelle Lawless well.

PART I

THE MURDER

"Other sins only speak; murder shrieks out."

—John Webster, *Duchess of Malfi* (1623)

On September 12, 2006, Joshua Charles Kezer sat near the prison telephone, fidgeting a bit nervously while he waited for the time arranged for him to initiate the conference call. Lawyers had refused to take his case before. Why would he think it would be different this time? He already had been incarcerated, in jail or in prison, for more than 13 years, and he was tempted to lose hope.

At the same time, a group of lawyers in St. Louis were gathering around a conference table waiting for Josh's call from the Missouri state correctional facility in Jefferson City. I was one of them.

The lawyers had been joined by a small group of Missourians who believed Josh was innocent. Jane Williams was a retired social worker and minister's wife who had seen Josh in the prison chapel, the only inmate praying on his knees. "That's Josh Kezer; he's innocent," a friend had told her years before.

Jim Sullins was a retired sheriff's deputy, working in 1997 as a private detective. The waitress serving him at a diner seemed depressed, and he asked her what was wrong. She was Josh's mother. When she told him about her son's case, he volunteered to do some investigating and began collecting evidence.

Josh made the call as arranged. His voice on the speakerphone was firm and a bit animated: "I don't understand how I was convicted. I didn't do it. I didn't even know her. I was hundreds of miles away in Kankakee when she was murdered. And I had witnesses to back me up." The lawyers had read a summary of the case for Josh's innocence prepared by Jane Williams, which included evidence Jim Sullins had gathered. They were intrigued by what Jane had been able to put together but wanted to hear from Josh himself before they decided to represent him. Josh continued, sounding almost irritated, "You need to know something. One lawyer Jane found told me I failed a lie detector test. He decided he didn't want to help me." Only one of the lawyers at the table had any practical experience in criminal law, but they all knew that polygraph tests are not admissible for a reason. They're worthless because all they do is measure emotions.

On its face, the case against Josh seemed pretty solid. He had been convicted by a unanimous verdict of 12 presumably reasonable jurors who were out for their deliberations for only a short period of time. He was a member of a notoriously violent street gang, a fact that was in evidence at his trial and certainly had some effect on the jury. There was a young man who said he found the victim's body and testified at Josh's trial that he saw Josh near the crime scene and was frightened by him. There were several young men, Josh's acquaintances, sitting in a local county jail, who claimed he admitted killing the victim. And another young man who shared a cell with Josh after his arrest testified that Josh confessed to him too. Then, on the last day of his trial, there was a surprise witness, one of the victim's young female friends who testified she saw Josh harassing the victim at a Halloween party a week before the murder.

Some of this evidence was questionable from the start. The young man who said he saw Josh near the crime scene was known to local law enforcement at the time, mainly for driving drunk, and there was some question whether it was the young man or his identical twin brother who reported finding the body. After Josh's trial, that young man would be convicted of drug dealing and spend years in a federal prison, but these were facts the jurors didn't know. As is usually the case, the jailhouse snitches who testified that Josh confessed all received lenient sentences in exchange for their testimony.

A few of these snitch witnesses later recanted their stories about the confession in statements to one of Josh's lawyers. But the prosecutor at Josh's trial managed to rehabilitate two of those who recanted. He had one snitch witness testify that Josh's lawyer who obtained his recantation threatened him with harm in prison from Josh's fellow gang members if he didn't recant. And he had the other testify that the same young lawyer tricked him into signing a statement that didn't reflect what he actually said. That prosecutor, nicknamed Cool Breeze by Josh's defense counsel, was a young and ambitious, some would say unscrupulous, lawyer from the Office of the Missouri Attorney General, who used the Kezer case and other high-profile cases he won as a stepping-stone to a political career. Starting not long after Josh's conviction, he went on to serve five terms representing Missouri in the US House of Representatives, and in 2008, he was the Republican candidate for Missouri governor.

But what about Josh's alibi witnesses, the half a dozen people who would testify that Josh was in Kankakee, Illinois, 350 miles away, shortly before and shortly after the time of the murder? Cool Breeze used the confusion of one of them about the time of an alibi event as an opportunity to taint all of their testimony. He argued in closing that the young lawyer who, according to the jailhouse snitches, threatened or tricked them into recanting also fed the Kankakee alibi witnesses their stories but that one of them couldn't keep her story straight. Because of a legal maneuver by Cool Breeze, the young lawyer who obtained the recantations and the alibi testimony was prevented from testifying that these accusations were false. Given this silence, the jury likely concluded that the accusations were true.

All of these facts about recantations and the prosecutor's closing arguments were disturbing, but they would not do us any good in the kind of case we would have to file to get Josh freed. These facts and the arguments they could support had been made on direct appeal or were forfeited by not being made more than a decade before. We needed new evidence, and the new evidence had to be convincing enough to satisfy a very high standard of proof.

None of the lawyers, myself included, had done anything quite like this before. We all had been focusing for varying amounts of time on commercial litigation for corporate clients. At the end of the meeting, we shook hands with our guests, expressed guarded optimism, and resolved to do our best to set Josh free.

But to really understand what happened to Josh, it is important to go back to November 1992 and start from the beginning.

1

THE FIRST 24 HOURS

Early in the morning of November 8, 1992, a young girl's bloody body lay across the front seat of a car at the top of an interstate exit ramp in Southeast Missouri, a quarter mile from the safety of her home. She had been beaten on the head and shot three times. Her car, a maroon 1989 two-door Buick Somerset, was sitting in the right-turn lane of the exit ramp, just past the stop sign, as if poised to enter State Highway 77 heading east toward the Mississippi River. The car doors were closed. The motor was running, and the headlights and dome light were on.

Jerry and Ruth Householder had spent the evening of Saturday, November 7, at the Double Nickel Night Club in Miner, Missouri, where they had dinner and watched their daughter compete in a talent contest. At around 1:15 a.m., they left Interstate 55 on the Benton exit ramp and approached the murdered girl's car. Ruth was driving, and Jerry was in the passenger seat. Except for the lights of the murdered girl's car, there were no lights at the intersection or along the interstate and the intersecting state highway. The Householders stopped at the intersection next to the Buick, on its left, but from where they sat in their car, they could see no one inside. Jerry asked, "You want me to get out and take a look?" Ruth answered, "No, it could be somebody up to no good. We can stop at the sheriff's office." Ruth turned left onto Highway 77 and drove to the Scott County Sheriff's office in Benton, which was on their way home, to report what they had seen.

A short time later, or maybe it was before—that has never been made clear—a black S-10 pickup approached the murdered girl's car. The driver was Mark Abbott, a man known to local law enforcement for his DWI convictions and suspicion of drug dealing. He had an identical twin, Matt, and the two of them were notorious for claiming to be the other. On this particular night, Mark was drunk and driving without a license. As he claimed later, "I left the interstate the Benton way to take the back way home because I figgered the Scott City police would be waiting for me up ahead." He said he stopped at the top of the exit ramp and got out to investigate the car sitting there with its lights glaring and realized he had found a body.

Abbott claimed later that his first instinct was to leave the scene and go home. He hopped into his little truck and sped away, but as he drove, he thought, "I should go to the sheriff's office and tell them about this. But shit, I'm drunk, and I don't have a license." As he crossed the interstate, he saw the outdoor pay phone on the parking lot of a convenience store and gas station and got an idea. "There's that pay phone. I can call 911 from there." He parked next to the phone, which sat on a pole in the parking lot, and dialed 911 but got no dial tone. This time he thought, "I'm just gonna go home. Somebody else'll find her." He drove into Benton and north on State Highway 61 toward home, but he continued thinking. "What if I left my fingerprints on the car? Did I touch anything?" And then he hit on an idea, "Hey, I can tell 'em I'm Matt. He has a license."

★ ★ ★

There were a few businesses in the general vicinity of the Benton exit in November 1992, but nothing was open at that time of the night. The closest, the Cut-Mart convenience store and gas station, had closed around midnight. As the Householders turned left onto Highway 77 toward Benton, the only light came from their headlights, the lights of the Buick sitting on the exit ramp, and lights from the occasional vehicle passing through on the highway below. The night was clear and cold, but wisps of fog hugged the low-lying areas along the roads. The Householders saw no one around the Buick or near the intersection. The Scott County Sheriff's Office is located in a one-story building in the center of Benton, behind the courthouse, less than two miles west of the interstate on Highway 77. They saw no one driving or walking along 77. Ruth Householder later told investigators, "We were looking in particular for someone on foot because we thought the driver might have been having some kind of car trouble."

Deputy Jim Newman was the sheriff's dispatcher on the midnight to 8:00 a.m. shift that morning. He and Deputy Wes Drury, the jailer in the county jail, were the only ones officially on duty when the Householders arrived. Reserve Deputy Rick Walter and part-time Benton Police Officer Roy Moore were hanging around after their shifts, finishing paperwork and talking to Newman and Drury. Walter was 33 and a supervisor for a local construction company. He had received his reserve commission in 1989, after taking the required 120-hour course, and in November 1992, he was the county's chief reserve deputy. He did regular patrol work on weekends and helped with traffic 'and crowd control at special events. Years later, after he became sheriff of Scott County, Walter would play an important role in Josh's exoneration. Moore was 35 and worked for the Cargill Grain Company. He recently had received a degree in criminal justice from Southeast Missouri State University and had been a part-time Benton officer for about four months. Later that morning, Moore would provide a piece of information critical to proof of Josh's innocence.

The dispatcher sits in an office area behind a reception window just off the entrance lobby and in the early morning hours, doubles as a receptionist. Jerry Householder hung back while Ruth went up to the window to make her report: "There's a car at the top of the exit ramp from the highway. It's running and the lights are on. But it looks like no one's in it." The dispatcher's log shows she arrived at 1:25 a.m. Deputy Drury took down the information and relayed it to Deputy Newman. The Householders left and were home by 1:30 a.m.

Normally, Deputy Newman would not have had anyone on duty to respond to a report like this of an automobile apparently abandoned in the middle of the night and would have called a deputy at home, but Walter said, "I'll go," and Moore added, "I'll ride with him." The dispatcher's log shows them en route at 1:29 a.m. They drove to the interstate in Walter's personal car, retracing the Householders' path along Highway 77, and saw no one on foot and no suspicious vehicles on the way. It took only a few minutes to get there.

Rick Walter pulled his car in front of and facing the Buick. When he stopped, he left his headlights on. The glare of the two sets of headlights merged in the space between the two cars, and the exhaust from the Buick danced in the light they provided. Moore approached the Buick from the driver's side while Walter radioed the dispatcher to run the license plate number. Moore looked through the window and called excitedly to Walter. "Someone's inside. I think it's a girl, and she's hurt."

Walter ran to the passenger side and looked in the window. A teenage girl was draped across the center console on her right side, with her head on the passenger seat, her left arm hanging down to the floorboard, her right arm pinned under her torso, and her legs drawn up on the driver's seat toward her stomach. She was wearing a sweatshirt and button-fly jeans. The top four buttons on her jeans were unbuttoned, and the jeans were torn away on the back below her left buttock, exposing the back of her left leg to the knee. She was not wearing shoes. Bits of grass clung to her dark socks. Her head was resting partially on her purse. Her face was bloody, and her hair was soaked in blood. Walter called to her through the partially closed window. "Can you hear me?" But he got no response. He ran back to his car and called for an ambulance.

The door on the passenger side of the Buick was closed and locked, and the window was rolled up all the way. The driver's side door was closed but unlocked. Moore opened the driver's side door with two fingers and began checking vital signs. He felt the girl's neck for a pulse but got nothing. After Walter called for an ambulance, he approached the Buick on the driver's side and leaned into the car for a closer look. He saw a spent bullet casing on the driver's seat under the victim's left, upper leg. The girl didn't appear to be breathing, and he thought, "She's dead." He reached in the driver's-side door and turned off the engine. He passed the keys across the car to Moore, who used them to unlock the passenger-side door. When Moore opened the door, he saw a second spent bullet casing on the passenger side.

Walter and Moore began a careful search of the area surrounding the Buick. They shone their flashlights all around to see if they could find someone hiding nearby. On the pavement a foot or so from the left front tire, there was a puddle of liquid about six inches in diameter. In Moore's written report, he said, "It appeared to be transmission fluid, but on closer examination, was determined to be blood." There were blood stains on the hood of the car, and there was a dripping trail of blood over to the exit ramp guardrail. In the light of the flashlights, frost glistened on the tall grass covering the embankment leading down from the highway exit ramp. Where the grass had been disturbed, a darker pattern appeared in the light from the flashlights reflected off the frost.

★ ★ ★

After the Householders, Walter, and Moore left the sheriff's office, Deputy Drury did a quick security check of the jail, which was entered in the log at 1:31 a.m. While Drury was on the phone with the ambulance dispatcher, a young man he recognized, wearing a dark shirt with what he described in his report as "some type of design," came into the lobby. It was within a minute or so of Drury's 1:31 a.m. return from the security check.

The young man was one of the Abbott twins. He came to the reception window exclaiming, "I found a body. She was shot." During 1991, Drury had frequented Store 24, the twins' parents' 24-hour convenience store and gas station next to the interstate in Scott City, and both boys worked there at the time. Drury believed he could tell which twin was which when he saw them together, but not necessarily when he saw them individually. Drury's formal report of the event states, "I understood Mr. Abbott to give me his name as Matt," and "he said that he lived in the new trailer park just off Highway 61 south of Scott City and that he didn't have a phone." Drury told Newman it was Matt Abbott, and that is what Newman entered into the log. Whichever Abbott it was, he clearly was in an agitated state. Drury described him as "wound up." Newman said he was "shaken up," "off the wall," and "hysterical."

By the time the Abbott twin arrived at the sheriff's office, Walter and Moore already were at the scene and had reported finding the girl's body. Thinking the twin's report redundant, Drury told him, "Go home. Somebody will call Store 24 to get directions to your trailer if they need to interview you."

★ ★ ★

Shortly after 1:30 a.m., Deputy Walter went back to his car and radioed the dispatcher to see how much longer it would be before help arrived. At about the same time, a car approached on Highway 77 from the direction of Benton. Officer Moore walked toward the car. A young man got out and approached him. Moore said later, "I didn't see anyone else in the car, but I maybe wasn't looking closely." The man struggled with English and spoke with a heavy accent that sounded Hispanic. At several points, Moore asked him to repeat what he was saying. The man told Moore he needed gas for his car. Moore said, "There's no place around here that's open." He asked, "Where you headed?" Hearing St. Louis, Moore told him, "You have to go up the interstate 8 or 10 miles north." This was the 24-hour gas station and convenience store owned by the parents of the Abbott twins. The man asked, "What should I do if I run out?" Moore suggested, "Put on your emergency flashers and lift the hood. A state trooper will come along eventually and help you." The man went back to his car and drove down the northbound ramp onto Interstate 55.

In his report, Moore described the man as 25 to 30 years of age, between five feet five and five feet seven inches in height and weighing between 120 and 135 pounds. He had short, dark hair and a thin mustache and was wearing a blue and white pullover shirt and blue jeans. Moore gave a very similar description in an interview two weeks later. He described the car the man was driving as "solid white, a late-model small station wagon or possibly a hatchback style car." He described the car in the interview two weeks later as "white, possibly an Escort or a Toyota," "square," and "like a mini-station wagon or hatchback style." Because he saw no reason to suspect the driver, he didn't ask for his name or take down his license plate number.

Between 1:35 a.m. and 1:39 a.m., after the young Hispanic man in the white car left, a second man drove up, got out of his vehicle, and approached Officer Moore. He told him, "I was the one who found the girl in the car. Is she dead?" In his report, Moore described this man as a "white male between 25 and 30, approximately 5 feet 7 to 5 feet 9 inches tall, with a medium build, wearing a light-colored shirt and jeans." Later, Moore testified that the man was driving a car rather than a pickup, "about like a Monte Carlo or Buick, '80 to '85 or earlier." Mark Abbott drove a small pickup truck.

Because Moore had just seen the Householders at the sheriff's office, he was skeptical of the man's claim that he was the one who found the body. He asked, "Have you been to the sheriff's office?" The man said, "Yeah, I talked to Deputy Drury." Moore used Walter's radio to check the man's story, and Wes Drury told him it wasn't necessary to have him appear at the sheriff's office. Then, Moore advised him, "You can either go back to the sheriff's office and give any additional information you have, or you can go home and wait to be contacted." The man said, "I'll be available if you need me." Then he left.

Chief Deputy Tom Beardslee was at home, asleep, when he got the call from the sheriff's dispatcher about the car at the exit ramp. He lived off Highway 77, east of Benton proper and close to the interstate. That night, he could see the lights of the Buick and the emergency vehicles from home. Dressing quickly, he arrived at the scene at 1:39 a.m. and began coordinating the activities of the medical and law enforcement personnel.

An ambulance from the North Scott County Ambulance District arrived at 1:46 a.m. One of the EMTs from the ambulance placed heart monitor electrodes on the victim's right and left upper chest. There was no sign of life, and the victim was officially pronounced dead. The EMTs believed she had died only a short time before they arrived.

★ ★ ★

The Buick was registered to Esther Lawless. The victim's driver's license identified her as Angela Mischelle Lawless. She was the daughter of Esther and Marvin Lawless, who lived just outside the Benton city limits, about a quarter of a mile east of the interstate. Not surprisingly, in a county of small towns, many of those at the scene at least knew of the Lawless family. Roy Moore had gone to high school with Marvin Lawless.

Most of those who knew the victim called her by her middle name. Mischelle Lawless was 19, born on August 2, 1973, in Sikeston, 15 miles to the south, but she grew up in Benton. She had two younger siblings, a brother, Jason, who was 15 and a sophomore at Kelly High School, and a sister, Valerie, who was 12. Mischelle graduated from Kelly High School in 1991, and after a year of restaurant work, she had just started her first year as a nursing student at Southeast Missouri State University, commonly called SEMO. The university has its main campus in the City of Cape Girardeau, in the next county to the north, about 18 miles from the Benton exit on the interstate. While in school, Mischelle continued to work part-time to earn extra money at a Sikeston Shoney's Restaurant. She was a commuter student, living at home at the time of her death. For two weeks at the end of October, she had rented a trailer in Sikeston with another girl, but the other girl was homesick and spent only a few nights there. The arrangement wasn't working, and both girls moved back in with their parents—Mischelle a little more than a week before she died.

There seemed to be nothing in Mischelle's life to suggest that it would end with her murder. She had been a Girl Scout and was a member of the Future Homemakers of America and Students Against Drunk Driving. In high school, she sang in the chorus and volunteered as a candy striper at St. Francis Medical Center in Cape Girardeau. On her application at St. Francis, she wrote that she was thinking of becoming a nurse because she "wanted to help people." Along with the rest of her family, she was an active member of the Unity Baptist Church, and at the university, she was involved in the Baptist Student Union. Mischelle was intelligent, a pretty and popular girl, with lots of friends and an active social life. There was no obvious reason anyone would want to kill her.

Scott County Sheriff Bill Ferrell arrived and assumed overall command at approximately 2:00 a.m. He decided to go to the Lawless residence personally to notify the family of Mischelle's death. At 2:45 a.m., he called Deputy Brenda Schiwitz at home and asked her to meet him there. She arrived at 3:00 a.m., and the sheriff and Scott County Coroner Scott Amick already were there. The sheriff left Deputy Schiwitz with the grief-stricken family and returned to the crime scene. There was, of course, little that Deputy Schiwitz could do to comfort them. They were just beginning to come to terms with the fact they had lost a daughter and a sister. Mischelle would not become a nurse and live out her life's plan of helping people. She would never marry and give her parents grandchildren.

Shortly after the sheriff left the Lawless residence, the family's pastor, the Reverend Dale Huff from the Unity Baptist Church, arrived. He had married Marvin and Esther Lawless and had baptized Mischelle and her brother and sister. He was there to provide whatever solace the family could find in their faith. Then, Reverend Huff and the coroner accompanied Marvin Lawless to the crime scene.

★ ★ ★

The Missouri State Highway Patrol dispatcher at Troop E sent Sergeants Jim Keathley and Dennis Overbey and Corporal S. J. Hinesly to begin the crime scene investigation. The two sergeants took photographs and videotaped the car and the area around it, using flashlights for illumination outside the reach of headlights. They collected blood-swab samples from the hood of the Buick, the puddle next to the left-front tire, several other areas of the pavement around the car, the shoulder of the road, and the guardrail. They followed the trail of trampled grass by flashlight down the embankment and into the field between the highway and the service road and found more blood. In several places, larger areas of grass near the blood were mashed down as if someone had lain there. At 103 feet, they also found and photographed a footprint in the soft ground. The trail of blood and trampled grass ended there.

The law enforcement personnel at the crime scene could tell immediately from looking at the spent casings found in the Buick that Mischelle had been shot inside the car with a .380 caliber or 9 mm semi-automatic handgun. A semiautomatic ejects the empty shell casing each time a shot is fired. The location of the spent shell in the front passenger compartment of the car indicated that the killer's gun hand was inside the car, either through the partially open window on the driver's side or through the open door, and that the ejecting shells had bounced off something inside. The size of the casings indicated the type of ammunition. The diameter of the .380 caliber and 9 mm casings is nearly identical, but the standard powder load for a .380 shell is less.

The sheriff decided to begin interviewing witnesses while the highway patrol conducted the crime scene investigation. He already had the name of one of Mischelle's boyfriends, Leon Lamb, from Marvin Lawless. At 4:00 a.m., Ferrell and Deputy Schiwitz headed south on Interstate 55 to interview Lamb, their first witness.

Not long after Ferrell and Schiwitz left, a tow truck from Satter-field's Body Shop and Wrecker Service arrived to take the Buick to the Satterfield's facility in Sikeston. While the tow truck driver was preparing the Buick for towing, Marvin Lawless arrived at the scene again. He gave Deputy Beardslee a business card from the T-N-T Tanning Studio in Sikeston. On the back was the name of Lyle Day, another of Mischelle's boyfriends.

★ ★ ★

At 4:30 a.m., Ferrell and Schiwitz arrived at a trailer on Kinder Street, where Lamb lived with his mother and grandmother. Lamb was handsome, six feet tall, 180 pounds, and athletic. He was 20 years old and worked at Stan's Food Mart in Sikeston. Asked about his relationship with Mischelle, he said, "I dated her for about two and a half years, but I broke up with her because it wasn't working." Asked when he last saw her, he told them, "Last night around 7:00 on the parking lot at the Midtowner Mall in Sikeston. She was out with Lelicia O'Dell. I saw them walking toward Vince Howard's car. He's black. Later, I saw her riding up and down Malone in Howard's car. Eric Shanks was in the car too. He's white."

When they asked what he did then, he said, "I went home. I was up late practicing taekwondo. Mischelle knocked on the door around midnight. She was drunk. We talked for a while, and then we had sex in my bedroom." Another question: "What time did she leave?" He said, "I think it was around one, maybe a little before. She was in a hurry. She was carrying her shoes and her bra, and I don't think she even buttoned her jeans. I told her to go home, but I don't know if she did." The distance to the Benton exit where her body was found is about 15 miles, which she could have traveled in 15 minutes or less.

The sheriff asked Lamb, "Do you have any guns?" Lamb said, "Yeah, I keep a .38 that belongs to my mother in my bedroom." It was a .38 Charter Arms revolver, not an automatic. The sheriff asked, "Which one of these cars outside is yours?" Lamb told him, "It's the '68 Mustang." The sheriff said, "Do you mind if we search it?" Lamb answered, "No. Go ahead. I have nothing to hide." The search yielded nothing suspicious.

★ ★ ★

The highway patrol investigators finished their examination of the crime scene around 5:20 a.m. Scott County Coroner Scott Amick removed Mischelle's body from the scene to the Amick-Burnett Funeral Home in Sikeston. Sheriff Ferrell and Deputy Schiwitz observed the coroner's preliminary examination of the body, which revealed wounds to the back and top of the head, face, the left side under the arm, and the right breast. Schiwitz made an inventory of the contents of Mischelle's bloodstained purse. She called Marvin Lawless to get more information. "Did Mischelle carry a wallet? We didn't find one in her purse." He told Schiwitz, "She has a brown and black wallet about six inches long and an inch thick."

Schiwitz also asked, "Does she carry any credit cards, or does she usually pay in cash? If she pays cash, do you know how much she was carrying?" He answered, "The only credit card she has is from J. C. Penney's. I don't know how much cash she had." Schiwitz told him they found a savings account passbook in the car that showed she closed her account on November 6 and withdrew $914. "Yeah, that's right, but she gave me $800 for car repairs and kept about $100 to pay bills. I don't know if anything was left by Saturday night."

Dr. Michael Zaricor began the autopsy at 8:30 a.m. at Mineral Area Regional Medical Center. Mischelle was five feet tall and weighed 95 pounds. Her eyes were brown and her hair reddish brown. Dried blood covered most of her face. Dr. Zaricor concluded that the cause of death was three gunshot wounds. One shot entered the left side of Mischelle's face at the cheek and exited the back of her neck on the left side at the hairline. Another shot entered the lower left side of her back, exited near her right breast, entered her right forearm, and lodged just under the skin. These two shots caused considerable damage, but Mischelle might have survived them, at least for a while. The "killing shot" entered the back of her head on the left, cut through her brain stem, and lodged behind her right eye. This shot would have caused death instantaneously. He recovered the slugs behind her eye and in her right forearm and gave them to Corporal Hinesly.

Under the heading of "Incidental Findings," Dr. Zaricor noted that there were two curvilinear lacerations near the top of Mischelle's head, consistent with blunt trauma. These wounds would have caused profuse bleeding, but they weren't life threatening. He also noted several fingernail marks on the back of her right hand and right wrist. Internal examination of pelvic organs revealed no signs of pregnancy. Corporal Hinesly took fingerprints for elimination purposes. He also obtained samples from a rape kit and a gunshot residue kit and blood and urine samples for further analysis.

★ ★ ★

At daybreak, Deputy Beardslee returned to the crime scene with Deputies Shoemaker and Chambers to look for any evidence they might have missed earlier. They found nothing of significance.

At 6:50 a.m., highway patrol Sergeants Keathley and Overbey began processing the Buick at Satterfield's. The third shell casing was under a pair of boat shoes. In the center console, they found five rings, including a Kelly High School class ring. In the back seat, there was evidence of a recent automobile accident: a neck brace, a note of a doctor's appointment, and some medical records. The third bullet, the one that had passed through Mischelle's cheek and out the back of her neck, hadn't been found. The highway patrol officers returned to Satterfield's later to look for the missing bullet and discovered a hole in the headrest. They cut a square around the hole, removed a section of the seat's padding, and dug out a slug. The inventory of ballistics evidence was complete.

★ ★ ★

The entry points of the bullets and their trajectory within Mischelle's body revealed in the autopsy suggest her position when each shot was fired. The shot through the left cheek and out the left rear of her neck into the headrest followed a horizontal path and probably was fired first as she sat upright in the driver's seat looking at the killer. Dr. Zaricor noted a nine centimeter by eight centimeter pattern of stippling on the bare skin around the cheek entrance wound, which indicates the bullet was fired at close range. Gunshot residue on her palms found later in lab tests suggests she placed her palms out near her face, as if trying to ward off the bullet.

The other two shots, into her back and the back of her head, must have been fired after Mischelle turned to the right and started to fall across the console. The path of the bullet that lodged behind her right eye was horizontal, suggesting that it was fired when she was in a more upright position. The path of the bullet from the left side of her back to the right breast was 60 degrees upward, indicating the bullet likely was fired down on her from behind and above as she lay on the seat. Dr. Zaricor noted a smaller, 4.5 centimeter by 3.8 centimeter, area of stippling around the entrance wound on her back.

The blood trail outside the Buick was from Mischelle's head wounds, but investigators weren't able to determine whether it was made on the way down the embankment, on the way back up, or both. The fingernail marks on the back of her right arm and wrist were made when the attacker grabbed her at some point in the struggle, the head wounds by blows from a gun butt or some other hard object delivered somewhere along the trail of blood.

Rick Walter always sensed there was more than one person involved in the murder. Rumors and speculation in the years to come contained accounts with multiple attackers, including a woman making the fingernail marks on Mischelle's arm. Yet there is no doubt it was possible for a single, armed man to overpower the diminutive teenager, despite her martial arts training. Her father told investigators she had advanced "only two levels from beginner and wasn't very good."

★ ★ ★

After the inventory of the Buick was completed, the sheriff and Deputy Schiwitz began looking for Lelicia O'Dell. Lelicia was 17 and had dropped out of high school. She and Mischelle had met and become good friends about a year before, while working together at Shoney's. She was the homesick friend who had shared a trailer with Mischelle. Ferrell and Schiwitz found her at Chantelle Crider's house. The three girls had planned to go out together on Saturday night. At the last minute, Chantelle's boyfriend, who was in the military, arrived in town, and Chantelle begged off to be with him. According to Lelicia, "We met at Chantelle's around 7:30 or 8:00, I guess, before we went out."

Except for some time discrepancies, Lelicia confirmed what Leon Lamb had told Ferrell and Schiwitz a few hours earlier. "We ran into Leon around 10:00, on the parking lot near the taekwondo school. We got in Vince's car to go riding around with Vince and Eric Shanks. Mischelle left her car there, and me and Mischelle got into the back seat. We rode around with them for a half hour or so. We went to Sonic and cruised up and down Malone. We had one beer each; a guy named Mike gave them to us." Deputy Schiwitz asked, "Are you sure it was only one beer?" Lelicia admitted, "Well, maybe it was more like two or three." Lelicia said, "Mischelle asked me to spend the night at her house, but I said 'No, I have to be to work at six in the morning.' Then she asked me, 'Can I spend the night at your house?' I told her, 'I can't have anyone sleep over because my bedroom just got painted and I'm sleeping on the couch in the living room.'" Then Lelicia paused and eventually said, "I guess she'd still be alive if I let her sleep at my house."

So Mischelle dropped Lelicia off at her home on Montgomery Street around midnight and left. Lelicia told Ferrell and Schiwitz, "There were some blacks outside who yelled at me when I got out of the car. The last thing I said to Mischelle was 'Be careful.' She waited until I got inside before she drove away." Lelicia didn't know where Mischelle went.

★ ★ ★

Deputy Drury called Store 24 around 2:15 a.m. to get directions to Matt Abbott's trailer. The clerk on duty couldn't help him, so Drury called Larry Abbott, the twins' father, at home. When Drury mentioned the location of the trailer park that "Matt" had given him, the elder Abbott said, "You must mean Mark; Mark is the twin who lives in the park off Highway 61."

Mark Abbott lived in a trailer park his father had developed and owned in partnership with another man. Tom Beardslee tried to interview Abbott there early the morning of Sunday, November 8. He first arrived at 9:24 a.m. but got no answer at the door. He returned at 10:15 a.m., with the same result. Finally, he returned with Wes Drury at 12:45 p.m., and they found Abbott at home, with a woman they assumed was his wife. When Abbott came to the door, Drury called him Matt, and Abbott responded, "No, I'm Mark. I told you last night I was Mark." Beardslee learned early on in his career that it pays to record witness interviews, so he recorded the interview with Abbott and typed a transcript himself.

Abbott told the two deputies he was 23 years old. Beardslee asked him what he was driving when he found the body, and he pointed to the black Chevy S-10 pickup in front of the trailer. Asked for his best guess as to when he found the body, he said, "About 10 after one, something like that." He described what he saw when he pulled up next to the car.

> The lights were on, the interior lights were on, and I could see somebody there. I thought somebody's drunker than hell, you know, laid over is what I thought. And ah, I got out; man, I got to get this off the road. I got out and reached in there and grabbed her, but when I did, I didn't even notice the blood or nothing. What I thought it was, here is a little something. I thought it was a guy, and I thought the person threw up on herself, you know, is what I was thinking when I picked her up; she was cold and bloody. I said, "Oh shit, I got to get the hell out of here." So then, I got on the way home, and I turned right around and came back to you.

Beardslee was puzzled. He had been to the crime scene. He had seen that the driver's-side window was only partway down and knew that the door was closed when Walter and Moore arrived. Abbott would have had to get his whole upper body through the partially open window— far enough to reach Mischelle's upper body in the middle of the car— to be able to lift her as he described.

Beardslee didn't think it was possible to do what Abbott was claiming he had done. He gave Abbott an out, asking him if the driver's-side door was open, which led to the following exchange.

ABBOTT: It was. . . . I just reached in the window; it was closed.

BEARDSLEE: The window partway down?

ABBOTT: The window was all the way down.

BEARDSLEE: All the way down?

Abbott could have admitted he opened the door if that is how he got inside the car. There would have been nothing wrong with doing that; in fact, it seemed to be the more sensible way to help someone sprawled across the seat inside. Beardslee wondered why Abbott insisted he had done the seemingly impossible.

Abbott added a gratuitous detail. "If it wasn't for the rings and stuff on her hand, I seen the rings on her hand, you know (unintelligible), you couldn't even tell that was a girl. She was in bad shape." Mischelle wasn't wearing any of her collection of rings. They were sitting in the center console. And her hands weren't readily visible. One was under her torso, and the other was resting on the floorboard.

When Beardslee asked Abbott if he saw "any other cars or any other people in the area," he responded:

> Well, when I come up the exit, some guy, looked like a hitchhiker, he looked like he jumped off in the ditch. You know right (unintelligible) that exit. I thought that son of a bitch thought I was . . . that was before I got to the car, I thought to myself, that son of a bitch thought I was trying to hit him or something with a vehicle. He jumped off, completely off that damn ditch, and I thought about that later.

Abbott described this man as "about 5 foot 10 or 11" and wearing "a gray or blue-gray sweatshirt and lighter-colored jeans." To Beardslee, it was as if he had just invented that detail of his story.

Toward the end of the interview, Wes Drury jumped in with a question. He thought he had heard Abbott admit earlier that rather than stopping to report finding the girl in the car, he drove past the sheriff's office, out of Benton on Missouri Highway 61 toward Scott City and home.

DRURY: You said you headed home after you checked her.

ABBOTT: Right here to the house.

That might explain why he arrived at the sheriff's office six or seven minutes after the Householders left, even though he was at the interstate exit, by his own estimate, 5 or 10 minutes before them. When he realized what he had said, he backpedaled a bit.

DRURY: How far did you get before you went back?

ABBOTT: I basically went straight there. I think I went right there. I was headed home (unintelligible) the Benton way.

BEARDSLEE: Sixty-one?

ABBOTT: Yeah. I thought I better get up there, that girl might be alive, you know.

Beardslee thought Abbott was lying. He was nervous and couldn't look Beardslee in the eye, and key details in his account were implausible.

After the interview concluded, Beardslee asked Abbott to come to the sheriff's office to give elimination prints. Abbott thought that was a good idea. "My prints might be on the door." He seemed to be trying to explain away in advance some evidence implicating him in the murder that had not yet come to light. Early Sunday afternoon, after his interview with Mark Abbott, Beardslee went back to the crime scene with Deputy Shoemaker to search for some evidence of the pedestrian Abbott said had jumped out of his way as he approached the exit ramp. He thought they might find a footprint left by the man or skid or braking marks left by Abbott's tires. They found nothing.

Beardslee had more questions. Abbott was acting suspiciously, and he needed to question him further in an interrogation room in the sheriff's office. He asked Abbott to meet with him for a follow-up interview in a couple hours. When Beardslee and Drury left Abbott's trailer, Beardslee called ahead to inform Deputy Schiwitz of his suspicions and Abbott's arrival, which he expected to be in a couple of hours. He told her he was going to the crime scene again and would arrive to interrogate Abbott as soon as he was finished. Abbott didn't wait. He went straight to the sheriff's office to be fingerprinted. When Beardslee arrived, Deputy Schiwitz was standing in the hall, and Abbott was in a closed-door meeting with Sheriff Ferrell.

While he was still there, he was interviewed again about the events of the night before, this time by Deputy Schiwitz. She noted later that Abbott "was so nervous and so upset by what he had just witnessed that he wanted to get the report made and get gone."

Abbott told Schiwitz he stopped behind Mischelle's car and waited for a short time. Then, not seeing anyone in the car, he got out of his vehicle and approached the car on the driver's side. Schiwitz's description of what Abbott said he saw when he did that is similar to the account Beardslee recorded, including his account of reaching through the window, "which was rolled down."

He said he was scared and drove around Mischelle's car to go to the pay phone on the parking lot at the Cut-Mart, directly across the interstate from the crime scene. Then, he added another detail he hadn't told Beardslee and Drury or anyone else in law enforcement. He was dialing 911 when a man in a small white car drove up and stopped next to him. "He asked me to take him to get gas. I thought it was strange. He was driving a car. Why did he need to go with me? I was scared, and I drove away fast. I was driving, and he was still talking to me." Schiwitz asked him to describe the man. According to her report, Abbott could only say, "He had a dark complexion."

2

THE INITIAL INVESTIGATION

Mischelle Lawless's funeral at the Unity Baptist Church on Tuesday, November 10, was attended by an overflow crowd of more than 300 people, including many of her young friends and acquaintances. Reverend Huff officiated, and burial was nearby in the church cemetery. Deputies from the Scott County Sheriff's Office mingled in the crowd, to show sympathy with the Lawless family but also because it was standard procedure in a murder investigation. Killers have been known to attend the victim's funeral, out of guilt or for some perverse motive.

People in and around Scott County were stunned by the murder. In an interview in the *Southeast Missourian* the day after Mischelle's death, Dale Estill, the night manager at the Sikeston Shoney's where she worked, described her as "a real, sweet girl." He said, "We're in a state of shock and disbelief." Fellow students at SEMO described Mischelle as "really friendly," "bubbly," and "always smiling and joking around." Some professors dismissed class early after brief comments about the murder. One administrator spent most of the morning talking to faculty and "spent quite a bit of time with one of Mischelle's professors who was especially distraught."

Mike Parry, the director of the Baptist Student Union, and his wife had gotten to know Mischelle at a church camp about five years before. Parry said she was "a very loving person" and that he and his wife had kept in touch with her since that summer. He said, "I was devastated, for me personally, for the students that knew her."

Denise Lincoln met Mischelle when Mischelle started eating lunch at the Baptist Student Union. She found Mischelle to be "reserved at first," but said, "She stayed after lunch and made friends with other students, both male and female. A lot of people were interested in reaching out to

Mischelle and including her in the Baptist Student Union family, and that was beginning to happen."

The day after the murder, Sheriff Ferrell told the *Southeast Missourian* that authorities believed Mischelle was beaten outside the car and shot while she sat in the front seat. The sheriff's office was pursuing alternative theories—that Mischelle knew her killer or that it was a random act of violence. Ferrell would not speculate about a motive, but he said it wasn't likely robbery. "We can't determine whether anything is missing." He stressed that motorists should not be concerned about traveling around Scott County. "I think this is an isolated incident. I don't think anyone has any reason to be frightened going up and down the interstate."

But people were frightened. Mischelle wasn't the sort of person anyone would expect to be murdered. If it could happen to someone as normal as Mischelle, it could happen to them or to their children.

Benton Mayor Paul Stuckey, who owned an insurance agency in Cape Girardeau, knew the Lawless family well. He told the newspaper, "A car wreck you understand; this you can't understand." He said the town's parents were very upset; they were warning their children not to stop for anybody. "I've got a 17-year-old daughter. That's what I'm telling her when she's going to Cape." But he added, "Of course, you've told them before." In another interview with the newspaper a few days later, Stuckey emphasized that murders don't happen in Benton. "I'm 49 years old and in Benton I can't remember a murder. We don't have anybody that gets angry enough at somebody to shoot them."

In a tiny town like Benton, with a population of 576 in 1992, the violent death of a resident is a personal tragedy for everyone who lives there. The murder of Mischelle Lawless was constantly on everyone's mind and a daily topic of conversation. The predominant view seemed to be that Mischelle knew her killer and that he was someone local, living among them and perhaps even participating in these daily conversations. The key fact suggesting this conclusion was that the driver's-side window of the car she was driving was rolled partway down. Driving along the interstate, on a November night with a temperature near 32 degrees, certainly she would have had the window all the way up. Why would she open the window when she stopped at the dark and lonely intersection if not to talk to someone she knew? Mayor Stuckey claimed the town's residents weren't concerned about a danger to themselves from a random killer. "It's not a madman running loose. I think our community feels like whoever killed the little gal knew her."

★ ★ ★

Despite the view expressed by Mayor Stuckey that Mischelle knew her killer, much of the early emphasis in the investigation being directed by Ferrell and Schiwitz was on the possibility that the murder was a random incident, perpetrated by someone Mischelle didn't know, like the person or persons who had abducted Cheryl Ann Scherer from Scott City 13 and a half years before. Just prior to noon on April 17, 1979, Cheryl Ann had disappeared from her job as cashier at the Rhodes Pump-Ur-Own gas station in Scott City during an apparent robbery. There were no witnesses and no real clues. Cheryl Ann was the same age and almost exactly the same height and weight as Mischelle Lawless.

In 1984, Sheriff Ferrell had interviewed Henry Lee Lucas and Ottis Toole, serial killers who had traveled the United States in the 1970s and early 1980s committing random murders. Toole and Lucas were in Scott City when Cheryl Ann disappeared, and they told police they had kidnapped and killed a girl in the area around that time. Shown a picture of Cheryl Ann, however, Lucas said it wasn't the girl, and both men had a history of confessing to crimes they didn't commit. Ferrell never had enough evidence to charge them, and they died in prison, leaving the disappearance of Cheryl Ann unsolved.

The sheriff's office received more than a hundred leads in the first week of the investigation, and there was no shortage of other sightings that Sunday morning of unidentified men on foot in the vicinity of and near the time of the murder.

Roy Easter, a Benton resident, came to the sheriff's office on the Monday morning after the murder to report a mysterious pedestrian near the crime scene. He told Deputy Chambers he had seen a man on the side of the road at the trailer sales lot around 1:25 a.m. Sunday morning as he was driving home on Highway 77 from a pool tournament in Charleston, Missouri. He described the man as "white, about 6 feet to 6 feet two inches tall, with light-colored, shoulder-length hair, and wearing a thin, dark-colored jacket." Easter also thought he remembered seeing a car sitting at the stop sign for the interstate exit ramp, about where Mischelle Lawless was found, and wondering whether the car was going to turn right on 77 and come toward him or turn left into his lane in front of him.

Kathy Korver, a registered nurse with the Job Corps, called and talked to Chambers not long after he finished interviewing Roy Easter. Korver said she and her husband were traveling south on Interstate 55 Sunday morning about a half mile north of the Benton exit within view of the flashing emergency lights, probably sometime after 2:15 a.m., when two young men ran out from the median in front of their car. "I had to slam on the brakes to avoid hitting them. Both men were in their 20s, about 6 feet tall, with a medium build. I could see the one closest to the car clearly in the headlights. He was wearing a bright blue shirt, blue jeans, and a thin jacket, and he had dirty dishwater blond hair that looked like it was cut very badly."

Justin Tanksley reported he saw a man in front of Glyn Ferrell's trailer sales lot the night of the murder as he was driving his girlfriend home on Highway 77 between 1:00 a.m. and 1:15 a.m. He described the man as white, six feet tall, with a medium build and dark hair. He remembered seeing two cars sitting at the exit where Mischelle was found, parked one behind the other with their lights on, as if waiting at the stop sign for traffic to pass.

None of these sightings led investigators to a suspect. The men Abbott, Easter, Korver, and Tanksley described could have been locals, or they might have been just passing through. But none of the witnesses could provide an identification of someone in particular. There isn't much hope of identifying a suspect under those circumstances, especially one who soon might have been hundreds of miles away, without a lucky match of physical evidence in a law enforcement database tying the person to the scene.

★ ★ ★

The investigation soon began to focus on men from the area who knew Mischelle and on finding a reason one of them might have had to kill her. Investigators interviewed her family and closest friends and people who worked or went to school with her and the men those people mentioned.

On Wednesday, November 11, the investigative team met at the sheriff's office to discuss initial results of the investigation and to start developing a list of suspects. Those present included Sheriff Ferrell; Deputies Beardslee, Schiwitz, and Chambers; and two state patrol officers, Sergeant Overbey and Trooper Don Windham. Windham wasn't at the crime scene the night of the murder but was assigned to the investigation soon after and became the lead investigator for the highway patrol.

This group went around the room suggesting names for the list. Mischelle's primary boyfriends, Leon Lamb and Lyle Day, were at the top. Lovers are natural suspects, and Lyle Day already had hired a lawyer, a fact that was duly noted. Three other young men who had dated Mischelle were on the list: Jim Copeland, Jeff Owens, and Jeremy Turner. Ferrell wanted to give Mark Abbott a polygraph. He also suggested Copeland. His phone number was found at the autopsy, handwritten on a piece of paper in Mischelle's clothes. Beardslee mentioned both Abbott twins. He was suspicious of Mark Abbott because of his implausible statements and nervous demeanor in the Sunday interview, and no one was sure yet which of the twins had found the body, had come in to report finding it, or had re-appeared at the crime scene. Vince Howard and Eric Shanks weren't on the list.

After the first few days, Trooper Windham and Deputy Schiwitz took the lead for their organizations, doing most of the important witness interviews together. Windham was young and eager to advance, with a bachelor's degree in criminal justice from SEMO. Deputy Schiwitz started with the sheriff's office under the previous sheriff, John Dennis. Tom Beardslee was nominally the chief deputy, but Brenda Schiwitz had gained Bill Ferrell's confidence, especially with crimes against women, which she was making something of a specialty.

Beardslee had little to do with the investigation after the first day. Bill Ferrell generated little paperwork related to the Lawless case, but as anyone familiar with the department could tell you, he kept track of every detail and directed everything behind the scenes.

★ ★ ★

In their search for someone who might have had reason to kill Mischelle, investigators were able to piece together the last months of her life from interviews with friends and family and from entries in a journal she had started keeping at the beginning of 1992. What Mischelle wrote in the journal confirmed much of what investigators heard from other sources and fleshed out portraits of two key suspects, Leon Lamb and Lyle Day, but it also revealed a side of Mischelle that was much subtler and more wholesome than the happy-go-lucky party girl image she seemed to project.

Mischelle was close to her family. There are journal entries about buying gifts for family members and chauffeuring her brother and sister around the county. Occasionally, she noted an argument with one or the other of her parents, but these were of a variety that was typical of someone her age straining for independence but still living at home.

Mischelle was religious, if not overly so. She didn't record theological musings in the journal. But she recorded regular Sunday church attendance, either with her family or with Leon Lamb, occasions when she sang with the church choir, and hanging out at the Baptist Student Union.

An important use for the journal during most of the year was to chronicle the ups and downs of her relationship with Leon Lamb. The very first entry, on New Year's Day, was typical of the good days in the relationship. She went over to Lamb's house, and they talked, ate, watched rented movies, and "loved." She ended the entry with the observation, "Made me feel loved today & I am really happy. [Heart symbol] him! Great first Day of 1992."

The problem with Leon was that he didn't show Mischelle the same level of devotion that she showed him. If she went over to his house and he made her dinner and paid attention to her, she was ecstatic. If they just "loved" and he "was a butt" and ignored her the rest of the evening, she was miserable. At the beginning of 1992, they had been dating for about two years already, and it was obvious Lamb was beginning to get restless. On January 4, she told him she thought she was pregnant, and he said he "doesn't want it." On January 10, he told her he felt "like his life was passing him by," and she wrote, "I love him so much & it hurts."

As the year went on, the relationship deteriorated further. They fought, sometimes physically, typically, by Mischelle's own account, with Mischelle landing the first blow and Lamb shoving her defensively. Lamb told her several times that he wanted to cool down or break off the relationship. Each time, they stopped seeing each other for a few days but got back together again as if nothing had happened. During the brief breakup periods in the late spring and early summer, Mischelle went riding with other boys or even on an occasional date, but it seemed she was more interested in making Lamb jealous than in developing a relationship with someone new. Then, in the middle of July, they broke up for an extended period. When she went to see him on July 12, he told her to leave him alone. She hit him and left. She wrote in the journal, "I'm not sure I want him back." When she stopped by his house on July 19 to drop something off, she ended up staying, and they "loved." Afterward, he "said we couldn't do this."

For the next six weeks, there was an occasional mention in the journal of missing Lamb, running into him and having a strained conversation, seeing him with another girl, or seeing the other girl and threatening her but nothing to indicate she had made up with Lamb. She recorded regular encounters with new boys, on a vacation trip and as the school year at SEMO began. She seemed to be compensating for the loss of Lamb, but none of the relationships during this period turned into anything serious. She described casual dates and noted a few times when someone kissed her. Occasionally, these encounters looked like they might lead to something significant. On July 20, for example, she met a boy named "Greg" and wrote, "Kissed and stuff. I could love him." The next day, she wrote that she had a dream about him, but that was the last time his name appeared.

Then, there was "Mark." She mentioned in passing in her diary on July 2 that she met someone by that name at the Purple Crackle, a night club in East Cape Girardeau, Illinois. On August 6, she wrote that she went there again and "took Mark and Jocko home, kissed and he asked me out." It isn't clear which one kissed her and asked her out or whether she went out with him. There are two more entries referring to Mark, on August 28 and September 3. Mischelle wrote on September 3, "Stayed @ Mark's." Some in law enforcement have speculated these entries were a reference to Mark Abbott.

August 23, 1992, was Mischelle's first day of college, and her journal entries started to reflect the lifestyle of a college coed. If these flirtations were intended to help Mischelle forget Lamb, they weren't having that effect. On August 31, she had a busy day socially. She saw "Lee" and "Jared" at school and then went with "Chad" to his place and talked. She wrote that she came home at the end of the day, "[D]id nails. Thought about Leon & cried. I miss him."

During this college period, Mischelle still worked at Shoney's and kept her old friends from there. At SEMO, she went to class, skipped class, had lunch at the Baptist Student Union, studied for tests, went to fraternity parties, and met a boy on the football team she liked. She also cruised Sikeston with Lelicia and Chantelle and with Vince Howard and Eric Shanks, and she attended "motel parties" with the "Shoney's gang." There are lots of references to drinking alcohol at both ends of the interstate, occasionally to excess. But nowhere in the journal during that period is there a reference to using drugs.

On October 4, according to her journal, she went cruising with Lelicia, "Kenneth," and "Eric," drinking and "stealing road signs." On October 9, they found a trailer they liked for rent in Sikeston. On October 15, she and Lelicia paid a deposit on the trailer in Sikeston, and they moved in gradually over the course of the next several days. But this stab at independence didn't last long. Lelicia only spent one night at the trailer, and Mischelle was back living at home within two weeks.

Halloween fell on a Saturday night that year. Mischelle got the rest of her things out of the trailer and went to pick up Lelicia and Chantelle. They put on glitter and went to a party at what Mischelle thought was John Worley's trailer outside Benton. Mischelle wrote of the party in her journal, "Lelicia left & came back. Drank & flirted and stuff. Todd Mayberry liked me. When we left kissed almost everyone. Took Lelicia home & Chantelle and I snuck out & went to McDonald's & cruised. Couldn't find Lyle so went home to Chantelle's."

Mischelle started to see Leon Lamb again sporadically at the beginning of September, recording a few apparently sexual encounters with him here and there in her journal. About the same time, she started to note an interest in Lyle Day—casual at first but progressing in October into a sexual relationship. Also about the same time, she started to record in her journal or tell friends about occasional incidents in which her flirtations with other boys may have ended up as something more serious. On October 7, she went to a Sigma Tau Gamma party at SEMO. According to the journal, a "guy" whose name she may not have remembered "kidnapped me & we had fun." She spent the night with him at the fraternity house. "Got sick. Snuggled. He's gorgeous." She joked about it later, perhaps with some embarrassment, and referred to the boy in conversation with friends as the Kidnapper, but she apparently didn't see him again.

Laura McMullin was a friend who knew Mischelle from working at a Bonanza Steak House and attended SEMO with her. She said Mischelle was getting wilder and wilder the last few months of her life—as Laura put it, dating a lot of different guys and "having sex" (whatever that might mean) with "most of them." This image of Mischelle as a promiscuous flirt is potentially misleading. It may be that she was involved in sexual encounters, but if her journal is any indication, she had no real interest in anyone but Leon Lamb until fairly late in the summer of 1992, when they stopped seeing each other for about six weeks. There is no clear evidence in her journal that she had intercourse or any kind of serious sexual relationship with anyone during those six weeks in July and August when she wasn't seeing Lamb or with anyone other than Lamb and Lyle Day in the fall. Even then, the sexual relationship with Day was restricted to the last several weeks of her life and was something she went into gradually, in an apparent attempt to get over her attachment to Lamb.

According to Lelicia O'Dell, Mischelle was having "sex" with three boys at the end of her life, Leon Lamb, Lyle Day, and Jeremy Turner, her date that last Friday night, November 6. Turner confirmed that a date on November 6 for dinner and a movie had occurred. There is no doubt about the truth of Lelicia's statement as to Lamb and Day but not with Turner. Turner was a SEMO student. Mischelle met him in August when she started college, at a party at the Sig Tau house. Her August 26 journal entry reads, "Jeremy showed, ate Chinese, saw Lethal Weapon III. Chased me down on way home, he's ok, but rather stay friends. Next day, hid from Jeremy—lots of fun." After August 26, Turner saw Mischelle at places like the Purple Crackle and Sig Tau parties, but it's unlikely that they dated seriously.

A few weeks before her death, she came into Broussard's Restaurant in Cape Girardeau, where Turner worked, with her mother, and he asked her to go on a hayride. She made the excuse that she had been in an automobile accident and begged off. Mischelle came into Broussard's again on November 6 with her mother to have dinner, and Turner asked her to go out with him after he got off work. This time she said she would. Turner told Sergeant Overbey they met at the Sig Tau house. They went to the Billiard Center, back to the Sig Tau house, then over to Jessie Roberson's house, where they sat around drinking until about 11:45 or midnight. Turner and Mischelle left Roberson's to pick up a friend who had a flat tire and returned again to the Sig Tau house, where according to Turner, Mischelle "went into the bathroom to make herself throw up. I kissed her goodnight, and she left in her car. That was the last time I saw her. I invited her to a Sig Tau party the night she was killed, but she didn't show up." Sergeant Overbey asked Turner to account for his time on November 7 and the early morning hours of November 8. While Mischelle was cruising around Sikeston with Howard and Shanks, Turner was working at Broussard's. "I got off work at 11:30. I went to the Billiard Center with Day Alexander, to Alexander's house, and to the party at the Sig Tau house. I left the party at 2 in the morning and went home to my parents' house. I didn't leave Cape Girardeau the whole night."

Mischelle's last journal entry was on November 5, the Thursday before she died. She had lunch with her mother, tanned, and closed her bank account, to have money to pay her father for repair work on her own car. It was her mother's birthday, and later, she took her mother to eat again at Steak 'n Shake to give her the presents she bought. She wrote that she "saw Lyle" but didn't elaborate. The promise in the journal for November 5 read, *"The Lord will keep you from all harm—he will watch over your life; the Lord will watch over your coming and going both now and forevermore.* Psalm 121: 7, 8."

★ ★ ★

Bill Ferrell grew up around law enforcement. His father was a deputy for John Dennis in the 1950s, and he spent much of his spare time as a teenager hanging around the Scott County Jail and the sheriff's office. After starting out at a tire and salvage business, he went to work in 1971 for the prosecuting attorney and the sheriff as an investigator. Turning to politics, he was county assessor for a term and then, in 1976, ran for county sheriff and won. He held the office until his retirement in 2004, and in 1992, he was in his early 50s and already had been sheriff for 15 years.

In Missouri, a rural county sheriff, especially a longtime sheriff, is likely to be the real head of all law enforcement activity in the county. Most of the small municipal police forces in the county were dependent on and subservient to the sheriff's office. Even the highway patrol deferred to Ferrell's authority. They knew better than to conduct an investigation in his county without notifying him and getting his approval.

Ferrell's 1992 bid for reelection had been his toughest race yet. The August Democratic primary was a nasty affair. In April, the state auditor's office had released an audit of Scott County government that was critical of Ferrell's operation of the county jail, and Bud Mills, Ferrell's opponent, had made good use of the audit. Mills and his supporters criticized Ferrell harshly, and Ferrell claimed that threats had been made against him and his deputies.

Ferrell had been providing meals for the prisoners himself at a fixed amount per day and then submitting invoices to the county commission, seeking reimbursement for his services. But he provided no receipts proving his expenses and not even an accounting of the number of meals served. The auditor recommended that the bills from food vendors should be submitted directly to the county for payment and until it happened, that the sheriff should provide documentation supporting the food expenses he claimed. But Ferrell argued that submitting food bills directly to the county would result in higher costs for meals because if the county paid all expenses, Ferrell would have no incentive to keep the cost down. He kept costs to a minimum by using unpaid jail trusties to prepare the meals and pocketed the difference between the amount he charged the county and the amount it cost him to feed the inmates. This is not unusual in rural Missouri, and many voters thought of it as a legitimate way for a sheriff to supplement his income. The audit report also noted that the reimbursements were deposited into Ferrell's personal checking account, but Ferrell countered that he had paid the expenses out of his personal funds and was merely being repaid.

Although many have always seen Ferrell the way Josh and the Lawless family now see him, to the voting majority of Scott County at the time of Mischelle's murder, Ferrell seemed more like a kindly, almost fatherly friend and advisor than a policeman. Like most men his age, he was a little overweight and had a pleasant, friendly face. He rode around the county in a pickup truck with his dog. His only uniform was blue jeans and cowboy boots, topped by a white cowboy hat, and he never carried a gun. "I don't want to be intimidating unless it is really necessary." His hobby was competitive calf roping, and he liked to take his horse and dog to visit local kindergartens and vacation Bible classes. He used the animals to get the children's attention, then gave them junior deputy badges and talked about being good citizens and having good manners. He brought the DARE anti-drug program to the county, and in 1978, he was instrumental in creating bumper stickers that read, "Have you hugged your kid today?" His home phone number was listed, and he liked to advise county residents in legal trouble "because they had no one else to turn to."

3

DIGGING DEEPER

Interstate 55 runs 964 miles from Lakeshore Drive in Chicago to Interstate 10 in LaPlace, Louisiana, just outside of New Orleans. Scott County, Missouri, straddles Interstate 55 in the southeast quadrant of the state along the Mississippi River, which forms the county's eastern border, approximately halfway between St. Louis and Memphis. The county has a roughly rectangular shape, tilted slightly toward the southeast, in the general direction of the flow of the winding river. It is bordered, north to west to south, by Cape Girardeau County, Stoddard County, New Madrid County, and Mississippi County.

Scott County is predominantly rural. It has an area of 421 square miles and a population of about 41,000, not quite enough to fill the Cardinals ballpark in St. Louis if the entire county made the two-hour trip north. About half of these people live along Interstate 55 in and around the county's two largest towns, Scott City and Sikeston. Benton is the county seat—the site of the 33rd Judicial Circuit Courthouse, which serves Scott and Mississippi Counties, the Scott County Sheriff's Office, and the Scott County Jail.

Until early in the 20th century, much of Scott County was part of a vast swamp that stretched south into Arkansas. Most of that swamp was drained, at that time by a system of canals and levees for agricultural use, but the county still contains residual pockets of swampland, especially in the southern part and along the Mississippi and its tributaries. Cutting across the county from northeast to southwest is Crowley's Ridge, a nearly 200-mile-long geologic formation, named for one of the first Europeans to settle in the region. The ridge rises as much as several hundred feet above the broad plain that sweeps away on both sides. It begins at the Mississippi River south of Cape Girardeau above the town of Commerce, crosses the county in a southwesterly direction surrounding Benton, bends south into Stoddard County and across the St. Francis River near Malden into Arkansas, and finally arcs south and then east back to the Mississippi near the Arkansas town of Helena. Miles across in places, the ridge is flanked by areas that are drained by narrow rivers and not very long ago, were covered by lakes and bogs with names like Black Mine Swamp and Hatchie Coon Sunk Lands. Beyond this plain, away from the Mississippi to the north and west, wooded hills rise up and blend into the beginnings of the Ozark Mountains.

★ ★ ★

Scott County had relatively little violent crime in the early 1990s. Crack cocaine was a problem in poorer black neighborhoods, like Sunset Addition in Sikeston, and the woods were full of young men cooking methamphetamine, the new hillbilly heroin. There was a Southeast Missouri Drug Task Force, which Sheriff Ferrell had helped establish in January 1990, aiding overwhelmed rural law enforcement offices dealing with the growing challenge. Sheriff Ferrell was quoted in 1997 as saying, "Years ago, I predicted it would be the biggest problem we had . . . but I still didn't realize what it would turn out to be. It snowballs, but it's underground and you don't know what you've got until it's too late." But at the time Mischelle Lawless was murdered, the drug trade was conducted in Scott County by and large without open violence. Murder of any kind was a rarity. In the previous 16 years that Bill Ferrell had been sheriff, his office had investigated only 10 murders. And all of those had been run-of-the-mill, solved in a week or so with the arrest of some obvious suspect who knew the victim. But there was an asterisk on Ferrell's perfect record of cleared murder cases. Cheryl Ann Scherer didn't make the official Scott County murder statistics because her body was never found, but there was little doubt that she was dead.

★ ★ ★

The majority of Scott County's workforce is employed at city jobs. There are industrial plants around Sikeston and Scott City; motels, restaurants, and service stations for travelers on Interstate 55; and the usual array of schools, grocery stores, and shops scattered in the population centers throughout the county. But away from the interstate, along the state highways and county roads, there are cotton, rice, and soybean farms and businesses that support them.

Scott County revels in its rural image. Billboards along Interstate 55 tout the down-home cooking at Lambert's Café in Miner, just off the interstate near Sikeston, which bills itself as the "world-famous Home of Throwed Rolls." The list of Sikeston special events advertised on the county website features annual events like the Cotton Carnival, the Jaycees' Bootheel Rodeo, and the Redneck Barbecue.

Scott County's official motto is "Where north meets south and east meets west." According to the county's website, this slogan:

> summarizes many attributes of this unique Southeast Missouri county. The bustling industries of the northern part blend into the southern area, rightfully known as "where Southern Hospitality begins in America." With the mighty Mississippi River flowing on its eastern edge, the county marks the beginning of the American west and its great pioneering spirit where a neighbor helps a neighbor.

Since 1803, when Lewis and Clark traveled, down the Ohio and up the Mississippi, to begin the exploration of the trans-Mississippi "West," the Mississippi has been the traditional border between the East and the West. And the farther south you drive in Missouri on Interstate 55, the more "southern" the state becomes. The north certainly meets the south somewhere in southern Missouri south of Cape Girardeau, and it makes as much sense for that place to be on Crowley's Ridge in Scott County as anywhere else. As the fall cotton harvest approaches, along the state highways and county roads below the ridge, fields white with cotton bolls stretch away toward the horizon.

Missouri was a slave state before the Civil War. Although it remained in the Union, the former governor became a Confederate major general and many of its citizens, particularly outside St. Louis, sided with the Confederacy. Confederate cavalry under General John Marmaduke invading Missouri in the spring of 1863 followed Crowley's Ridge to avoid the swampy lowlands to the east and west, on their way to briefly besiege the Union supply depot at Cape Girardeau. They retreated back along the ridge after failing to capture the town. Most of Scott County was under martial law and, in effect, occupied enemy territory during the war.

Today, Scott County's racial makeup is approximately 88 percent white, 10 percent African American, and 1 percent Hispanic. Despite their Confederate sympathies, few Southeast Missourians were slaveholders at the time of the Civil War. A migration of black residents started in the 1920s, when local farmers planted cotton on reclaimed swampland to replace the cotton fields that were being destroyed in the South by the boll weevil. At that time thousands of black farmers and field laborers moved north with their families. Sunset Addition, now known simply as Sunset, sprang up on the western edge of Sikeston when these newcomers established a segregated enclave of small houses and shacks. In the early days, Sunset was poor, but thriving. It had its own businesses, churches, and schools to serve its residents. By the 1990s, it had lost that sense of community and become an area known for drugs and violence. Scott County has had something of a history of racial animosity and rough justice. The last lynching in Missouri, of a black man named Cleo Wright, took place at Sikeston in 1942. Having been accused of assaulting a white woman and nearly killing an arresting officer, Wright was dragged through the streets and burned alive. The prosecuting attorney in Scott County tried unsuccessfully to get indictments of the leaders of the mob.

Racism is far more subtle in Scott County today. Blacks and whites are wary of one another, but Scott County is no different from any big northeastern city in that respect. If anything, people in small towns—black and white, rich and poor, native born and immigrant—are thrust together more than in big cities, living in closer proximity and more likely to attend the same schools. There was nothing out of the ordinary about Mischelle Lawless's casual friendship with Vince Howard. Still, some found this relationship distasteful, and race fueled some of the speculation about the identity of Mischelle's murderer and his motivation. There were those who thought she was killed by a black man, and there were others who thought she was killed by a white racist because she went cruising with Howard.

★ ★ ★

Forensic evidence gathered from Mischelle Lawless's body and the crime scene was sent to the Southeast Missouri Crime Laboratory at SEMO in Cape Girardeau. The director of the SEMO Crime Lab was Dr. Robert Briner. The SEMO Lab sent some of the evidence to the FBI Laboratory in Washington, DC, for further testing.

Whatever the amount of alcohol Mischelle had consumed over the course of the evening and however it might have affected her, she wasn't legally drunk at the time of her death. Gas chromatographic analysis of a sample of her blood taken at the autopsy showed less than .05 percent alcohol by weight. In addition, results of toxicology tests of a urine sample were negative for a broad array of drugs: amphetamine, marijuana, cocaine, opiates, PCP, barbiturates, and benzodiazepine.

There was no outward indication Mischelle had been raped. The long tear in the back of her left pant leg likely was the result of her struggle with an attacker, but it didn't necessarily indicate the attack was sexual. A vaginal smear from the rape kit taken at the autopsy yielded no intact human sperm, but tests for the presence of prostatic acid phosphatase (PAP) were positive, which is considered presumptive evidence of the presence of human seminal fluid. That, too, was consistent with what Leon Lamb had said about having intercourse with Mischelle shortly before her death, even though there was no DNA evidence to identify the seminal fluid as belonging to him. The killer may have intended to rape Mischelle, which the rip in her jeans suggests, but if so, it appears he wasn't successful.

All of the blood in the trail leading from Mischelle's car, along the pavement and down the embankment in the grass, belonged to Mischelle. Two samples of scrapings of a red substance from under her right and left fingernails were detected. Tests for genetic factors yielded both A and B reactions, suggesting a mixture of at least two blood types from at least two different people. Mischelle Lawless was type A and was assumed to have been the source of the A antigen, but Mischelle couldn't have been the source of the B antigen. And it also is possible that the source of the B antigen wasn't even human blood because B antigen can be found in bacteria or soil.

Nevertheless, the working assumption in the initial stages of the investigation was that Mischelle had scratched the killer or someone who was present and assisting the killer during a violent struggle. Blood typing could exclude suspects as the source of the B antigen, which could have come only from someone with type B or AB blood, not from someone with type A or O, which was still a large segment of the population.

Samples from Mischelle's fingernail scrapings were sent to the FBI Laboratory. Using relatively primitive methods compared to those available today, the FBI developed a partial DNA profile from the scrapings that narrowed the search to 7 percent of the population at large—about 25,000,000 people in the United States. It could be used to eliminate individuals but not to identify a specific person.

The latent fingerprints and palm prints lifted from Mischelle's car were of limited value. Most of the fingerprints were too smudged to be useable, and all three useable fingerprints belonged to Mischelle. There were three useable palm prints on the hood of the car, but they could have been left by Mischelle too. There was no way to make a comparison because her palm prints weren't taken during the autopsy. Mark Abbott's palm prints were taken, and they didn't match the palm prints on the hood of the car.

Andy Wagner was a ballistics analyst for the SEMO Crime Lab. He examined the three slugs from Mischelle's murder and concluded, based in particular on the groove impressions, that they probably had been fired from a .380. Wagner eventually compared bullets fired from about a dozen guns, including one belonging to Marvin Lawless, without finding a match with the three slugs in Mischelle's murder.

★ ★ ★

The Abbott twins were nice-looking boys, with an athletic build and a certain rough country charm. In 1992, Mark was a little heavier, but the brothers were difficult to tell apart. They were part of the popular crowd in high school. Growing up, they seemed to have everything going for them. The family was prosperous. In addition to Store 24, Larry and Reba Abbott owned rental property around the county, including a share of the trailer park where Mark lived. Reba had a housekeeper to help with domestic chores. As young adults, the twins had steady employment. Matt was part owner, with another brother, Larry Jr., of Interstate Manufacturing in Dexter. They built automatic cotton carts for John Deere, which cotton farmers used to haul raw cotton to market. Mark attended SEMO briefly and worked mainly in the family businesses and was working at Interstate Manufacturing and doing maintenance of rental property at the time of the murder.

But by late 1992, when the twins were 23, their lives started to show signs of going off track. Both of them liked to drink and carouse and were regulars at local night spots. The drinking and carousing led to scrapes with the law, mostly minor ones at first. A few years before, Matt had been sentenced to five years' probation for stealing a three-wheeler when he was drunk. The night of Mischelle Lawless's murder, Mark had several DWI arrests under his belt and was driving without a license. There were suspicions Mark and Matt were involved with drugs. Scott City police officers contacted as part of the investigation were very familiar with Mark. They thought it odd that he reported finding Mischelle Lawless's body given what they perceived as his animosity toward law enforcement.

Mark Abbott told investigators that he spent the latter part of Saturday, November 7, and the first hour of November 8 at Country Nights, a honky-tonk in Sikeston.

> I worked on rehabbing some family rental property until about 10:00. Then I went to Country Nights. I think I got there around 11:00. I was dancing with Heather until about 1:00. I was pretty drunk, and I had a suspended license. So I got off 55 at Benton to take 61. Those asshole Scott City cops were trying to catch me driving, so I took the backway home.

Glenna and Heather Pierce confirmed that Mark Abbott had been with them at Country Nights. They left there at closing, about 1:00 a.m., but they were vague in their recollection of when Abbott arrived and left.

If he did leave around 1:00 a.m. as he claimed, he could have arrived at the Benton exit around 1:15 a.m., give or take a few minutes. If Leon Lamb's estimate of when Mischelle left his home is accurate, Abbott might have been driving not far behind her on the interstate, and he could have arrived at the murder scene not long after she was shot—unless, of course, as Deputy Beardslee suspected, he was there when she was shot and had some involvement in her death.

Deputy Schiwitz and Trooper Windham went back to Abbott on November 23 to review with him his account of the night of the murder. He insisted he didn't know Mischelle, and he expressed a willingness to take a blood test and a polygraph exam. Abbott expanded, however, on his earlier account of the encounter at the Cut-Mart, for the first time providing descriptions, although fairly general ones, of the man looking for gas and the car he was driving. According to Schiwitz's typed report of the interview, "the driver wasn't a Negro, but could have been Hispanic or Mexican as he had a dark complexion" and "had black hair, with sides and back longer." According to Windham's report, Abbott described the man as "a dark skin toned male, possibly Hispanic" who was clean shaven and less than 20 years old. Also according to Windham's report, Abbott said Kevin and Terri Williams told him Ray Ring wanted to talk to him, and based on that, he thought the man "could have possibly been Ray Ring."

Before this November 23 interview, Abbott had described the car only as small and white. On November 23, according to Windham's report, he said that the car was newer looking and had a shape something like a Saab, with "a spoiler or something" on the back. Schiwitz and Windham drove Abbott around after the interview looking for a similar car, and he identified a Mercury Merkur XL4-TI with a spoiler as "possibly the vehicle he had seen."

Abbott said the man stopped behind his truck, about six feet away from where he stood at the phone trying to make a 911 call. He wasn't sure if anyone else was in the car, but he thought there might have been. While still in the car, the driver said, "I'm out of fuel—I've got to go with you." Abbott later said he thought the use of the term "fuel" was unusual, but he didn't say the man spoke with an accent. He claimed that the man scared him and that he answered, "screw you," jumped in his truck, and sped to the sheriff's office.

There was a rough similarity between Mark Abbott's account of the man at the Cut-Mart and Roy Moore's report of the man, presumably Mexican, in a small white car who stopped at the murder scene and asked, in broken English and a thick accent, where he could find an open gas station. The only significant difference between the two descriptions was that Moore said the man had a thick accent. Brenda Schiwitz noticed the connection. She interviewed Moore on November 24 regarding his report.

After Abbott reported the incident to the sheriff's office, he said he didn't go home. Instead, he said he drove directly to the Pierces' home in Cape Girardeau. Heather said he arrived "around 2 a.m., shaking and talking excitedly," and told her about finding a girl dead. "I touched the body. Where's the bathroom? Is there blood on my hands? I gotta wash my hands." According to Heather, Abbott fell asleep on a couch talking to her and left early in the morning but apparently, still didn't go home. At least, Deputy Beardslee didn't find him there on the two occasions he stopped by Sunday morning.

Abbott continued to be considered a suspect. Deputy Chambers asked the Scott City police what sort of guns his father owned and found out that David Beck, the former Scott City police chief, had sold Larry Abbott an Astra .380. But the elder Abbott didn't get a permit for the gun and returned it.

There is no record of anyone asking Matt Abbott near the time of the murder where he was in the early morning hours of November 8. In a deposition almost a year later, he claimed, "I don't remember what I did that weekend. It didn't stand out in my mind at the time, because I didn't hear about the murder until a few days later." Of course, he was the one who showed up at the crime scene driving a sedan instead of a truck.

4

GETTING DESPERATE TO CHARGE SOMEONE

M arvin Lawless told Trooper Windham that Mischelle went with him Saturday afternoon, November 7, to buy a Ping-Pong table and to help him deliver it to a good friend. "We came home and ate supper. Mischelle left around 6 to go to Sikeston for a night out with friends. My wife and I went to bed around 11. We were asleep when the sheriff arrived." He also said, "Mischelle had a curfew, but we didn't really enforce it. She tried to get home around 1. She either was home around that time or called to let us know she was going to be late. She always knocked on our bedroom door to let us know she was home."

Marvin Lawless wasn't pushing any particular suspect in his discussions with investigators. To his knowledge, his daughter wasn't having problems with anyone, and he couldn't think of anyone who would want to kill her. "I saw Leon a lot over the years. He's a good guy. Leon was the one she loved and wanted to marry, but I know he wasn't ready for a commitment." He said, "I never met Lyle Day. Mischelle knew him from T-N-T Tanning in Sikeston. He was in an accident of some sort, and he's a semi-cripple. Mischelle went out with him some but she didn't really care for him—she cared for Leon." Still, Lawless had no particular reason to suspect Day.

★ ★ ★

Some of Mischelle's best female friends were Lelicia O'Dell, Chantelle Crider, and Laura McMullen. Lelicia and Chantelle were both 17 and lived in Sikeston. They knew Mischelle from the Sikeston Shoney's; their relationship was based primarily on socializing with young men around Sikeston. Lelicia told investigators, "We drink alcohol, mostly beers, but we don't use drugs." She remembered that Mischelle talked to Leon Lamb in the parking lot just before they went driving around with Vince Howard and Eric Shanks, but she said, "I didn't hear the conversation."

Laura McMullen was 20 and lived in Benton. She was a student with Mischelle at SEMO, and they had worked together at a Bonanza Steak House. "Mischelle told me the sex was better with Leon than anyone else." But Mischelle didn't socialize with Laura in the way she did with the other two friends. "We went to college events and to the Purple Crackle across the river in Illinois. But I was dating a Marine." She told Don Windham that Mischelle and her other two friends "rode around the Malco parking lot, and I didn't care for that at all."

Chantelle and Lelicia disliked Lyle Day and thought he killed Mischelle. Laura didn't like Day either, but she said, "I can't imagine anyone would want to kill her." All three girls liked Leon Lamb and considered him Mischelle's true love. None of them suspected him of murder.

★ ★ ★

Leon Lamb met Mischelle in 1989 when they were both in high school and working together part-time at a Bonanza Steak House. They started dating, according to Lamb, in November or December of that year. Lamb was a year ahead of Mischelle in school. He didn't attend college after graduating the following spring, and he was working at Stan's Grocery at the time of Mischelle's murder. He and Mischelle had a common interest in martial arts, and he was one of her instructors in taekwondo.

According to what Lamb told investigators, he and Mischelle first became intimate in February or March of 1990. Over the course of more than two and a half years, "She told me a few times she was pregnant or had a miscarriage. She was faking it. I almost always used a condom. I think she was just trying to get me to say I would marry her, but I wouldn't do that." Told that Mischelle was taking birth control pills, he said, "I didn't know that." Eventually, he decided he needed to cool off the relationship. He told investigators, "I knew she was going through a lot at the time. I didn't really know her anymore. She was pretty much childlike and immature." He said she told him again that she was pregnant "about the time they broke up," but in any event, he said, "I knew it wasn't true."

Lamb claimed, "I stopped dating Mischelle about two months before her murder, but we still met for sex two or three times a week. It was usually at my house, like on the night she was killed." Mischelle's journal entries are more or less consistent with Lamb's characterization of their relationship during the fall of 1992, although he may have exaggerated the frequency of their meetings. After six weeks of being apart, they started a relationship again at the beginning of September. They were together at taekwondo on September 1, and he asked her over to his house.

According to Mischelle's journal, they talked and "loved" for the first time since July, and she showed him her tattoo, which she had acquired since they broke up. Afterward, at home, she wrote, "He still loves me. I know." On September 7, after returning from a float trip, she went to see him "wasted." They talked and "loved," and she wrote that she loved him.

But nothing really had been resolved while they were apart. If anything, the relationship had gone downhill. On September 8, Mischelle went to see Lamb. They talked and "loved" as they had done frequently in the past, but afterward, he made it clear where she stood. "Said we couldn't do this anymore. Why not!? I will get him back somehow." The next day, she heard from friends that he was with another girl. "He has hurt me so bad now. Called him when I got home. I wish I could die. I still love him—I have no idea why." A day later, she went to see him. They talked, and she put lotion on his infected finger. But the visit didn't go as planned, and she wrote, "Turned me down. I'm so mad—someone he doesn't know over me." On September 11, they argued when she went to his house again, and she decided she was going to "leave him alone."

For a couple of weeks, the only mentions of Lamb in Mischelle's journal were of occasional hostile encounters in public, with him and "Stephanie D.," the girl she thought he was dating. On September 21, for example, she wrote that she "dragged him out of" a bowling alley and "punched him," "saw him later at Rick's Deli, scrapped" and "got thrown off," and afterward went to his house and "yelled." On September 28, Mischelle went with Lelicia and Chantelle to the Cotton Carnival, and they ran into Lamb. Lelicia and Chantelle wandered off, and Mischelle went with Lamb to his house, where they "loved." But that was the last such entry for a few more weeks. On October 15, he told her he wanted his keys back, so she went to his house and got her lamp and ashtray. But then on October 22, she stopped by his house, and they "loved." He spent the night at her trailer on at least one occasion during this period. As far as the journal entries indicate, they "loved" one more time, on November 4, and then, according to Lamb, on the night she died.

Lamb claimed that on the last night, although Mischelle didn't say she was afraid of anyone in particular, "She asked me to let her spend the night or to drive her home. She never did that before." Lamb denied he argued with Mischelle in the parking lot in Sikeston the night she died. "She just asked me how I did in a Taekwondo tournament that day." Asked if it bothered him that Mischelle was hanging around with Vince Howard, he admitted, "I told her a long time ago to stay away from him. But it wasn't because he's black; it's because he's bad news."

Lamb clearly disliked Shanks and tried to direct suspicion toward him. In a re-interview with Schiwitz and Windham on November 16, he claimed Shanks was a "big liar" who relied on Howard to protect him when he got into fights. "Both of them use drugs. I have a gut feeling they killed Mischelle." But Lamb admitted he never had seen either one of them with a gun. Lamb had a similar suspicion about Lyle Day: "Day's a drug user too, and he's been strange since his accident. I think he could have done it. She told him she was pregnant. That could be his motive."

Trooper Windham contacted Lamb again to get a blood sample. The FBI Lab's partial DNA profile later excluded him as the source of the fingernail DNA. Even though Lamb was the last person known to have seen Mischelle alive, he was never considered much of a suspect. Everyone close to Mischelle, both friends and family, said he couldn't have done it, and he didn't seem to have a motive.

★ ★ ★

Deputy Jerry Alley interviewed Lyle Day on November 8. He told Alley he had been dating Mischelle for about a month. "I told her I didn't want to go steady; I would only see her for sex." Then, while they were riding in his truck on November 4 or 5, he wasn't sure which, she told him she may be pregnant. He was upset. "Are you sure it's mine? I can help you pay for an abortion. I'm not ready to be a father." According to Day, Mischelle got very angry. "I won't have an abortion; it's against my religion." Then she jumped out of his truck and headed on foot in the direction of the T–N–T Tanning Salon. "I drove around the block and couldn't find her. I caught up with her at T–N–T." He insisted, "That's the last time I saw her."

Chantelle and Lelicia knew that Mischelle had told Day she was pregnant. Both girls knew Day became very upset when he heard the pregnancy news and wanted Mischelle to have an abortion. Of course, Day already had told an investigator about this incident himself and having a girlfriend claiming to be pregnant apparently was nothing out of the ordinary for him. According to his friend Darrell Best, "Two other girls made the same claim—and they were just jerking him around."

Day's father hired a lawyer for him. On November 13, Sheriff Ferrell and Deputy Schiwitz interviewed Day with the lawyer present at the lawyer's office in Sikeston. Ferrell gave Day a Miranda warning. Day readily admitted that Mischelle told him she might be pregnant by him and described the fight they had a few days before her death while riding in his truck. He claimed, "Mischelle was more serious about the relationship than I was."

Lyle Day was 18 years old at the time of Mischelle's murder. He lived with his parents just outside of Sikeston on Double H road. In September 1991, at the beginning of his senior year in high school, he drove into a telephone pole and was in a coma for a month. Some witnesses described him as "slow" and being "more moody" and "volatile" as a result of the accident. He also had a kind of limp, dragging his bad leg behind him. As a result of the accident, he didn't graduate from high school. At the time of the murder, he was unemployed and on Social Security disability, taking GED classes occasionally and hanging out at T-N-T Tanning in Sikeston.

Day met Mischelle at a bowling alley. "I left T-N-T to go there to get a soda. We talked, and I tried to sign her up for tanning sessions. I gave her a T-N-T card, and she started coming in pretty regularly." Day didn't officially work at T-N-T, but he liked to hang around and occasionally helped out by cleaning the beds and trying to attract tanning customers. The owner, Andy Stone, let him use the tanning beds in exchange for his help. Mischelle started hanging out at T-N-T. Day told investigators, "I think she had a crush on Andy." In any event, she became friends with Stone's wife, Tammy, and even started going to church with her. Some witnesses described Stone as Day's friend, but after Mischelle's murder, Kathy Fodge, who dated Day herself for three or four weeks, said she overheard Stone telling Day, "I don't want you coming around here anymore."

Mischelle first mentioned Day in her journal on September 15, four days after she wrote that she was going to leave Lamb alone. She went to a Shoney's motel party, and Day "walked me to my car and kissed me." The relationship developed slowly. On September 20, she saw Day on the Malco lot in Sikeston when she was out with friends and "he kissed me." The next day, she went "riding" in Sikeston and saw him again. She rode with him and "we kissed." This was the same evening she fought with Lamb at the bowling alley. On October 2, she went cruising in Sikeston with Lelicia, and they took Day along. As the journal indicates, they had lots of fun that night: "Ran through field. Lost my shoes. Came home. Lelicia spendin the night. She has the hick ups."

On October 4, Day told Mischelle that Leon Lamb was saying that she was "just a little Ho" and that he was using her for sex. Lamb denied it the next day when Mischelle confronted him, and she was briefly angry at Day and didn't see him for a few days. Then, on October 9, she went cruising with Lelicia after they found the trailer they were going to rent and, as she put it in the journal, Day "kidnapped" her.

According to her journal, Mischelle talked to Day on October 12 and 13 and after her accident, on October 14, and she got into an argument with him on October 15 because "he threw a cigarette at me." Then, on October 16, she took him to see the trailer she had just moved into, and for the first time, she wrote in her journal that they "loved." The following day, she rode around and got drunk with Vince Howard and Eric Shanks, and they dropped her off at her car, where she passed out behind the wheel with the motor running. Day happened to have been parked nearby. He saw her when he returned to his truck, woke her, and brought her home. She wrote, "I really like him."

The next entry, on October 22, mentions that she talked to Day and that he "hurt my feelings." Later, she went cruising with Chantelle and Lelicia. Then, she stopped by Lamb's home, and they "loved." She talked to Day on October 23 and had him spend the night at the trailer on October 24. They rode and talked on October 25, and she wrote in the journal, "Really like him." According to Mischelle's journal, she and Chantelle Crider looked for but couldn't find Day after the Halloween party they attended.

There is nothing in Mischelle's journal for the last week of her life that helps explain her murder. November 1 was a Sunday. Mischelle went to church, and afterward, Day came by her house. They left for a while to have a serious talk, and she told him she really liked him. They kissed, and he kissed her hand. On Monday, November 2, she told Day she loved him, and he shrugged it off. But Mischelle didn't seem too upset by his reaction. She wrote in her journal, "Found phone # left on my car—hum." Then, as she wrote in the journal on November 3, "Got Chantelle & we chopped down sign & fell in ditch. Lyle & 2 friends got in w/us & cruised. Stole cotton. I like Lyle a lot."

November 4 was a Wednesday. Mischelle went to class and had lunch at the Baptist Student Union, and Chantelle went with her to physical therapy. She went over to Lamb's, and they "loved." The description in her journal of her visit with Lamb seems matter of fact, with none of the desperate intensity that characterized her feelings about the relationship earlier in the year. Later, she talked to Day on the phone from home and wrote, "Still being a butt so I didn't tell him."

The journal ends on Thursday, November 5, and as to Day, Mischelle wrote only, "Saw Lyle." There is nothing about Day asking her if she was sure the baby was his or offering to help pay for an abortion. There is no doubt the incident happened; Day told investigators about it. So did Kevin Garrett. He and Joey Adams gave Mischelle a ride to T-N-T Tanning on November 5, when they saw her walking down the street, obviously upset about something, and without a coat. Garrett said

Mischelle told them, "I'm mad at my boyfriend. He tried to hit me and wanted me to have an abortion." Day showed up at the parking lot at T-N-T looking for Mischelle. He told Garrett, "I hate her, but I want to make sure she got back to her car."

★ ★ ★

Richard Ray Ring was 19 and worked at Little Caesars Pizza in Sikeston. He had one white and one African American parent. Investigators were casually interested in him because he was a friend of Mischelle's boyfriend, Lyle Day. Ring reportedly was with Day the night of the murder and could provide Day with an alibi.

On November 19, Sheriff Ferrell suddenly focused on Ray Ring as a suspect, not just as an alibi for Lyle Day. Sheriff Ferrell had him come to Benton the morning of November 19, and with Trooper Windham present, he interrogated Ring personally. He gave him a Miranda warning at the beginning of the interview and later asked for a blood sample.

Ring said he knew who Mischelle Lawless was but claimed he had never talked to her. "The last time I was in Benton was three or four months ago. I passed through on my way to John Worley's party in Commerce. Mischelle was there." He added, "The party got busted; John Worley's parties always get busted."

Ring knew who Mark Abbott was but didn't like him.

> Mark Abbott is a racist. I dated one of his ex-girlfriends a few times, Laura Bailey. She told me he said he would kill any black man who dated a white girl and any girlfriend of his who dated a black man. He has some real asshole friends. I wouldn't be surprised at all if they killed somebody. You might want to look at Kevin Williams and Gary Arnzen.

According to Ring, "They all smoke marijuana, get drunk, and then want to fight."

Ring said Lyle Day was a good friend. Day had told Ring about the possibility he had gotten Mischelle pregnant. "But he told me about three other girls who told him the same thing, and they are all still alive."

Ring was able to give Ferrell and Windham a fairly detailed alibi for the night of the murder. "I went to a party with Lyle Day and Gene Haynes at Gene Tidwell's house in Matthews. We had Gene's sister's car and had to return it by one. Then we went to Hardee's in Sikeston. I didn't want to go back to the party, so I started walking home after Lyle and Gene left. Two friends from Little Caesars stopped and gave me a ride home." Ring said his roommate, Larry Koout was home and awake when he arrived. He said, "I want Larry out of the apartment; he went crazy and tried to stab me two days ago."

Later, Theresa Haynes confirmed Ring's story. "I was worried they would wreck my car. It was 1:05 by the VCR clock when they finally arrived."

★ ★ ★

Vince Howard and Eric Shanks weren't on the original suspect list compiled by investigators on the fourth day of the investigation. When he was asked who, in his opinion, killed Mischelle, Leon Lamb told Deputy Schiwitz and Trooper Windham, "I think it was Shanks and Howard." Asked why he thought that, he said, "I don't know; there's something about them I just don't like." Both men were bodybuilders. Howard was the bigger of the two, but both were muscular enough that they were rumored to use steroids.

★ ★ ★

Vince Howard was a month shy of his 28th birthday at the time of the Lawless murder. He graduated from Sikeston High in 1984 and started college at SEMO, playing on the football team, but he injured his hip and quit school. After three operations, he was in good enough shape to be able to enlist in the Army Airborne, training at Fort Benning, Georgia. In 1987, after two and a half years in the Army, he re-injured his hip in a jump and received a medical discharge with a 30 percent disability. The same year, he married Astrid, a woman he met in Europe. In 1992, they had one child, a boy who was about a year old at the time, and were living in Sikeston. Howard was unemployed and collecting a monthly disability check. In a deposition the following year, he described himself as "a retired disabled veteran."

Deputy Schiwitz and Sergeant Overbey interviewed Howard on November 20. He told them he met Mischelle through his "buddy" Eric Shanks and had known her "about three or four months. She's just a friend. I wouldn't even describe her as a close friend. She liked to talk a lot, and I guess I was willing to listen." He claimed, "I never was with Mischelle alone, only with Eric and Lelicia. I only rode around with her one time before the night she was killed, and I never asked her out." Asked if he owned any handguns, he said, "I don't have one. I wouldn't have one in the house because of my son."

Howard said his wife was at work until 1:00 in the afternoon on November 7. After she got home, "I went out and spent the rest of the afternoon at a pool hall in Sunset. Eric called me at home early in the evening so we could plan our Saturday night out. I picked him up about 6:30." Asked what his wife thinks about him spending so much time away from home, he said, "Astrid doesn't like me hanging around with Eric; she thinks he's cheap because he lets me buy the beer." But that night Shanks broke tradition and bought a twelve-pack. Later, Howard bought another twelve-pack.

Howard said he and Shanks drove around Sunset and other parts of Sikeston for a while. "Then Mischelle and Lelicia flagged us down at the Sonic about 8:30." They parked Mischelle's car at the taekwondo studio and were about to get into Howard's Buick when "a boy in a red car whipped onto the lot." When Mischelle came back, she said it was her boyfriend and that he was drunk. "Lelicia called him Leon." After Leon left, Lelicia got in the back seat with Eric, and Mischelle sat in the front with Vince. "Eric bought a six-pack in bottles for the girls. They wanted to go to Sunset, but I told them they shouldn't go there."

Howard told the deputies:

> We rode around the Sonic, and then we went to Eric's house. We sat in my car outside until 10:00 or 10:30, and the girls used the bathroom. Then we rode around again for 10 or 15 minutes and came back to Eric's and parked behind his house. Lelicia and Eric kissed a bit. I just listened to the radio and to Mischelle talk. She told me she smoked two doobees in Cape with some guy on Friday night. But mostly we talked about her problems with her boyfriends, that Leon fella we saw earlier on the parking lot and Lyle Day. She told me that "Lyle is only screwing me because he wants to; he doesn't really like me."

Howard said Shanks had to go to work early in the morning at Parker Farms, so they took the girls back to Mischelle's car around 11:00 or 11:30. Then, he took Shanks home and went home himself. His wife was in bed with their son. "I told her to scoot over, and I got in. I didn't leave the house again that night. I was asleep when Deputy Alley came to my house in the morning."

Asked if it bothered his wife that he rode around with girls, he said, "She didn't know about it until Deputy Alley showed up Sunday morning. She got mad and told me to stay away from Eric." Howard denied rumors he cleaned out his car Sunday morning. "I got my son's car seat and jacket out of the trunk. I put them there so we would have room for anyone we picked up." Asked who he thought might have killed Mischelle, he told Schiwitz and Overbey, "I heard a black guy named Don Atkinson was with her. I also heard about another black guy named Curtis was with Lyle that night. I heard Curtis killed Mischelle for Lyle."

★ ★ ★

Charles Eric Shanks was 24 in November 1992. Deputy Schiwitz and Trooper Windham interviewed Shanks on November 19. He attended Sikeston High and was a cadet in the Sikeston police with Theresa Haynes. At one time, he worked with Leon Lamb at Stan's Grocery. He worked with Mischelle at the Sikeston Shoney's for a few months in 1992 but quit the Shoney's job in August and went to work at Parker Farms. He had a DWI conviction and charges for distributing liquor to a minor. He didn't drive and did not have a car so he depended on others like Vince Howard for transportation. He told the two investigators, "I guess I knew Vince for seven or eight years. We met playing basketball; one of my friends introduced us. Now we lift weights together, and sometimes we cruise around Sikeston looking for girls." Shanks deflected the suggestion Howard might have shot Mischelle after he took Shanks home. "He carries a baseball bat for protection, but as far as I know, he doesn't have a gun."

Schiwitz and Windham were at least considering the possibility that Shanks could have killed Mischelle. Scott Stone told Sergeant Overbey he was at a party in the early summer of 1992 when Shanks pulled a gun and pointed it at Lyle Day. "I think it was a .38. I took it away from him and removed the bullets." Schiwitz and Windham asked Shanks what guns he had. "I have a 12-gauge Mossberg pump action shotgun and a .22 rifle, and my father owns a .357. But we only use them for target shooting and hunting."

Shanks told the two investigators he had known Mischelle for a couple of years. He described her as "wild" and said she "liked to talk." He said, "We went out a few times. I think that made her boyfriend mad. Mischelle and Lelicia took me to their trailer once, that's all." In a deposition the following year, he denied that he ever had sex with Mischelle.

Shanks told pretty much the same story as Howard about the time they spent with Mischelle and Lelicia the night of the murder. They saw the two girls driving in Mischelle's maroon car around 8:00. The girls flagged them down, and they parked the two cars near the taekwondo studio. "Mischelle's boyfriend zoomed onto the parking lot as the girls were about to get in Vince's car, and he stopped pretty far away. When Mischelle came back, she said she told him he could come along with us, but he didn't want to. He almost hit another car when he left." Shanks thought Lamb looked "disappointed" and "angry" but said Mischelle told him, "He's just drunk."

Shanks said the four of them rode around in Howard's car for two or three hours. Shanks claimed, "Me and Vince were drinking, but the girls weren't." Shanks said, "We stopped at my house twice—the first time was about 10:00 or 10:15. Mischelle talked to Vince about her problems with her boyfriends. We left my house the second time and dropped the girls off at Mischelle's car around 11. Vince took me home about 11:30."

5

THE TRAIL RUNS COLD

In the months immediately following Mischelle's murder, Sheriff Ferrell and the investigators from the sheriff's office and the highway patrol tried what they could to catch the killer. They canvassed the area around the interstate exit, talking to people who lived in the houses strung out along Highway 77 and the residents of a nearby trailer court. Early Sunday morning, a week after the murder, 22 officers from the sheriff's office and the highway patrol stopped 200 vehicles at roadblocks on Interstate 55 and State Highway 77. About 1 in 10 of the motorists had traveled the same route at the same time the week before, but no one saw anything that helped solve the mystery of Mischelle's murder.

By the end of the first month of the investigation, Sheriff Ferrell was beginning to get frustrated with the lack of results. Under the headline "Month-Old Murder Investigation Stalls," he was quoted in the *Southeast Missourian*, "We've talked to everybody two or three times. We had some suspects that were stronger than others, but we've never had a serious motive. It's starting to look as if it was a random, interstate, no-reason, no-motive killing."

Ferrell started to contact law enforcement in neighboring Missouri counties and beyond, searching for similarities between Mischelle's murder and other murders around Missouri and elsewhere.

★ ★ ★

The day after the murder, Marvin Lawless hung red silk flowers around the stop sign next to the spot where his daughter had died. Mischelle's grandparents erected a cross nearby. As the weeks passed, the family waited patiently for news that her killer had been caught but heard nothing. There was an outpouring of support for the Lawless family at first. Friends sent cards and letters and telephoned. They established a reward fund, hoping to get information about the killer, but everyone fell back into daily routines as the months passed. Marvin Lawless eventually returned to his business of buying and selling cars, and Esther Lawless went back to her job at a dental office. But as Marvin Lawless told the *Southeast Missourian*, "I just can't get back to life until this is done."

The Christmas season of 1992 was an unhappy one for the Lawless family. Mischelle's father told the *Southeast Missourian* that the family hung their stockings as always and distributed the gifts they had bought before the murder, but Mischelle's death overshadowed everything. On December 30, he said, "We want to know just why and then who. And if I knew those two things, I am satisfied I wouldn't feel any less pain, but at least I would know the situation behind the crime. I sit here daily and wonder who could it have been and what motive they could have had to do something like this. What threat could she have posed to anyone?"

At first, he had expected a quick arrest, but after nearly two months of waiting, he was reconciled to the possibility that it would be a long time before the crime was solved. "I am willing to look at the long haul. I am the type of person that doesn't just quit. I don't care if it takes 10 years; I am going to hope that this person is brought to justice."

The investigation slowed as the months dragged by. There were hundreds of tips in the first weeks, but most of the information was useless speculation. One radio station even reported erroneously that a suspect was in custody and had confessed. But before long, the flood of information slowed to a trickle.

In an interview in the *Southeast Missourian*, Sheriff Ferrell said he still worked on the case for some time every day. Yet with few new leads to investigate, the number of officers assigned to the case had shrunk from 10 to 3, including Don Windham. Sheriff Ferrell explained the reduction in the effort in a December 31 *Southeast Missourian* article. Although they continue to follow leads, "We just don't have anything new."

Ferrell didn't know that the boy he would soon charge with the murder was back in town, visiting his mother after Christmas and reconnecting with acquaintances he had made the previous summer, nor did he know that those acquaintances would end up together in the Cape Girardeau County Jail within a month and offer Ferrell what he desperately needed.

★ ★ ★

As 1992 rolled over into 1993 without an arrest for Mischelle's murder, frustrated investigators started going back over ground they had covered before, looking for something they might have missed. On January 6, Deputy Schiwitz and Trooper Windham re-interviewed Lelicia O'Dell. Windham asked her, "Did Mischelle break up with anybody or did she reject anybody who asked her out or was there anybody she humiliated in some way?" Lelicia mentioned Todd Mayberry. She described an incident at a keg party at what she referred to as John Worley's trailer near Commerce on Halloween night, 1992. "Mischelle was drunk and kissing Todd, but when she sobered up, she told him to get lost. He went crazy. He called her a bitch and a slut and told her he would beat up every boyfriend she had." Mayberry knew Mischelle slightly. He was 22 and lived in Commerce, but he grew up in the Benton area and went to the same schools as Mischelle, two years ahead of her. This was the same party and the same Todd Mayberry that Mischelle mentioned in her journal, without writing anything about Mayberry calling her a bitch and a slut.

Schiwitz and Windham interviewed Mayberry on February 1. He was working at O.P.X. Trucking near Benton as a security guard. He said he knew who Mischelle was; they went to school together. "I didn't have anything to do with her until that Halloween party, and that was the last time I saw her. We were drinking together and kissing, and she suddenly got up and said she had to go home. I didn't shout at her."

Mayberry insisted he had nothing to do with Mischelle's death. "I didn't even try to contact her after the Halloween party. I was at a party at Jason Grogan's the night she was murdered. I don't have a clue what happened to her." At the end of the interview, he agreed to give a blood sample. Although he was type B, the FBI's partial DNA profile excluded him.

★ ★ ★

None of the individuals considered in nearly three months of investigation was a suspect Sheriff Ferrell felt he could charge with the murder. Except perhaps for Mark Abbott, every suspect had something to indicate he wasn't the killer—exclusion by forensic evidence, lack of access to the type of weapon used, or some sort of alibi.

Perhaps the most glaring problem for the investigation was the lack of a motive. There was the notion of jealousy or a lovers' quarrel with boyfriends, Lamb or Day, or of a spurned would-be lover like Mayberry. Ray Ring said Mark Abbott had said he would beat up any girlfriend who went out with a black man. But there was no indication at the time that Abbott knew Mischelle or had ever seen her with Howard.

Then, there were the contradictory drug theories—that Mischelle was involved in drug dealing or that she had angered drug dealers by interfering in their operations. Other than the story about smoking "doobees" with Jeremy Turner the night before her death, there was nothing indicating Mischelle had any involvement in drugs.

It was starting to look like the killer may have been someone outside the circle of Mischelle's friends and acquaintances, with no obvious connection to Mischelle or her death. It may even have been someone passing through the county, serendipitously meeting her, and moving on without leaving a trace.

Then, Sheriff Ferrell got what he was looking for. Prisoners in the Cape Girardeau County Jail started coming forward with stories about a boy they knew from Kankakee, Illinois, they said had confessed to the killing. Pretty soon, the investigation was back on track and moving forward rapidly.

PART II

THE ARREST AND PROSECUTION OF JOSHUA KEZER

"Our 'beyond a reasonable doubt' burden of proof in criminal cases is intended to protect the innocent, but we know it is not foolproof. . . . No matter how careful courts are, the possibility of perjured testimony . . . and human error remain all too real."

—Justice Thurgood Marshall, US Supreme Court, *Furman v. Georgia*, 408 U.S. 238, 366–367 (1972)

6

JOSH KEZER

After several weeks of a false spring, the latter part of February 1993 turned unusually cold in the area of Southeast Missouri around Cape Girardeau. At the time, four young men who knew each other were being held in the Cape Girardeau County Jail—Shawn Mangus, Chuck Weissinger, Kelly Church, and Steve Grah. Mangus whispered to Weissinger in the pod, "Psst. Come here. I've got an idea." Weissinger looked at him and said, "What?" a little too loudly. Mangus responded with an urgent tone but under his breath, "Quiet! I don't want anybody else to hear this." Weissinger whispered this time, "Hear what?" Mangus launched into his proposal. "You hear about the Benton girl? The one that got murdered down off the interstate?" Weissinger said, "No. Can't say I did." Mangus continued, "Well I heard they've got no leads. We're facing felonies and looking at long sentences." Mangus paused and looked cautiously at Weissinger. "Why don't we say Josh Kezer told us he did it? Trade that for a deal." Mangus could see the scowl on Weissinger's face. "Don't worry. He didn't do it. He was up in Kankakee at the time. He'll be able to prove it, and they'll let him go. By then we'll have our deals."

★ ★ ★

Joshua Charles Kezer was a handsome kid, 17 years old at the time of Mischelle's murder. But looking back years later at a picture of himself with his mother in late 1992, he was amused by the image of hair high on top of his head and hanging down a little in back, a hairstyle no doubt fashionable at the time, at least around Kankakee and Cape Counties. He was skinny but not extraordinarily so and strong for someone with his build. He had a wry smile when he was smiling, which he did easily when he had reason to be happy. But much of the time he had little to be happy about.

Josh was born at Riverside Hospital in Kankakee, Illinois, on February 16, 1975. His father, Charles Edward Kezer, was born in 1950 to parents with German and Austrian roots. Charles Kezer was a Vietnam combat veteran from a blue-collar background who grew up in the Kankakee area, which includes the neighboring cities of Bradley and Bourbonnais.

> My dad dropped out of high school to help support his family and ended up getting drafted into the Army and sent to Vietnam. He smoked marijuana pretty regularly and he experimented with psychedelics and harder drugs. Nothing like heroin, cocaine, or crack, but drugs common to his era. From what I understand, drug use was pretty common in the '70s and in 'Nam. That was where he got the nickname "Crazy Charlie." I don't know what he did to get that nickname. He never spoke to me about Vietnam. He really didn't want to talk about it. I wish he had, but I understood. Something bad happened to him there.

Later in life, when a conversation Josh had with his father strayed into that topic, the elder Kezer, his kidneys failing, began to cry. To his son's knowledge, whatever horrors he had seen went with him to the grave. "One good thing that came of his time in the Army was his training as a mechanic. That became his life's work." At the time of his son's arrest, Charles Kezer repaired, detailed, and sold used cars from the yard in front of his house.

Josh's mother, Bessie Joan James, was born in 1955 in Hollywood, California, during a brief period her parents, Hadley and Jane James, spent there. Josh's maternal grandparents were originally from Southeast Missouri. Hadley was the son of a blacksmith, and as Josh describes her, "Jane was a church girl who picked cotton." After California, the family moved to Kankakee. Hadley worked as a mechanic at a nuclear power plant, and Jane worked at several factories in the area. Bessie Joan, who went by Joan or Joni, spent her youth in Kankakee. She was still a teenager when she met Charlie Kezer, who was five years older, wild and charming, and had seen something of the world.

The nickname "Crazy Charlie" followed the elder Kezer when he got out of the Army. Somehow, he never went to prison, but he was well known to local police departments. In one story that Josh was able to confirm with his mother and grandmother:

> My father was chased around the city by Kankakee police. The City of Kankakee had just purchased new police cars, and the police used them in the chase. I don't know what started it, but during the chase, one

by one, each of the new police cars got damaged. My father ended up trapped on a bridge over the Kankakee River with dented police cars parked at both ends. He didn't surrender. He smiled, saluted the cops, dove into the river, and swam miles downriver to a spot near where my mother was living with her parents.

The police thought they knew who had saluted them.

They knew my father was dating my mother, so they went to my grandparents' house to get him. My Gramma always had a soft spot for my father. For all his faults, she believed he had a good heart. When he knocked on the door, soaked from the swim, she said, "Hello, Charlie" and let him in. She gave him some dry clothes, told him to hide, and told the police she hadn't seen him when they showed up. Later she drove him home, crouched down in the back of her car. I was surprised to hear that because she was such a religious woman.

When the police came to his house, he was watching a Yogi Bear cartoon and smoking a joint (which he continued smoking when they forced open the door), and he claimed he had been home all day. Despite their suspicions, the police couldn't prove it was Charlie Kezer who damaged their new police cars because he wasn't driving his own car that day. "Without a dented car linked to my father, the police couldn't prove who was driving the car. They couldn't arrest him, and he didn't spend a night in jail." Josh gets a glint in his eye every time he tells that story. Charlie Kezer was a character, and like his grandmother, Josh loved that about him.

Both of Josh's parents struggled with drugs and alcohol abuse.

My father was an alcoholic and drug addict. He was really rough, to put it politely. He had a rough childhood. He brought back demons from Vietnam. He had PTSD, and he never quite adjusted. He only overcame his alcoholism late in life. When drunk, my father was Hyde. When sober, he was Jekyll. My father was physically abusive; my mother was emotionally abusive. Both my parents were what could be called difficult people. They took no shit from anyone and were proud of it. They reminded me of a line from an Eminem song, "Maybe that's what happens when a tornado meets a volcano."

Perhaps not surprisingly, given the strength of their personalities, the marriage wasn't a happy one. They were divorced before Josh was old enough to have any memory of living as a family. Josh wasn't close to his father's family. "I got really close with my mom's family, especially my three male cousins. Jason and James Smith were sons of my Aunt Kathy. Michael 'Bunk' Whisker was the son of my Aunt Debby."

When Josh was in fifth grade, in the middle of the school year, his mother moved him to Southeast Missouri, to the little village of Arbor, just outside of Delta in Cape Girardeau County. As Josh describes Arbor:

> It wasn't anything like Kankakee, which I thought of as a kind of Little Chicago. My mother was taking me home to my roots, but it didn't feel like home. I'm sure there was more to it, but it felt like the entire town consisted of my great grandfather's house, a couple houses next to his, his blacksmith shop, and a few other homes up in the hills. Is that a town, or even a village? It didn't feel like home. My mother and I took care of her elderly grandfather. We lived in his house. Years later, after he passed away and I was incarcerated, my grandparents lived there.

Josh finished fifth grade in Delta, a few miles down the road from Arbor. "We were related to too many people in Delta. Let's just say dating girls became stressful. A growing boy can only be told so many times, 'No son, she's your cousin.'"

After fifth grade, Josh's mother moved them to Chaffee, which was just under 10 miles away, across the county line in Scott County. Josh attended sixth grade in a different school district, but the change didn't help much with Josh's sense that he didn't belong. "I thought of myself as a kid from a relatively big city in the North. Then I was all of a sudden in a tiny town in the South. And I flunked sixth grade. Up to that year, I got all As and Bs." Josh's mother didn't believe Josh really flunked. She became irate because she thought the school didn't want them there.

Josh and his mother moved again, this time to Cape Girardeau. Josh considered Cape Girardeau to be more like Kankakee. A little bigger. A little less backwoods. He repeated sixth grade at Hawthorne School in the Cape Girardeau District. He did well and advanced to seventh grade with ease. He also excelled at athletics, setting a record posted in the school gym for the 600-yard dash that lasted for at least 20 years. "One of my mother's friends told her my name was still there while I was in prison. My mother told me it was the first time anyone had said anything good about me in years."

From time to time, Josh had what passed for a girlfriend at that age. One of them was a girl named Stacy Reed. "I did well in seventh and eighth grade. I joined the track team, and I was very fast. To this day, I've never lost a one-on-one foot race. I started daydreaming about being in the Olympics. I had friends and started to feel like I belonged." But that didn't last long. "Our homelife was unstable. We moved again to Jackson after eighth grade." Jackson is a town on the western outskirts of Cape Girardeau near Interstate 55, which has its own school district. "I joined the wrestling team, and I was really good at it. I had friends again."

Early in 1991, in the middle of ninth grade, Joni Kezer's substance abuse caught up with them. She had to go into a rehab program for 30 days and found Josh a temporary home, which happened to be outside the Jackson school district. "I thought it was a cousin who took me in, but it was just one of my mom's friends from work."

Days before Josh's 16th birthday, the principal called him out of class. "He found out I wasn't living inside the Jackson district boundaries. My living arrangement was supposed to be temporary, but for some reason the principal didn't care." In addition, there was a teacher who reported him being late. "When we got to his office, he gave me a choice. 'Quit or I'll kick you out.' I said, and I'll never forget this, 'I'm not going to quit. I'm not going to find myself sleeping under a bridge a year from now.' So he kicked me out but wrote down that I quit. I was getting As and Bs and Cs, and he kicked me out."

Josh moved back in with his mother when she got out of rehab. He got into some minor trouble with juvenile authorities in the next couple of months. "I punched a kid in the mouth for calling me a son of a bitch. I think I was acting out. I wanted to be in school and, maybe subconsciously, blamed my mother for the fact I wasn't in school. But I couldn't tolerate someone calling my mother a bitch. That's how I took it."

Josh's probation officer consulted with his mother and suggested he go to Kankakee to live with his father. In the summer of 1991, Joni Kezer called Charlie Kezer.

> "Come get your son. He needs his father." My father insisted I get back in school, but I didn't want to do that. I was already a year behind because of repeating sixth grade, and I lost another half year when I was kicked out of ninth grade in Jackson. I aged out of junior high sports, which was my main interest in school at the time. I didn't want to be the new kid again. And I didn't want to be going to school with much younger kids anyway.

Josh's father said he had to get a job if he wasn't going to be in school. Josh knocked on doors and put in applications around Kankakee, but no one would hire him. Jason Smith and Michael Whisker weren't much older than James and Josh, but they were in prison. So Josh hung out with his other cousin, James Smith. They spent every day together and became best friends. James was in a local speed metal band, and Josh partied wherever the band partied. "James and I drank, smoked pot, and jammed. Every day. All day." According to Charlie Kezer, they were "young, dumb, and full of cum." Josh told me, "I imagine I was a lot like my father when he was that age."

In early February 1992, just before his 17th birthday, Josh moved back to Cape Girardeau. He wanted to be close to his mother again. Joni Kezer seemed to have her life in order. She attended Alcoholics Anonymous.

> Still, I couldn't live with my mother. I didn't like her live-in boyfriend, and he didn't like me. He was violent, and he mistreated her. He knew I would hurt him if I saw him hurt her. My mother arranged for me to stay with some friends of hers, but after a few weeks, the friends decided I was a bad influence on their younger child and kicked me out. The truth is they were overwhelmed with a teenage boy they weren't prepared to have live with them.

Then, Josh rented a basement apartment from a family he had come to know. One day Josh discovered they broke into his apartment and went through a chest his mother had gotten him. Josh confronted them, and they argued. Josh left the house and called his mother. By the time Josh and his mother returned, the police were there. The family told the police everything in the house belonged to them and Josh was no longer welcome. "For the next several months, I drifted from place to place around Cape Girardeau and from Cape to Kankakee and back. I was homeless. A little over a year after I told the principal in Jackson that I'm not going to find myself living under a bridge a year from now, I found myself doing just that." During this time, Josh got to know three of the young men who would get him arrested and charged with murder.

Josh wasn't in school, and he had no regular employment. He had a few part-time jobs that he lost for various reasons. "I was fired from McDonald's because I was working for Hardee's at the same time and because of a leather jacket. The jacket was stolen before I worked at McDonald's. I found it in the basement locker room and stole it back. It was the same brand and size, and I could identify it by some repairs on the inside my mother had done." Another employee claimed it was his jacket and complained to the manager. "When the manager told me to give the jacket back, I explained that it was mine, that it had been stolen, and I wasn't giving it back."

A few days later, Josh got fired from Hardee's. He was hanging on the back of a truck with Shawn Mangus and Kelly Church. They called it gravel surfing. When the driver saw Mangus and Church in his side mirrors, he accelerated, and they jumped off. Josh was in the middle and hung on when the truck sped up. "I held on and hung 10 for as long as I could, but eventually ate gravel. I limped into work later that day. The manager told me to go to the emergency room when I told him I slipped on grease and twisted my knee, but he fired me anyway because he didn't believe my explanation."

Josh isn't proud of what he did to lose another job. He was working for SEMO security selling tickets to a concert parking lot. "I thought I could make some extra money if I kept a small amount of the proceeds. I thought they wouldn't notice, but they did notice and fired me. I was a hustler, but my hustle wasn't working." Josh wasn't prosecuted, possibly because SEMO security wasn't sure it could prove he was the one who kept the money.

During this period, Josh's life was out of control. He dyed his hair black and spent most of his time hanging out along Broadway, at the Billiards Center, around Capaha Park, and near SEMO.

> I drank alcohol and experimented with drugs. I stayed with boys and girls I met, sleeping on couches or in their basements. Sometimes, their parents knew I was in the house, and sometimes, they didn't. Sometimes, I slept in abandoned houses, at laundromats in apartment complexes, or in friends' cars. I slept in hospital waiting rooms. At times, I slept outside, in the park or under the bridge on the river. Most of the time I didn't sleep much at all.

Despite this vagrant lifestyle, Josh had no trouble with the law. There was nothing on him in Scott County records. In Cape Girardeau County, he appeared several times in police reports as a victim or a witness to an incident, but that was all. As Josh described it, "I was wild, but I wasn't unruly."

In one such report, in April 1992, he was with Kelly Church at Wink's convenience store when Brian O'Kelly, a boy Josh and Kelly knew, came in and invited the two of them to fight. "The manager told him to leave the store, but he just stood there and cursed at her. He finally went outside, but he stayed on the parking lot yelling at us inside. When the manager told him to leave the parking lot, he yelled, 'Fuck you bitch; suck my dick.'"

She had had enough and called the police. O'Kelly was gone by the time the officers arrived, but they interviewed the manager, Church, and Josh. They caught up with O'Kelly at Cape Central High School, where he was a student, and issued a municipal summons for peace disturbance and trespassing.

Josh's mother seemed to be getting her life together. She graduated in May from SEMO with a major in psychology and a minor in criminal justice, with a golden sash for honors. Josh told me, "I attended her graduation, and I was proud of her."

★ ★ ★

Josh spent most of his time with Kelly Church. At the end of May, they met two girls from Benton, Amanda Drury and Christy Naile. The girls were cruising Broadway and picked them up. Josh happened to get in the back seat next to Amanda. "I thought Amanda was pretty. Soon, the four of us were getting together regularly. I didn't have a car and neither did Kelly. I didn't even have a driver's license. Christy had a little white car, and she drove us around. Occasionally, she would let me or Kelly take the wheel."

Once Roy Moore, the Benton officer, saw him sitting alone at a gas station before dawn. "I guess he wanted to find out who I was and what I was up to. I told him I was waiting for my girlfriend to wake up so I could go see her. He was nice about it and didn't judge me. He gave me a ride in his patrol car. He saw I was cold and gave me a windbreaker he had in the back."

The romance between Josh and Amanda got fairly serious as those things go with 16- and 17-year-olds. Amanda's mother lived in Sikeston, but Amanda stayed in Benton much of that summer with her grandparents, Glenn and Margie Proctor. "The Proctors didn't like me. They thought I was dirty, which I probably was. I was moving from place to place and living outside a lot." Josh wasn't welcome in the Proctors' house, and they told Amanda so. Josh called Amanda collect, and Margie Proctor refused to accept the charges. Amanda secretly ran up big bills talking to him on the telephone.

Despite the obstacles of Amanda's grandparents, Josh managed to see Amanda regularly. A typical date involved Amanda and Christy driving up to Cape Girardeau to find Josh and Church. "We would cruise Broadway, go somewhere, and cruise some more. Then, we would drive up to Cape Rock Park overlooking the river, and we would have sex in Christy's car or somewhere alone."

As the summer progressed, Amanda began to rethink their relationship. "In the beginning, I think she was attracted by my image as a rebel. I was living on the streets while most of the other 17-year-old boys she knew were living at home with their parents. Eventually, I think she started to be embarrassed by me. I had no money and no car. I wasn't as independent as I liked to pretend." Their last date was on August 2, to the REO Speedwagon concert at the Benton Raceway. During the concert, they argued. "I thought I was in love, and I got very possessive. I was angry that Amanda was talking to other boys." That was the last straw, and Amanda left without him. "I was devastated by the rejection and had a hard time letting go."

Josh moved back to Kankakee in September and settled in again with his father. It wasn't long before Josh drifted into a gang, the Latin Kings. His slightly older cousins, Michael Whisker and James' brother Jason, had already been members for years. For Josh, being in a gang was the equivalent of friends hanging with friends in the neighborhood. "Where I lived in Kankakee, just about everybody was in a gang."

The Latin Kings started in Chicago in the 1960s and spread to other cities around the country, a predominantly Hispanic gang with a fair-sized mix of other ethnic groups. Members dealt in drugs, robbery, extortion, just about every crime imaginable, and they had and have a reputation for extreme violence, a reputation that by all accounts is well deserved. The gang had core members and others who were on the fringes in a kind of probationary status. "I was one of those on the fringes. I got the gang's crown tattoo on my back, but my cousins protected me from the most violent parts of gang life. I didn't have a violent initiation, and I wasn't involved in serious crimes." Josh took part in fights with other teenagers over turf and slights and insults, but he didn't do anything that got him in excessive trouble with the police. "Gang membership gave me a sense of belonging and a self-confidence I never had before. I was somebody to be feared, not just for myself, but also for the gang that would stand with me in a fight. I was good with my hands, and I liked to fight, so why not fight with the Kings?"

Charlie Kezer knew his son was in a gang and didn't like it, but he overlooked a lot. They began arguing, and occasionally his father disciplined him physically, which according to Josh, "Wasn't out of the ordinary for that part of Kankakee." Then one night, Josh was on the phone with a girl and wanted a little privacy. He took the phone into his bedroom and closed the door on the phone cord, something his father had told him repeatedly he didn't want him to do.

> My father snapped. He pushed open the door and yelled, "Keep the fucking cord out of the door!" I yelled back, "It's my phone! Fuck you!" My father punched me in the mouth. We wrestled around the room, smashing into the walls. At one point, my father had me bent

over with my right arm pinned behind me, yelling through tears, "Please stop; I'm sorry." But I didn't stop. Instead, I reached with my left hand and grabbed a large porcelain sculpture that I shattered on his knee. At that point, my father let me go. Looking back on it, I was wrong. He was doing the best he could, and I didn't make it easy on him. I still feel bad about that.

His father's girlfriend already had called the police. When they arrived, his father wanted him arrested. "Fortunately, they didn't arrest me. I think they were concerned about me. Instead, they asked me if there was some place they could take me, and I moved in with my cousin James and his mother, my Aunt Kathy."

Josh did get arrested in the nearby town of Bourbonnais. He was out drinking with friends. They were at an apartment complex, and Josh got into an argument with a girl and her friends.

The girl and the boys she was with were bullying and threatening my friend, and I intervened. The girl spit in my face. There was some shouting and shoving, and the girl was doing most of it. Somebody called the police, and the girl and her friends claimed I shoved her. I told the cops all I did was push the girl away when she attacked me, but they didn't believe me because I was in a gang. They arrested me on a juvenile charge of assault and took a mug shot, but I was released before the end of the day.

Josh got a job at Wendy's and at a local restaurant as a prep chef. He moved into an apartment he shared with friends. "Around that time, I realized that I was tired of being a rebel. I wanted a more normal life. I scaled back my involvement in the Kings. I was looking for a way out." Sometime in November 1992, Josh invited an Army recruiter to his apartment. "Back then, I wanted to be a Navy Seal and thought you could take any route in the military to get to the Seals. I was going to choose the Army out of respect for my father's service in Vietnam. After everything I'd been through at a young age, I believed I had the physical ability and mental determination required." The recruiter sat on the floor in Josh's apartment with Josh and some of his Latin Kings friends. "We were all interested in leaving the gang, but the recruiter said we weren't what the Army wanted. We were crushed." The recruiter told Josh it was because he lacked education. Josh's father was skeptical of that explanation and suspected it was because Josh and his friends were in a gang. His father hadn't finished high school, but the Army wanted him for Vietnam. But

Charlie Kezer was proud of his son for trying and told him so. Josh and his father were talking again. Charlie even gave Josh a couch for his apartment.

Josh's mother visited Kankakee for Christmas that year. "I tried to cook a roast for her and her boyfriend and burned it to a blackened crisp. We laughed it off and had a great time together. We spent Christmas Day together in Kankakee at my mother's parents' house. We took photos of everybody. It was like we were a family again."

Josh enjoyed spending the Christmas holidays with his mother so much that he decided to surprise her by coming down to Cape Girardeau after Christmas. Josh paid Murray Meents to take him. "My mother was glad to see me, but I didn't stay with her for long." Joni Kezer's abusive boyfriend didn't want him around. Josh was out on the streets in Cape Girardeau again, looking for old friends and making new acquaintances, but now he was a Latin King. "Murray left me in Cape without explanation. Looking back now, I guess it was because he left the scene of an accident and had to get out of town."

Josh ran into Kelly Church on the street, and Kelly took him to a party at a house on Morgan Oak Street. The house was rented by Josh's old girlfriend from grade school, Stacy Reed. "That's where I got reacquainted with Shawn Mangus and Chuck Weissinger."

Later in January, someone called the Cape Girardeau police to report a young man lurking around a house with a gun, which he was pointing at another young man like he was going to shoot. It was Josh. He was "playing guns" with "Goose" Pengiel and another friend, armed with a realistic looking BB gun. As the patrol car approached, Josh ran into Pengiel's house. "I was frightened and just reacted without thinking." When the officer called to Josh to come out, he showed him the BB gun. Exasperated, the officer confiscated the gun but didn't charge Josh.

The case involving Josh's arrest for the apartment complex incident kept getting continued, and it was on the docket again. Josh's mother drove him up to Kankakee for the hearing, but the complainant asked for another continuance. Josh's mother asked the judge about a deal in which Josh would plead guilty and agree to go to Teen Challenge and leave the Latin Kings. The judge liked the deal and agreed.

Teen Challenge was a Christian residential program for troubled teenagers in Cape Girardeau with a long-term facility near St. Louis. New entrants are processed in Cape and bused to St. Louis for a stay that lasts 12 months. "When my mother dropped me off at Teen Challenge, I had every intention of staying. She believed Teen Challenge could help me, and I agreed. I needed to do something to reset my life." But Josh wasn't prepared for what followed. "It turned out that the husband or brother of the teacher who got me kicked out of school in Jackson was assigned to walk me through the facility and introduce me to all that Teen Challenge had to offer. My trauma of getting kicked out of school was triggered. We didn't get along, and I left the day after I was admitted."

Josh went to where his mother was living, but his mother couldn't let him stay. He tried to explain to her why he had left, but she was exhausted and afraid of her boyfriend. She expected him home any minute and needed Josh to leave. "Her boyfriend had a nice rifle sitting on the floor against a wall. It seemed like an aggressive move for an abusive boyfriend. I was angry that my mother was picking her boyfriend over me. I took the gun and broke it into pieces, and my mother, in tears, threw me out." Joni didn't know what would become of Josh. She knew her boyfriend would beat her, and she was afraid. "Looking back at that, I'm ashamed of my behavior. My mother needed more from me. I needed more from her. We just didn't know how to give each other what we needed at that time."

A few days later, Josh called his father and asked if he could come home to Kankakee, but his father said no. Instead, he took him to the Teen Challenge facility near St. Louis. Teen Challenge took him back, but Josh was "homesick" and left again. Someone drove him to the Greyhound bus station, and he bought a ticket to Kankakee. His father told him he could stay if he agreed to get a job and stopped hanging around with the Latin Kings. He got a job at K-Mart and "ramped down" his activity in the Latin Kings. Things were coming together for Josh. "It took us a while, maybe because we were a lot alike, but my dad and I were in a good place. And my life was in a good place. I was working and had planned to get my GED." It was early February 1993, and Josh was home in time to celebrate his 18th birthday at his father's house.

7

WITH FRIENDS LIKE THESE

Shawn Eric Mangus was 17. He and Kelly Church had been charged together in connection with a drug deal gone bad. Mangus sold a man some LSD at the man's apartment. The man took too much and had a psychotic episode. Mangus pulled a gun, forced the man to write him a check to pay for the drugs, and tied him while he tried to figure out what to do next. The man got loose somehow. He took the gun away from Mangus during a fight that spilled into the parking lot. When the Cape Girardeau police arrived, they arrested Mangus and charged him with first-degree robbery and armed criminal action. Church's role in the drug deal and ensuing events was unclear, but he was with Mangus and was charged as well.

On February 27, a deputy at the Cape Girardeau County Jail notified Trooper Windham that Mangus wanted to talk to someone investigating the Lawless murder. Windham and Deputy Schiwitz interviewed Mangus on March 1. He told them, "I know a guy named Josh Kezer. He told me he killed the Lawless girl."

Josh had been living in Southeast Missouri when Mangus first met him late in 1991. Mangus and Josh rented an apartment with Sebastian Cole on Broadway in Cape Girardeau for a few months in early 1992, before Mangus went to jail in Poplar Bluff. He didn't see Josh again until January 1993. According to Mangus, that was when Josh confessed to the Lawless murder, at an apartment on Morgan Oak Street in Cape Girardeau rented by Stacy Reed.

On March 10, Sheriff Ferrell and Trooper Windham interviewed Mangus, and Mangus put the interview down in writing. About Josh's confession, Mangus wrote:

> He asked if he could trust us about something that was bothering him, if he told us. He asked me if I knew anything about a girl getting killed

at the Benton exit. I told him I didn't know anything about it. He said, "somebody had me kill her, or shoot her, or hurt her," but I do remember him saying he shot her. He appeared to be crying, but the room was dark and I couldn't tell. Mangus said he asked Josh if he was serious, and Josh said he was. Asked if Josh was bragging about the murder, Mangus said, "He was more sorry than bragging."

Windham told Mangus he would talk to Morley Swingle, the Cape Girardeau County prosecutor, and say that Mangus was assisting in his investigation. On April 26, Mangus pled guilty to a reduced charge of stealing, a class C felony, and received a sentence of one year, with credit for time served. He could have gotten much more. The minimum sentence for first-degree robbery, a class A felony, was 10 years.

★ ★ ★

Windham and Schiwitz interviewed Charles Paul Weissinger at the Cape Girardeau County Sheriff's Office on March 3. Weissinger was 24. He had gotten out of prison late in the previous November but at the time of the interview, was on his way back on a charge of burglary and theft. At first, Weissinger seemed reluctant to talk. He said he knew who Josh Kezer was but insisted they were just acquaintances. When first asked, he denied knowing anything about a killing on the interstate near Benton. Eventually, he said he heard Josh say he shot somebody, a girl, but he thought Josh said it was in Benton, Illinois, not Missouri.

Windham and Schiwitz obtained a handwritten question-and-answer statement from Weissinger on March 9. He said he saw Josh in the first or second week of January 1993 at Stacy Reed's apartment on Morgan Oak. He had been at Stacy's most of the day with Shawn Mangus when Josh arrived in the early evening.

Q. Did Josh mention anything about having killed a girl on I-55 near Benton, Missouri?

A. Yes.

Q. What did he say and who to?

A. To Shawn, he said he had to get something off his chest and said he had shot a girl up off the highway at Benton.

Toward the end of the statement, Weissinger opened up a little. He said he thought Josh was capable of murder because of "the way he acts and he carries guns and has the worst temper I probably have ever seen." He claimed he had witnessed Josh "with 22s, 25s, 32s, 38s, 9 mm, or .380s, through [*sic*] aways or so it would seem."

After making these statements, Weissinger received a three-year sentence. He could have gotten 10 years as a prior and persistent offender. His lawyer told him he must have given up some "good information" to get such a deal.

★ ★ ★

Later, Steve Grah wanted to get in on the action. He said to Mangus, "Hey, man, can I say I was there too when Josh confessed?" Mangus was a bit perturbed. "No. You'll just fuck it up. I already said me and Chuck were the only ones there and they should talk to Kelly because Kelly is his good friend. I don't even think Josh likes you. Why don't you just say Josh showed you a .380?" Hearing that, Grah made up his own story.

Schiwitz and Windham first interviewed Steven Allan Grah on March 3. Grah was being held on a $50,000 bond, charged with beating a homeless man who later died from his injuries. He had a record already for aggravated kidnapping, attempted armed robbery, assault with a deadly weapon, armed violence, violation of probation, possession of a controlled substance, and burglary and had spent three years in Joliet and Menard prisons in Illinois and five years in Missouri prisons. At the time of the interview, he was a few weeks short of his 28th birthday.

Grah was from Chicago, where he supposedly became a member of the Latin Kings. His street name was Bacardi. He told Schiwitz and Windham, "I ran a gauntlet of gang members who were beating me for my initiation. Josh told me his initiation was shooting a man in the face with a .380 in South Kedzie in Chicago. He has a .45, a .357, a .22 automatic with a black finish and a sawed-off shotgun. He always carries a gun in his waistband, around back. He keeps a knife in his front pants pocket." Asked if he thought Josh was capable of murder, Grah said, "Yeah. I do. He's nuts. I saw him slap a girl once with his backhand."

Grah said that Josh hung around with Mangus, Weissinger, and Stacy Reed, getting high. "He doesn't have a car. A fat girl he knows lets him use hers." Asked to describe the car, Grah said, "It was white with damage on the right rear. I saw Josh leave a party with the fat girl once and drive to Sikeston to buy an OZ of marijuana." The fat girl Grah described apparently was Christy Naile.

In Kankakee, as Grah told it, "Josh was 'Chief Enforcer One.' He enforced the rules of the gang, which might include killing someone, slapping someone, raping someone." Grah didn't know about any of this firsthand. He was repeating what he said Josh had told him. Asked if Josh ever bragged about shooting someone, Grah answered, "He said he'd been asked to go to the Disciples neighborhood on Kedzie, and he did. He confronted a Spanish Cobra. They exchanged gang signs, and he pulled out a .380 Beretta and shot him in the face and walked away." The interviewers asked if Josh ever bragged about shooting someone else. Grah answered, "No. He said this was how he got in the gang was by shooting the guy." They asked if Josh ever mentioned going to Sikeston. Grah said Josh went there to buy dope. "I asked him for a ride, and he said no because he and a girl named Mischelle were going to pick up an OZ. I'm not sure of the girl's name."

Grah said he saw Josh at Stacy Reed's with a gun. "Josh showed me a .380 Beretta. It was in his waistband. He said, 'Check out this new gun I have.'" Unlike Mangus and Weissinger, Grah didn't claim Josh confessed he had killed Mischelle Lawless.

After agreeing to provide information about Josh, Grah's bond was reduced to $3,000, and he was released from the county jail. Eventually, he would plead guilty to killing the homeless man and receive a 10-year sentence.

★ ★ ★

Kelly Church was another one of the lost boys who knew Josh Kezer from the streets of Cape Girardeau. Church was 17 when they interviewed him in the Cape Girardeau County Sheriff's Office on March 12. He said the last time he saw Josh "he was sleeping at Stacy Reed's house on January 6, 1993."

Q. Did you see him in November or December of 1992?

A. Yes, on Broadway in Cape Girardeau, but it's hard to remember exact dates because he comes and goes so often.

Q. How long between his visits to Kankakee, Illinois, does it take him to return to Missouri?

A. Usually about two weeks.

Q. How does he get from Kankakee to here?

A. Murray Meents brought him the last time, but I'm not sure of the times before.

It was Murray Meents who drove off after an accident and was arrested for leaving the scene. Then, the questioning turned to the topic of murder.

Q. Did you hear Josh brag about shooting anyone?

A. Josh said he's in a gang called the Latin Kings and that he was going to get the gang's help to kill some people screwing with his mother. Josh said he was going to kill Amanda Drury's dad because he wouldn't let Josh see Amanda. Josh also said he met a girl on Broadway Street in Cape Girardeau that fucked him over and he was going to kill her.

Q. Do you know the girl's name?

A. No.

Q. When did he say he was going to kill her?

A. In November or December of 1992.

Q. Where did he tell you he was going to kill a girl from Benton?

A. At Stacy Reed's house in front of me and Shawn Mangus.

He didn't know if Josh was capable of killing someone, but he knew he had a temper. "Josh is screwed in the head. He does things like throw a beer bottle at someone who looks at him funny."

The charges against Church were dropped not long after the last interview. He went to Kentucky to live with his mother and disappeared from the case.

★ ★ ★

Stacy Ann Reed was 18 when Schiwitz and Windham interviewed her at her new place on Albert in Cape Girardeau. She told them she had dropped out of school and was unemployed. She said she joined the Latin Kings in December and claimed that "the Master," the head of the gang in Illinois, had initiated her. Her gang name was Kelo. She had stars and gang signs and the words "Latin Kings" written on her tennis shoes and jeans. Her head was shaved all the way around above her ears, with long hair on the top of her head, and she wore a cap tilted to the left side.

Stacy had known Josh for about seven years, since they were at Schulz School together, and she reconnected with him when he was visiting from Kankakee after Christmas. "He stayed with me in part of December and part of January, at my place on Morgan Oak at Spanish Street.[1] The last time I saw him was in February. He's in the Latin Kings. He drinks liquor and smokes cigarettes, but as far as I know, he doesn't drop acid or smoke pot." Asked if she thought Josh was capable of murder, she said, "He has a temper, but I don't think he's violent. But he did tell me he went to Teen Challenge in

Illinois for attempted murder. Maybe that's true, maybe not." In any event, she said she had never seen him with a gun.

Stacy said, "Josh usually comes from Kankakee with a boy named Murray in Murray's blue car. When he's in Cape, he hangs with Kelly Church and boys I only know by nicknames—Pop I and Coon. Pop I looks like Popeye the Sailor, and Coon is part black." Stacy told the investigators, "While Josh was staying with me, he met Steve Grah. He heard Steve was talking about being a Cape Latin King, and he didn't believe it. Josh doesn't like to hang with the local Latin Kings who are my friends, like Steve and Bo Garcia. He says they're not the real thing; they're just wannabes." Years later, Josh would explain to me that he met Grah at Big Al's and disliked him immediately.

Stacy didn't know much about Amanda Drury, but she said Josh told her they were supposed to get married.

★ ★ ★

After Shawn Mangus and Chuck Weissinger pointed a finger at Josh, the investigation turned to the task of finding a connection between Josh and the little white car that Mark Abbott said he saw at the Cut-Mart. They knew about Josh's relationship with Amanda Drury during the summer of 1992 and about the fact that Josh and Amanda frequently rode with Amanda's friend, Christy Naile, in a little white car. On March 4, 1993, Deputy Schiwitz interviewed Christy Naile at her home in Benton. She was a 17-year-old student in her senior year at Kelly High. She said she knew Josh and recounted the story of his relationship with Amanda the previous summer, including the night of their breakup at the REO Speedwagon concert. She said she knew Kelly Church and drove Josh, Kelly, and Amanda around Cape Girardeau that summer in her white Plymouth Duster.

Deputy Schiwitz asked her where she was the night of Mischelle's murder. "I went to a movie in Sikeston with my boyfriend. I picked him up in my car at his home in Morehouse. Then, I drove him home after the movie. I got home around midnight." Christy's mother, who was the clerk of the circuit court in Benton and present for the interview, confirmed that fact. "The next morning I went to visit Amanda, who was spending the weekend with her grandparents in Benton. My mother called there to tell me about the murder."

Christy didn't think anyone could have taken her car without her knowledge after she got home at midnight. "I got up the next morning, and my car was parked where I left it the night before." But she did mention that she kept a set of spare keys in a magnetic box that was attached to the car under the rear bumper. Amanda knew about the spare keys. In fact, "in the middle of last October, while I was at a party at Amanda's mother's house in Sikeston, I discovered that the keys weren't in the box. Later that night, Amanda handed them to me without explaining why she had them." About a month before the interview, the keys had disappeared again, "right after I visited Amanda in Sikeston, and I haven't seen them since."

Christy saw Josh in late December, for the first time since the previous summer. "He left a note on our front door that my sister found the next morning. He came to the house again later that day. Josh was trying to find Amanda, and he kept asking questions about her. He also told me he joined a gang." At first, she didn't remember what the gang was called, but she recognized Latin Kings when Schiwitz suggested that name. "Josh told me there was some kind of initiation, but he didn't tell me what he had to do."

Deputy Schiwitz explained that a car fitting the description of Christy's car was seen near where Mischelle Lawless's body was found immediately after the time of death. She added, "I might ask your permission to look at the car, and I might ask you to take a polygraph." The next day, Sergeant Overbey obtained consent from Christy's mother to process her car. An evidence technician located several tiny spots on the driver's-side and passenger-side armrests that reacted to luminol, indicating the possible presence of blood. They took samples for further analysis by a lab.

On March 5, Sheriff Ferrell, Deputy Schiwitz, and Trooper Windham interviewed Amanda Drury. She told them, "My boyfriend [Randy Eskew] and I spent last night with friends, but we don't have a permanent address." Amanda said, "Josh and I rode around last summer with Christy in her car, and Christy sometimes let Josh drive. Josh knew Christy had a spare key; she kept it hidden in a magnetic box. We were with Christy once when she locked her keys in the car and used the spare."

★ ★ ★

On March 11, Windham and Schiwitz showed Mark Abbott a photo lineup of Josh and five other young men. The picture of Josh, obtained from the Bourbonnais, Illinois, police, was the mug shot taken of him when he was arrested in the confrontation with a young girl and her friends. He was shirtless, standing in front of height indicators, with a sign across his chest that read "Bourbonnais, Ill. Police." The photo was faxed to the Scott County Sheriff. It was the only one that was black and white and the only one that obviously was a mug shot. According to Windham's written report, Abbott identified Josh "without hesitation" as the young man with a dark complexion he saw at the Cut-Mart. After the photo lineup, Windham and Schiwitz showed Abbott eight Polaroids of small white hatchback-style cars. One of the cars belonged to Christy Naile. Abbott picked Christy's car as the one the young man at the Cut-Mart was driving, the young man he had just identified as Josh.

★ ★ ★

With the reported confession and Mark Abbott's identification of Josh and Christy Naile's car, Sheriff Ferrell thought he had at least one person who was involved in Mischelle's murder. On March 11, the same day Mark Abbott identified Josh and Christy Naile's car in photo lineups, Scott County Prosecutor Cristy Baker-Neel applied for a warrant for Josh's arrest on a charge of second-degree assault, alleging that on or about December 25, 1992, he "attempted to cause physical injury to Randy Dale Eskew by means of a deadly weapon." The date of the incident was wrong, but something did happen.

Kelly Church told investigators that Josh had come to Amanda's new boyfriend's house, where she was living with her boyfriend and his family, and had a late-night shouting match with her boyfriend's father. Josh only went to see Amanda because a few days earlier, Christy said Amanda wanted to see him. Her boyfriend was named after his father, whose name was Randy Eskew. The elder Eskew filed a complaint about the incident sometime after the event. Investigators located the three young men who were with Josh that night: Kelly Church, David Pengiel, and Randy Wilson. In interviews, all three said Josh had a verbal altercation with Eskew's father. They differed only in a few details, mostly as to which of the two had started the shouting and threats. All three said Josh and Eskew's father both said they had a gun.

As Josh described the incident, it didn't happen the way it was reported. It may have happened in early January or on New Year's. Pengiel drove Josh, Wilson, and Church to the Eskews' home. All four boys went up to the door. Eskew's father called for his gun. His wife brought it, a long-barreled rifle or shotgun. Pengiel, Wilson, and Church ran to the car. Josh backed away slowly; maintained eye contact; said that he had a gun, too; and put his hand in his jacket as if reaching for one. He said he had a gun because he was scared.

> I didn't have a gun. I did put my hand in my jacket and said I had one but only after Eskew's father pointed one at me. What was I supposed to do when he pointed a gun at me? Cower because he wanted me to? I was a King. I didn't cower. Police reports claim I started the shouting and threats. I didn't. Eskew claimed he didn't point a gun at me. He

did. I went there to see Amanda because I was told she wanted to see me. I didn't do what I was accused of doing. In retrospect, I shouldn't have went. But I was a kid. I did what kids do. I went to see a girl I thought wanted to see me.

On March 15, about a month after his 18th birthday, Josh was sitting on a couch at his father's house, recently returned from work at K-Mart, when the doorbell rang. He assumed the two men at the front door had come to look at one of the used cars his father offered for sale. Instead, the men, officers of the Illinois State Police in plain clothes, carried a second-degree assault warrant issued by the Scott County Circuit Court. When the men asked for Mr. Kezer, Josh told them that was his father but that he could help them. He put on his jacket and shoes. When he came outside to show them the cars, they spun him around, put him in an arm bar, and slammed him face-first against their car. He yelled to his father's girlfriend to call his father. Handcuffed and dazed, he was taken to the Kankakee police station, where he was allowed to call his father. Josh's father was told the bond likely would be 10 percent of $10,000. At first, the judge was willing to accept such a bond. His father came to court with the money, and he and Josh planned to drive to Scott County and clear up the assault charge. But the judge received a phone call on the bench and announced that Josh was to be held without bail for Missouri authorities on a governor's warrant. The judge questioned why Josh would be held without bail on an assault charge. He apologized to Josh and Charlie Kezer and told them there was nothing he could do. Josh had to be held.

* * *

A few weeks later, Trooper Windham and Deputy Dan Hinton went to Kankakee to bring Josh to Scott County. They left Kankakee with Josh on April 7. On the drive, the two officers conducted what amounted to an interview, and Windham wrote it up as a report a week later. Josh says he freely admitted he was a member of the Latin Kings, but he says other things were outright false or deliberately reported out of context. For example, the subject of guns came up, and Windham asked Josh if he was a good shot. He responded that the only time he had fired a gun was in the Boy Scouts, which was for a merit badge. Josh said he was told he was a good shot. Josh wasn't aware of the game Windham was playing. Windham reported Josh's claim that he was a good shot and associated it with Josh's gang activity. Josh wasn't aware of Mischelle Lawless's murder at the time. He didn't know that what Windham would later write would misrepresent what he had said. "They asked me about Amanda. I told them I still loved her and tried to see her on my last trip. The way I saw it at the time, I was charged with assault, but I hadn't assaulted anyone, so what did I have to fear? I was naive."

Toward the end of the interview, Windham changed the subject abruptly and asked Josh if he had killed Mischelle Lawless. Taken aback, Josh said, "No," and got very quiet. Windham kept asking questions, but Josh remained silent.

When they arrived at the sheriff's office in Benton, Sheriff Ferrell ushered Josh into his office. Windham came in and sat next to Brenda Schiwitz behind Ferrell. He started the conversation with Josh casually. "Would you like a soda? Do you need anything? Here, sit in that chair on the other side of my desk." Then, Ferrell's face turned red and contorted in rage. He rose up in his chair and came halfway across the desk, yelling, "YOU KILLED MY LITTLE GIRL!" Josh remembers that moment vividly. It was the turning point of his life. Ferrell produced a warrant for first-degree murder that he had obtained while Windham and Hinton were on their way to Kankakee.[1]

Josh was processed, fingerprinted, and allowed two phone calls. First, he called his Aunt Kathy. At first, his cousin James thought he was kidding and didn't believe him. When his cousin heard Josh cry and tell him he was serious, he got his mother on the phone, who told Josh she would contact his father, mother, and grandparents. He also called a senior member of the Latin Kings who could have helped him verify his whereabouts. He told Josh it wasn't gang business and hung up. That was the moment Josh decided he was no longer a Latin King.

Josh was arraigned a few days later, on the same docket with Jeffrey Rogers, a man charged with child molestation who would figure later in Josh's case. Josh pled not guilty. The record reflects that Josh was represented by a lawyer from the public defender's office, but the man standing next to him said nothing. Josh is convinced that he didn't have a lawyer at his arraignment and didn't have one until another inmate snuck him an application for representation weeks later. The judge set bond at $500,000 and scheduled a preliminary hearing for May 12. When a lawyer from the public defender finally met with Josh, he told him sympathetically, "You're going to need more help than I can give you." Josh would remember that later.

For a felony case to proceed beyond charge and arraignment in Missouri, there must be a finding of probable cause—either by a grand jury after the prosecutor presents evidence or by a judge after a preliminary hearing. A grand jury hears evidence in secret and indicts the person charged by issuing what is called a true bill. The prosecutor presents the evidence, which may consist of little more than sworn testimony of a law enforcement officer about what witnesses have said in interviews. The defendant's lawyer does not participate. A preliminary hearing is public, and defense counsel may cross-examine. As a practical matter, however, a preliminary hearing may be as perfunctory as grand jury proceedings but more transparent.

The preliminary hearing scheduled for May 12 didn't happen. Sheriff Ferrell was pushing Cristy Baker-Neel to present the case against Josh to the grand jury. In the spring of 1993, Baker-Neel was the acting Scott County Prosecuting Attorney, a relatively inexperienced assistant when she was appointed to fill the unexpired term of the elected prosecutor, who resigned suddenly partway through her term. She had one assistant prosecutor, who like her, had handled only minor criminal cases, and one investigator. Ostensibly because she needed more time to prepare, she had the preliminary hearing taken off the docket and began getting the case ready to present to a grand jury.

★ ★ ★

The murder charge against Josh was big news in the area around Scott County and Cape Girardeau. Television stations and newspapers on both sides of the Mississippi covered the story, with video and still coverage of Josh being escorted across the street to and from the county jail and courthouse. Marvin Lawless told the *Southeast Missourian* that Mischelle's family was relieved her killer had been caught and "now await prosecution to the full extent of the law." Her father said, "I don't think he was anyone we knew." Sheriff Ferrell could see no connection. "We have no knowledge that they knew each other at all. That issue has never been cleared up." No one could explain why Josh would have wanted to kill Mischelle.

Sometime later, Marvin Lawless called the sheriff's office with information that Josh had pulled a gun on his wife's cousin, the same Brian O'Kelly from the incident at Wink's convenience store where Josh and Kelly Church were the target of O'Kelly's threats. Deputy Schiwitz interviewed O'Kelly two days later. He claimed Church pulled a knife on him, something that didn't appear in the police reports. He didn't accuse Josh of doing anything and, in fact, said he had never seen him with a gun.

With all the publicity, Josh's face was soon well known. In the weeks that followed his arrest, citizens of Southeast Missouri began to come forward, claiming they recognized him from circumstances that had some bearing on his guilt.

Doug Brantley contacted the sheriff's office to claim Josh was the man who had threatened him and his wife and three relatives with a gun the previous Halloween outside the Billiards Center in Cape Girardeau. Brantley reported the incident to the Cape Girardeau police the following Monday. He described the drunk who threatened him as white, 150 to 160 pounds, between five feet six inches and five feet eight inches tall, and wearing a gray sweatshirt with front pockets and a hood, blue jeans, and dirty white tennis shoes. The report was filed away, and nothing came of it until Brantley said he recognized Josh as the teen who threatened him with a gun. Shown a six-picture photo lineup, he picked the same picture of Josh that Mark Abbott had identified, the only one that was obviously a mug shot.

According to reports in the sheriff's files, at least five people claimed they saw Josh at Mischelle's funeral. The young man they described was slim, about six feet tall, with dark hair worn back on the sides, and wearing dark jeans and a black leather-type jacket. He stood alone along one wall of the church and later stood apart from the rest of the crowd at the gravesite. He appeared nervous, constantly looking around but avoiding eye contact.

8

THE DEFENSE

Josh's mother's parents weren't satisfied with having their grandson represented by a public defender. And then there was what the public defender told Josh. They scraped together $50,000—all the savings they had—to hire Albert Lowes of the Cape Girardeau firm of Lowes & Drusch. Lowes was a respected 60-year-old lawyer with a general civil and criminal practice. He was born on a farm near Oak Ridge, Missouri. In 1950, right out of high school, he joined the Marine Corps. After the Marines, he attended SEMO and graduated from the University of Missouri law school early in 1959. He was a burly, bald man who filled a room with his presence. He liked good cigars and kept a well-stocked bar in the basement of his firm's office. He was what might be called "colorful"—but that doesn't really do him justice. He had a folksy, informal style of questioning, sprinkled with local geographic references and an occasional "ain't" or other grammatical lapse well designed to help him relate to Southeast Missouri witnesses and juries. He was blunt and far from politically correct, referring in depositions to a mixed-race acquaintance of Josh's as a "half-breed" and another as "dumber than shit." Then, there were his special names for things that no one else used. The sheriff's office was a "cop shop." Polygraph equipment was a "truth box." Taking a blood sample was "vampiring."

Cristy Baker-Neel was hesitant about the Kezer case, her first murder prosecution and one in which she faced a seasoned defense lawyer. On top of that, she was unsure of the strength of the case that she was being rushed to present to the grand jury. In contrast to most murder cases, there was no evidence the defendant knew the victim, and there was no physical evidence linking the defendant to the crime. Her whole case was based on the self-interested testimony of a few jailhouse snitches and a local drunk who told inconsistent stories of what he saw at and near the crime scene. But she pulled together the evidence she had and took it to the grand jury. There were 19 witnesses: Sheriff Ferrell and investigators from the sheriff's office and the highway patrol, including Brenda Schiwitz and Don Windham. There also were Dr. Zaricor and other forensic witnesses, Mark Abbott, Shawn Mangus, Steve Grah, Amanda Drury, and Leon Lamb. On June 29, the grand jury issued a true bill charging Josh with the class A felonies of murder in the first degree and armed criminal action. The true bill was presented to a circuit judge, who set Josh's bail at $1,000,000.

★ ★ ★

The prosecution has an obligation to voluntarily disclose any information or documents that are relevant to its case, including any evidence that might be exculpatory, that is, indicating the accused may be innocent. Pursuant to this obligation, the Scott County prosecutor provided the defense with copies of investigative reports compiled by the sheriff's office and the highway patrol. These included statements given by witnesses such as Abbott, Mangus, Weissinger, Church, and Grah. The defense also is entitled to make specific requests for documents and physical evidence and take depositions of investigators and other witnesses. Al Lowes filed his first motion to produce documents on July 7 and his first notice to take depositions on July 12.

Lowes had hired a May 1993 graduate of the University of Missouri Law School named David Rosener, and he put him to work on Josh's case before the July bar exam. One of Rosener's first assignments was to interview Shawn Mangus and Chuck Weissinger. Al Lowes put Josh's life in the hands of an attorney with literally no experience who technically wasn't even an attorney yet.

Rosener visited Mangus in the Cape County Jail several times over the course of the summer of 1993. During the first visit, on June 26, Mangus told him essentially the same story he had told the investigators—Josh confided in him and Chuck Weissinger in Stacy Reed's apartment some time before January 18, 1993, telling them that somebody had him shoot the girl in Benton. In the interview, Mangus had no explanation of Josh's motive, and he expressed skepticism about the confession, at least to the extent that he said, "I don't believe Josh is capable of killing someone for no reason."

Two days later, Rosener visited Weissinger at the Central Missouri Correctional Center in Jefferson City. He admitted right away, "That story we told about Josh's confession wasn't true. We were just trying to get a better deal. We didn't think it would get that far." Josh would learn years later from Weissinger's sister that Weissinger was motivated to tell the truth by pressure from his mother and her. They knew Weissinger was lying and wanted him to make it right. To his credit, he tried.

Weissinger gave Rosener a 10-page handwritten statement detailing what had happened. "I was in a cell with Shawn and Isaac Johnson.[1] I told Shawn I was facing 10 years as a prior and persistent offender. He said he knew a way I could do better for myself." Shawn said he already told them Josh said he killed the girl in Benton. "You can back me up." Weissinger liked the idea, and he and Mangus hatched a plan. "Shawn told me what to say to the police so our stories would be consistent." The common thread was that in January, in the bedroom of Stacy Reed's apartment in Cape Girardeau, Josh confessed to both of them that he killed a girl in Benton. According to Weissinger, "Steve Grah was in on the plan too. He was supposed to say he saw Josh with a .380."

Rosener went over the statement Weissinger had given to Deputy Schiwitz and Trooper Windham at the Cape Girardeau County Jail. Weissinger said that was the story Mangus had fed him. "Joshua Kezer never said this, and he never said that he killed a girl in Benton. Even though it was a complete lie, I decided to take Shawn's story and tell it to the police to see if I could also work out a deal on my sentencing."

Shortly after Weissinger discussed the plan with Mangus, he talked to a Missouri highway patrolman and "a sandy-blonde-haired female deputy" from the Scott County Sheriff's Department. "I told the two that I might be able to help them out with the Benton, Illinois, murder. The two police acted like they didn't want to talk to me yet. I then talked to Shawn Mangus and discovered that the murder happened in Benton, Missouri, and not Benton, Illinois. Shawn continued to fill me in on what to say, and I began to get the story, the lie, straight."

Weissinger said Windham told him that "he was good friends with Morley Swingle," the Cape Girardeau County Prosecutor, and that "although he couldn't guarantee anything, he would talk to Swingle for me and that he thought that Swingle would give me a better deal on my criminal charges in Cape County."

A few weeks later, Windham drove Weissinger to Benton to meet with Sheriff Ferrell. Weissinger told Rosener, "Windham and Ferrell had a stack of papers, which they left in my view that had Shawn's name and the statements that he had made to them about Joshua." He got "the feeling they just wanted me to say that either Josh did it or that he told me he did it. I did my best to tell them what they wanted to hear, even though it wasn't true." If he got a detail wrong while talking to them "about the fictious [sic] discussions with Joshua," they "would prompt or lead me with their notes from Shawn Mangus."

Weissinger said that although he told investigators he had seen Josh with several types of handguns, in fact he had never seen Josh "with any kind of gun." He said:

> The stories about Joshua that I told the police, Windham & Ferrell, were completely false. I only did it because I thought they would help me with my criminal charges and maybe get me a reward. I also know that anything that Steve Grah and Shawn Mangus said to the police about Joshua Kezer and killing a girl in Benton is a lie—they only said what they did about Josh to get a reduced sentence or a reward.

Weissinger also said Sheriff Ferrell told him that he would talk to "Swingle for me and that he would do his best to help me out."

Rosener visited Mangus several times again after he obtained Weissinger's recantation, but Mangus stuck to his original story about Josh's confession. Finally, when Rosener visited on August 10, Mangus confirmed what Weissinger had told Rosener in June.

> I have reviewed my June 26, 1993, statement [to Rosener] and must now come clean and tell the truth—specifically, Joshua Kezer never in any way said that he killed a girl in Benton or any other person for that matter. I have no reason to believe that Joshua Kezer has ever killed anyone. My statement of June 26, 1993, to Rosener and also my previous statements to the police that Joshua Kezer said to me that he had killed a girl in Benton are completely false—Josh Kezer never said this.

Rosener had John Holshouser, a guard at the jail, enter the interview room and witness Mangus's signature.

After the August 10 statement to Rosener, Mangus wrote Josh a note, apologizing for claiming he had confessed to the murder: "Josh, hey, I just wanted to write and let you know that I'm sorry for what has happened. I did what I did, there's nothing that I can do to change that, but I told them, and your lawyer the truth. I hope you'll find it in your heart to forgive me and Chuck. Take care of yourself and give your mom and grandparents my apologies too."

Mangus also sent Weissinger a letter:

> I talked to his [Josh's] lawyer today, and I wrote him a statement telling him the truth. I read your statement too, you didn't have to blame it all on me though, thanks, that really makes me look like a hell of a shithead, but at least we got the truth out. I feel much better now that

this shit is over with and out in the open. I'll probably be joining you before too long, since that can give me a new charge. I looked it up in the law library and it's a class B misdemeanor, but I already have two so they can pile all that up and turn it into a felony.

In another letter to Weissinger, Mangus wrote, "I talked to you know whose lawyer about a week after you did last, and I told them the truth too. You didn't have to blame everything on me though, wetback! you dirty fucker you! Oh well, I just hope those El Porkos don't charge me with obstructing justice though, that would suck."

With these recantations, the prosecution's case had started to unravel. The case against Josh started with Mangus and Weissinger claiming he confessed to killing Mischelle Lawless. Now, both of them were saying it was a lie.

★ ★ ★

About the same time Mangus decided to join Weissinger in recanting, other witnesses were emerging to take their place with tales of Josh confessing. For a time after being charged with the Lawless murder, Josh shared a cell in the Scott County Jail with Jeffrey Rogers and Samuel Wade Howard. Rogers was the accused child molester who was arraigned on the same docket with Josh. Howard had a prior conviction for unlawful use of a weapon and was locked up this time on a charge of first-degree murder in the shooting death of his father-in-law.

On August 6, Rogers sent word that he wanted to talk to Sheriff Ferrell. Rogers told Ferrell in an interview about another Kezer confession: "[Josh] told me he killed Mischelle Lawless. Another person was there when he did it, but Kezer didn't say who the other person was." When asked why Josh confessed, Rogers said, "I think he needed to tell someone what he did, and he confided in me because I'm older." To bolster his credibility, Rogers said, "I made a note of the conversation on a calendar in my cell." There was nothing entered on the calendar indicating a confession or even a discussion with Josh.

Rogers also said Josh talked in his sleep. "He has nightmares and talks crazy, saying things about his case." Rogers didn't go into any detail. He said he wanted to talk to his lawyer first. According to a memorandum of the interview, Ferrell advised him to do that and have his lawyer contact the prosecutor if they wanted to pursue the matter any further. Rogers said, "I'm afraid to talk while I'm in the Scott County Jail. Josh talks about being in a gang. I'm scared what some of his gang friends might do to me." Six days later, Rogers was granted a change of venue to Mississippi County, and he was transferred to the Mississippi County Jail in Charleston.

★ ★ ★

On August 10, Wade Howard told one of the Scott County jailers he had information about Josh's case and wanted to talk to Sheriff Ferrell. Ferrell wasn't available, so Schiwitz and Windham, recently promoted to corporal, interviewed him. Howard told them, "Josh confessed to me last Sunday. He said he shot the girl because she wouldn't go out with him." According to Howard, "He said another man was with him when he shot her but didn't mention his name. Then, he climbed up in his bunk and got real quiet." Windham asked Howard if he believed what Josh had told him. "I do. His nerves are bad, and he's real jumpy. He talks in his sleep and cries out 'Mischelle.'"

On August 23, after learning that Steve Grah had added to his claims about Josh, David Rosener interviewed him and obtained a written statement that was substantially more damning than the statements he had made to investigators in the spring. Grah said, "Josh pulled me outside of the party and took me outside alone and told me he killed a girl in Benton. . . . When Josh told me he killed a girl in Benton, at first I didn't believe him. I don't think Josh shot that girl at all but was just trying to act tough and be a big dog around me."

Grah was sure this happened in late January or early February because "it was just a couple of days before I got married, which was on February 2, 1993, and my wife had her baby on the fourth of February."

Al Lowes took Grah's deposition on August 24. Grah repeated the account of Josh confessing to the murder that he had given to Rosener. Lowes and Rosener were sure Grah was lying. They tried to find out what was going on by interviewing Grah's wife. On September 2, she gave Rosener a written statement: "In late August 1993, Steve Grah told me that he was fixing to get a $25,000 reward for saying that a 'Josh' shot the Lawless girl in Benton. I believe that Steve would lie to either get a reward or to help him get out of trouble. Steve always lies, and I'm sure he's lying about this Josh guy and Lawless."

★ ★ ★

The Office of Missouri Attorney General has a division created by statute that provides assistance to local prosecutors, particularly those in smaller, rural counties, including providing a special prosecutor to try complex or difficult cases. Cristy Baker-Neel asked the AG for help. She got an experienced special prosecutor who was well acquainted with Southeast Missouri in general and Scott County in particular. Kenny Hulshof entered his appearance in the case on July 27, 1993. He was a nice-looking, almost handsome man whose wire-rimmed glasses made him look scholarly.

Hulshof was born in 1958 in Sikeston and raised on his family's farm near Bertrand. He graduated from the same Kelly High School in Benton as Mischelle Lawless and went on to earn a bachelor's degree in agricultural economics from the University of Missouri and a law degree from the University of Mississippi. He returned to Missouri after law school—starting the practice of law as an assistant State public defender. When one of his clients was executed in 2001 for the 1986 murder of a state trooper, he asked to serve as a State's witness. After three years as a public defender, the newly elected Cape Girardeau County Prosecuting Attorney, Morley Swingle, recruited him.

Hulshof spent the next three years as an assistant in Swingle's office before joining the AG's office, led at the time by Republican William Webster. He made a name for himself by convicting Ray Copeland, an elderly serial killer, who with his wife, murdered five drifters who worked on his farm. Hulshof was beginning to specialize in small-town murder cases in 1992, the year Jay Nixon was elected attorney general as a Democrat.

★ ★ ★

Because of the awful nature of the crime and the heavy local news coverage, Al Lowes wanted the case moved out of the area for trial. The defense applied for a change of venue and change of judge on July 14, 1993, and the case was moved to Ste. Genevieve County and assigned to Judge Stan Murphy, who set it for trial to begin on January 28, 1994.

Ste. Genevieve County Circuit Court, part of the four-county 24th Judicial Circuit, is located in the town of Ste. Genevieve. Ste. Genevieve is a town of about 5,000, sitting on the west bank of the Mississippi, 73 miles north of Benton. The oldest municipality in the state, it was first settled by French colonials around 1735 and was moved two miles north to higher ground in 1785 after a disastrous flood. It was an offshoot of the older French settlements on the east bank of the river: Cahokia, Kaskaskia, Fort de Chartres, Prairie du Rocher, and St. Philippe. Its early Creole history is still on display in the poteaux-en-terre architecture of its oldest buildings, built with log walls set directly in the earth and a double-pitched hip roof surrounded by a stockade fence.

The Ste. Genevieve County Courthouse is not like the grander court buildings in some other Missouri counties. There are no towering Greek columns in front of the entrance, and the building does not dominate the town square. Built in 1885 of red brick with sandstone trim, the 36-by-48-foot Victorian-style courthouse looks like the home of a wealthy merchant.

★ ★ ★

Al Lowes began to take depositions in August 1993. He was at his folksy best with these witnesses, referring to Mischelle's friends and others in their teens and 20s as "young'uns." He hid beneath this disarming manner recurring themes aimed at proving Josh innocent.

THERE WAS NO PHYSICAL EVIDENCE LINKING JOSH TO THE CRIME

Dr. Briner of the SEMO Crime Lab, the State's primary forensic expert, readily confirmed that nothing forensic implicated Josh—no fingerprints, no blood evidence, no gun, and nothing on Mischelle's body, at the crime scene, on Josh's leather jacket, or in Christy Naile's car.

THERE WAS NO EVIDENCE JOSH KNEW MISCHELLE

Mischelle's friends; the "young'uns," such as Lelicia O'Dell; and the investigators who interviewed them confirmed that no one close to Mischelle had ever seen or even heard of Josh before he was charged with the murder.

THE SNITCHES WERE LYING

Lowes asked Deputy Schiwitz to acknowledge that Mangus and Weissinger were now saying their story of Josh's confession "was all a damn lie," and she answered, "That's what they said." She helped undermine Grah's confession story by contradicting his claim that the party at Stacy Reed's apartment was in late January or early February 1993. Lowes asked her when the party at Reed's occurred.

Q. That's in January or February?

A. January of '93.

Q. When did that sweet thing say this party went on?

A. Sometime before January 8th I believe is when she had to move out of her apartment so it was early January.

Q. She got her ass kicked out for not paying the rent, right?

A. That's what she said, yes.

ABBOTT'S IDENTIFICATION OF JOSH WAS QUESTIONABLE

With one witness after another, Lowes hammered away at the inconsistencies in Abbott's account of the night of the murder, including reaching through a partially lowered window to lift Mischelle and not telling anyone about the man at the Cut-Mart until his fourth conversation with law enforcement. Perhaps the biggest source of doubt about Abbott's identification that emerged from the depositions was Officer Roy Moore's testimony regarding his report of a Hispanic man driving a small white hatchback stopping at the crime scene and asking where he could find a gas station. Deputy Schiwitz said, "I can't be sure that Abbott and Moore were not talking about the same man," and she said, "Abbott wasn't sure either when I showed him Moore's report and asked him about the similarity."

THERE WERE OTHER LIKELY SUSPECTS

These other suspects included Lyle Day and Leon Lamb and even the J. J. who sold Mischelle's brother drugs.

THERE WAS NO EVIDENCE JOSH HAD DRIVEN CHRISTY NAILE'S CAR

Addressing Naile occasionally as "young'un," Lowes focused on showing that Naile supported the defense assertion that Josh couldn't have used her car to get to the place where Mischelle was killed because her car was in the same place she had left it the night before when she got up the next morning and the gas gauge hadn't moved.

★ ★ ★

Lowes was so sure Josh was innocent that he decided to arrange for him to take a lie detector test. The results would not be admissible as evidence in a trial, but law enforcement commonly uses them to decide whether someone is a likely suspect worth further investigation. Lowes hoped the prosecution would have second thoughts if Josh was considered to be truthful in his answers. Josh was happy to give it a try.

Josh was told Hulshof had approached Josh's defense about giving Josh a lie detector test. The implication was that Hulshof thought the case was weak and would drop it if Josh passed. But Hulshof was as committed to convicting Josh as Josh's defense was to defending him. The parties executed a standard agreement limiting the use of the results. Hulshof retained B. J. Lincecum to conduct the examination on October 7, 1993, at Lincecum's "Polygraph Suite" at the Sands Motel in Cape Girardeau, a sure sign of unreliability.

Josh told me he believes the polygraph exam was fixed. David Rosener wasn't allowed in the room. Lincecum and Josh were alone. Lincecum began by questioning Josh about unrelated crimes. Rosener counseled Josh to answer the questions honestly and to remain calm prior to entering the room alone, but Rosener and Josh didn't expect Lincecum to question Josh about other crimes. "I didn't understand why I was being asked about them. It felt like they were trying to pin everything on me." By the time Lincecum got to the four agreed questions, Josh was extremely nervous, and the test was primed to measure that emotion. He answered no to each of the four test questions:

1. Do you know for sure who killed Angela Lawless?
2. Did you kill Angela Lawless?
3. Right now, can you take me to the gun used to shoot Angela Lawless?
4. Were you there when Angela Lawless was killed?

Lincecum reported his interpretation of the test to Lowes and the prosecution in a letter, which stated simply: "It is the opinion of the polygraphist, based on the polygraph examination of Mr. Kezer, that he HAS NOT told the entire truth to his pertinent test questions." There was no explanation of what Lincecum considered to be "the entire truth" or why, and he provided no graphs of the actual results.

★ ★ ★

The trial was scheduled to begin in late January 1994. At a pretrial conference on January 4, Al Lowes made an oral motion for a continuance, and the judge gave him a new setting, with the trial beginning on June 13. The justification for the request was the two new witnesses who had come forward in August 1993 and claimed that Josh confessed, Wade Howard and Jeff Rogers. During this conference, the prosecution also revealed that Shawn Mangus told one of their investigators that his story of Josh's confession was false, confirming the recantation statement Mangus had given to Rosener the previous August.

David Rosener tried to talk to Howard after he was identified as another witness claiming Josh confessed, but Howard said, "I don't want to be interviewed until after I get my sentence." Eventually, the murder charge was reduced from first to second degree, and Howard was sentenced in January 1994 to 15 years. He talked to Rosener on February 15 and signed a statement, witnessed by a jail guard, recanting his earlier statement to Sheriff Ferrell. "When I talked regularly with Josh Kezer during the summer of 1993, Josh repeatedly told me and the other inmates that he didn't kill the Mischelle Lawless girl and that he was way up in Kankakee, Illinois, on the night she got killed."

Howard also stated:

> Later when the deputies took me to Sheriff Ferrell's office, I was in the room with Sheriff Ferrell and Deputy Brenda Schiwitz, and they told me they wanted a statement about Josh Kezer killing the Lawless girl. Sheriff Ferrell pressured and intimidated the hell out of me and made it clear to me that he just wanted me to say that Josh killed Lawless or that Josh said he killed Lawless or the like. Because I was afraid about what would happen, I just answered Ferrell's questions like he wanted to hear. I wasn't physically abused but I was really nervous.

Howard said that Josh told him "many times" that "he didn't have anything to do with the girl's murder." He stated that "Josh Kezer never told me that he shot and killed Mischelle Lawless. Anything that I told Sheriff Ferrell about Josh Kezer shooting Mischelle Lawless was something of a misunderstanding. And of course, Ferrell only wanted to hear one thing."

After Jeff Rogers transferred to Mississippi County, his lawyer continued to negotiate with the prosecutor regarding his testimony. Rogers would give them the name of the other person present at the murder with Josh as a sign of good faith, but he wanted something in return, a promise he would not be put into the general prison population if he was convicted. David Rosener tried to talk to Rogers in January 1994, at his parents' house in Benton, after he bonded out of the Mississippi County Jail, but Rogers refused to answer questions. Finally, on April 11, 1994, Rogers appeared for a deposition under the compulsion of a defense subpoena.

Al Lowes questioned Rogers, and Rogers answered the initial background questions. His full name was Jeffrey Wade Rogers, and he was 34 years old. His parents were Dale and Lulabelle Rogers. He had been employed as a truck driver but was disabled as the result of a work-related injury. He took Prozac, Desyrel, and Tylenol. He objected to Lowes's characterization of Prozac as "squirrel medicine." He knew Mischelle's parents, but he knew Mischelle only "vaguely." He had eight prior felony convictions, for burglary and stealing, and had been to prison twice. For about two months in the summer of 1993, he shared a four-man cell in the Scott County Jail with Josh; Wade Howard; and from time to time, another inmate.

Rogers stopped answering questions when Lowes started to get into what he told Sheriff Ferrell about Josh. Lowes explained that he was "trying to fish for some constitutional basis" for refusing to answer, and Rogers said, "Well, at this point I am negotiating with the attorney general's office and Scott County prosecutor's office on a deal and that's basically it. Advice from my attorney this morning, he just told me all I need to do is show up and not say anything, name, rank and serial number and that's what I'm going to do."

Lowes called this answer "bizarre" and asked, incredulously, "You claim you got some knowledge about the Lawless girl's murder or some conversation with the Kezer boy and you don't want to tell us about it?" Rogers answered, "Not at this time, no." Lowes asked if he needed time to improve his story, and Rogers said, "No. It's cut and dried as far as what I was told and what I know." Lowes asked if he was trying to work out something so "you don't have to go to the pen quite as long," and Rogers answered, "Or at all, if possible."

★ ★ ★

On June 7, 1994, Judge Murphy held a hearing on several pretrial motions, the most significant of which was a motion to disqualify David Rosener and Al Lowes from representing Josh in his trial. The judge kicked off the discussion by saying he hadn't had time to read the briefs and asking, "What is this all about?"

Hulshof answered, "Judge, in a nutshell, the defense counsel, Mr. Rosener, has made himself a witness in this case." Two of the witnesses who said Josh confessed to them, Mangus and Howard, had given Rosener statements recanting their original statements that Josh confessed to them.

Both were prepared to recant those recantations at trial. Rosener would be the only witness who could refute the testimony of either witness because he conducted both interviews alone. Hulshof argued that case law required that Rosener voluntarily withdraw from representing Josh or that the judge disqualify him. He argued further that the Rules of Professional Responsibility required that the entire firm, including Al Lowes, be disqualified. Hulshof called two witnesses to present facts supporting the motion.

Corporal Windham had gone to Louisiana with Luther Van Godsey, an investigator for the attorney general's office, two weeks before to see Shawn Mangus. Windham said he asked Mangus why he had recanted: "He said that he was afraid for his life because Mr. Kezer's attorney, David Rosener, had made insinuating statements that Mr. Kezer was contacting dangerous people within the gang and other dangerous persons and that he was notifying them that he would be testifying against Mr. Kezer and said that he was afraid for his life and that is why he retracted his statement."

Windham said, "Mangus agreed to testify if he was put in a witness protection program" and that arrangements had been made for him to come to Ste. Genevieve for the trial. On cross-examination, Lowes asked Windham if he told Mangus he could be charged with a crime if he admitted his original statement to investigators was a lie. Windham said, "I probably did," and Lowes responded, "I bet you did."

Godsey testified about the recantation Wade Howard provided to Rosener. "I visited Howard in March at Church Farm and showed him a copy of the statement he gave Rosener. He told me, "It wasn't what I said." Rosener wrote it as they talked. When Howard told Rosener it was wrong, Rosener told him "to initial the statement where it was wrong and he would change it later," which Rosener didn't do.

Godsey said Howard told me, "If I didn't believe him, that I should just listen to the tape." Godsey said, "I told Howard there was no tape." He confirmed what Howard told him instead by listening to Howard's end of a telephone conversation in which Howard confronted Rosener about the claimed inaccuracies in the written statement.

After all the testimony was finished, Lowes said emphatically, "Mr. Hulshof overlooks the fact that Rosener ain't a witness, he ain't gonna be a witness, and we ain't gonna make him a witness. There are other people that can take these people to task on these things, the statements, and we will do it in that manner." Lowes argued further that to deprive Josh of counsel on the eve of trial by disqualifying his lawyers would deprive him of his constitutional rights. "It would probably be impossible for him to obtain additional counsel because I imagine his grandparents are plumb out of money."

The judge asked Lowes if he wanted to "make a record" with Josh as to whether he wanted to waive any conflict of interest that his counsel might have. Lowes said he did and called Josh to testify.

> Q. In any event, if there is any sort of conflict, do you freely, voluntarily, waive that?
>
> A. I want to keep you.
>
> Q. Okay. You unequivocally waive any sort of conflict, if any, that there is?
>
> A. If by waiving conflict means I keep you, yes, I want to keep you.

Judge Murphy went over the possible conflict in his own questions to Josh. He asked Josh if he understood that he "would be giving up forever any right to complain about ineffective assistance of counsel because of this conflict and this problem with Mr. Rosener having taken a statement in this matter on your behalf that might lead to the potential that he might need to testify in your behalf?" Josh said he understood. When the judge explained that he could get a public defender who could subpoena David Rosener to testify on his behalf, Josh said, "Yes, but I want to continue with him." After hearing those answers, the judge overruled the state's motion to disqualify Rosener and the firm of Lowes & Drusch. Josh remembered what the public defender in Scott County had told him: "You're going to need more help than I can give you." "What I knew was my family was broke. My grandparents had given everything they had to Lowes. I didn't believe a public defender could help me. I wanted to go home. So I told Lowes and Judge Murphy I understood. I didn't understand."

9

THE TRIAL

Despite the setback with Mangus and Howard, Al Lowes went into the trial full of confidence. He still had Chuck Weissinger to testify that he had gotten together with Mangus in the Cape Girardeau County Jail and made it all up. And Lowes had alibi witnesses who would testify that Josh was in Kankakee, 350 miles away, the night of the murder and early the next morning.

The trial began on Monday, June 13. Josh's parents were there and two of his maternal aunts. The weather that week was springlike, without the heat and humidity of a Southeast Missouri summer. The daily highs were around 80, and the cool evenings were good for sleeping with windows open and air-conditioning off.

The first day was taken up with a final pretrial conference and jury selection.[1] There were the usual issues of jurors who had brushes with the criminal justice system and jurors who simply didn't want to be there. The judge dismissed jurors until there were 12 and two alternates. The trial continued the second day with opening statements from both sides. At the end of Al Lowes's opening statement, the judge declared a short recess. When the trial resumed, the prosecution began presenting its case. It spanned the rest of June 14 and part of June 15.

Much of the cross-examination of Deputy Newman was aimed at undercutting the credibility of Mark Abbott, the prosecution's star witness. Newman said, "Abbott didn't come in until the Householders were gone and Officer Moore and Deputy Walter arrived at the scene and called back a report," which suggested he hadn't come straight from the highway exit. He identified the Abbott twin who came in as "Matt" Abbott because that is what the night jailer, Wes Drury, said he heard.

Reserve Deputy Rick Walter said he was hanging around after his shift at the dispatcher's station when the Householders came in to report the car on the exit ramp. On cross-examination, he testified that "the window on the driver's side was between a quarter and halfway down."

★ ★ ★

Christy Naile said she knew Josh. During the summer of 1992, she rode around with him and Amanda Drury, who was his girlfriend at the time, pretty much every weekend. "The last time I saw him in the area before the murder was in the beginning of August. The next time I saw him was in December, around Christmas."

Christy said she owned a white 1985 Plymouth Duster. She drove Josh and Amanda in it that summer, but "I never let him drive." At most, he had been "under the wheel." She said, "I kept a spare key in a magnetic box in the wheel well in case I locked my keys inside, but I don't remember Josh ever being around when I used the spare key."

On Saturday night, November 7, the night Mischelle was murdered, Christy was in Sikeston with her boyfriend. They had driven in her car. "I got home about 12:10 or 12:15 a.m. When I got up the next day, the car hadn't moved from where I parked it, and the gas gauge looked like it was at the same level."

★ ★ ★

Lelicia O'Dell said she was Mischelle's best friend. They met when they were both taking classes at a martial arts school in Sikeston. She said, "Mischelle was dating Lyle Day most often, but she still dated Leon Lamb occasionally." She described the last night she spent with Mischelle. "We drove around for a while with Eric Shanks—I was dating him at the time—and Vince Howard, but nothing unusual happened. Around 11:00, they dropped us off at Mischelle's car, and we went to McDonald's. Then, we rode around by ourselves for a while. Mischelle took me home around midnight."

On cross-examination, Lelicia testified that she had never seen Josh before she saw him in the courtroom that day and that Mischelle never mentioned him. Then, Al Lowes tried to use his questions to suggest that Leon Lamb, Lyle Day, or even Mark Abbott could have killed Mischelle.

Hulshof immediately objected when Lowes asked Lelicia, "Now, were Vince Howard and Eric Shanks, were those both white boys?" Out of the hearing of the jury, Lowes explained that he intended to show that "Leon Lamb saw her and raised holy hell about her hanging around this black boy of this particular night." The judge sustained the objection, and

Lowes dropped the line of questioning. He asked Lelicia, "Lyle Day, he rode around in a little white Escort, didn't he, in late October and early November of 1992?" She said, "Yes." Then, Lowes asked about one of Mischelle's purported pregnancies.

> Q. Now, Mischelle told you some two or three weeks before she was killed that she had told the Day boy that she was pregnant, and he got rough with her?
>
> A. Yes, sir.

Finally, Lowes asked about a "guy named Mark" that Mischelle had mentioned several times in her journal. He asked if Mischelle had ever mentioned four incidents noted in the journal involving this Mark, including one in which she said that she took Mark and Jocko home from the Purple Crackle, that she kissed Mark, that he asked her out, and that she left him and returned to the Purple Crackle. Lelicia said, "No."

★ ★ ★

Leon Lamb's direct testimony was brief. He said that Mischelle was his girlfriend; that she had come by his house the night of the murder around midnight; and that after talking a while, they "got a little bit intimate" before she left around 1:00 a.m. On cross-examination, Lamb admitted that Mischelle had never mentioned Josh and that he had never seen Josh before he saw him when he came that day to court. Then, Lowes spent most of his questions suggesting that Lamb may have been the killer. In his folksy way, he tried to get Lamb to admit he was drunk and was angry with Mischelle the night she was killed because she was driving around with Vince Howard. When Lamb said he had one or two beers that night, Lowes asked sarcastically, "One or two beers all of Saturday night?" Then, he asked about Lamb's confrontation with Mischelle on the movie theater parking lot: "And didn't you then grimace at the little girl and call her aside and talk to her out of the presence of Lelicia and these two other boys?" Lamb said he "didn't remember it that way." Lowes asked Lamb if he ever told Mischelle she "shouldn't be hanging around a person like Vince Howard." When Lamb admitted that he had, Lowes asked:

> Q. Is that because he was a black man?
>
> A. No. I heard that he was bad news.

Lamb also admitted that at one time, Mischelle told him she was pregnant and that he wasn't happy about it. The judge cut off a question about
entries in Mischelle's journal and whether he knew she told witnesses she
was afraid of him and had accused him of pushing her around and giving
her bruises. Lamb didn't answer any of these questions, but the jury heard
enough to know what Lowes was trying to convey.

★ ★ ★

The prosecution called Mark Abbott to provide a key component of its
case. His testimony would place Josh an interstate's width away from
Mischelle's body within minutes of her death.

Abbott described what he did on the night of November 7, 1992,
before he found Mischelle's body. He said he arrived at Country Nights
in Sikeston around 10:00 or 11:00 p.m. "I ran into Heather Pierce, who
was there with her mother, Glenna, and I danced with both of them. I left
by myself around 1:00, when the place was closing. Then, I headed north
on 55 to go home." He admitted he had a lot to drink that night: "I really
don't remember, 5, 10, I don't know." He pulled up behind a car parked at
the top of the exit ramp, with all its lights on, including the dome light, and
the engine running. "I got out and went over to the car and saw somebody
lying across the front seat. I thought it was somebody passed out drunk, so
I reached in through the driver's window and picked the person up." He
said, "When I lifted the body, I saw the long hair covering the person's
face. It was all bloody, and I heard a gurgling sound."

Abbott said he left as soon as he realized what he had found and drove
across the overpass to the closest public telephone, which was hanging on
a pole outside a convenience store that was closed for the night. He parked
his truck next to the phone, got out, and tried unsuccessfully to call 911.
As he stood at the phone, a car pulled up next to his truck. It was a "kind
of sporty looking kind of car . . . white with louvers on the back window.
I could see the driver real good, but I could only see head shapes of the
others." The driver said, "We are going to have to go with you. We are
out of fuel." Then, Hulshof asked him who the driver was, and he pointed
to Josh and said, "Right there."

Asked how he responded, Abbott said he told the driver, "Screw
you," hopped in his truck and drove directly to the sheriff's office in Benton. When he entered the building, "Wes Drury was standing there, and
I told him that there was something wrong with a girl down there at the
exit." He said that Deputy Drury called him Matt, his twin brother's name,
as he was leaving, but he also said Drury asked, "Do you still live in the

trailer park outside Scott City, which was my correct address." He said, "I went back to the interstate for a minute or two when I left the sheriff's office because I was curious about what was going on. There were police cars there already when I got back."

Abbott said he went to see Heather Pierce in Cape Girardeau after he left the murder scene. "I arranged to do that at Country Nights. But I decided to go home instead, and then I changed my mind again."

Hulshof asked Abbott about his identification of photographs of Josh and Christy Naile's car the following March. He marked as an exhibit the picture array of six young men that Abbott had been shown and asked Abbott to indicate which one he picked as the driver of the car at the Cut-Mart. It was number three, the Bourbonnais, Illinois, mug shot of Josh, shirtless and looking nowhere in particular, with a gaze that was sullen and forlorn. Then, Hulshof showed Abbott the eight pictures of small white cars. Abbott identified the picture he said the man at the Cut-Mart was driving, the one that belonged to Christy Naile. But he said, "I didn't know whose car it was at the time, and I still don't know." It was one of three cars with louvers on the back window, although Abbott referred to the louvers as a spoiler when he said, "It was the spoiler I recognized."

Lowes hammered away at the fact that Abbott said nothing about seeing a man in a small white car at the Cut-Mart the first several times he talked to law enforcement. Lowes questioned Abbott about his claim that he reached through the driver's-side window to lift Mischelle's body. Abbott admitted, "I couldn't a done it unless the window was all the way down," but then he insisted, "It was."

Abbott acknowledged that he told investigators the driver of the car at the Cut-Mart was "dark complected and possibly Hispanic."

Q. Now, look at this boy sitting here today. Does he look the least little bit Hispanic to you?

A. To me, yeah, kind of.

Q. He looks Hispanic to you?

A. His shape not his tone.

Q. How many Hispanics have you seen that have blue eyes?

A. I don't know. I don't pay no attention to that.

Lowes returned to this theme a little later when he asked if "this Kezer boy qualifies, by your version, to be dark complected."

A. Not now, no.

Q. Well, do you suppose that he took some whitening pills or something?

A. Well, he might have been out in the sun; you might get dark too.

Lowes suggested another reason Abbott picked Josh from the photo lineup. Abbott agreed that Josh's photo "was quite obviously the only one that clearly showed that it had been taken with a police background" and "the fuzziest picture" in the array.

★ ★ ★

The prosecution continued with its case on Wednesday, June 15. The witnesses that day were the three young men who came forward while incarcerated and claimed they heard Josh confess.

Shawn Mangus was the first. He said he currently lived in Louisiana but used to live in Cape Girardeau, where he met Josh and Kelly Church. He admitted that he had been convicted of stealing in 1993 and had gotten a one-year sentence that he served in the county jail. He described an occasion when he was in an apartment with several others and he and Josh were in a backroom when Josh said, "I was the one who shot the girl that was found dead at the Benton exit." He brought this conversation to the attention of his jailers, claiming that it was "kind of hard to sleep not knowing if it were possibly true that this had happened, that he was the one that did it; it was kind of hard for me to sleep at night."

The prosecution anticipated cross-examination about Mangus's recantation. Hulshof asked Mangus about the statement he had signed for Rosener in August 1993. "It was false—Josh admitted killing that girl." He also said he agreed to sign the August recantation on the sixth or seventh visit from Rosener.

Q. Then why would you sign something that wasn't true, sir?

A. Well, because I was told that Josh was making phone calls and that I was in danger, and I was still sitting in jail and I was kind of scared at the time.

Q. Who was it that made those statements to you, sir?

A. Mr. David Rosener.

The jury would hear repeatedly during the trial that Josh was in a gang. It would not be much of a leap for the jurors to imagine that the "friends" who were frightening Mangus were Josh's fellow gang members.

Hulshof introduced a letter Mangus had sent to Josh, apologizing for telling investigators that Josh confessed, and asked him why he had written it.

> A. Well, he said that it would be a good idea if I wrote Josh and let him know that I had changed my story. He said that maybe I should apologize to him, is what he said.
>
> Q. Who told you that would be a good idea?
>
> A. Mr. Rosener.

Hulshof asked Mangus why he wrote letters to Chuck Weissinger, telling him that he had changed his story and had admitted that Josh hadn't confessed to them. Mangus said he wanted Weissinger to know that "I had turned my story around so that I wouldn't be testifying so that I wouldn't be snitching, I guess you would say, on Josh. Since I was still in jail, that was a bad thing to be."

David Rosener couldn't be a witness to challenge these claims because of the agreement Al Lowes had made in response to the prosecution's pretrial motion to disqualify Rosener and his firm from representing Josh. The jury would only hear that Rosener threatened a witness to get him to change his story. They wouldn't even hear that Rosener was barred from testifying in response. During a break, Rosener asked Hulshof, "Why are you doing this to me?" Hulshof answered, "Don't take it personally; it's just trial tactics." But it was personal to Rosener and Josh. Hulshof was attempting to put Josh in prison for what could be the remainder of his life. And he was willing to destroy Rosener to get it done.

Without another witness to the conversations between Rosener and Mangus, Al Lowes could do little more than poke away at Mangus's credibility.

> You originally were looking at first-degree robbery and armed criminal action and had a $100,000 bond you couldn't make. . . . Not long after you agreed to snitch, your bond was dropped to $3,000, and you got released. . . . And then the armed criminal action charge was dropped, and the Class A felony robbery charge was reduced to a misdemeanor drug possession and unlawful use of a weapon, isn't that right? . . . You were facing a minimum of 10 years on the robbery charge alone.

Mangus also admitted that a couple of state troopers flew down to Louisiana to talk to him after he signed the recantation statement for Rosener and that he changed his story back to the original version after that visit.

★ ★ ★

Steve Grah followed Mangus. He said that he had known Josh for a few months before his arrest and that both were members of the Latin Kings. He described a conversation he said he had had with Josh in the middle of January 1993, during a party at Stacy Reed's place on Morgan Oak Street in Cape Girardeau. He said Josh asked him if he could talk to him on the porch and when they got outside, Josh told him, "I killed this girl." Grah said he asked Josh, "Why did you do that?" and Josh responded, "I did it because she wouldn't take me home to Sikeston after a party." He also said that two days later, Josh showed him the .380 Beretta he said he used to kill her.

Grah claimed he offered to testify against Josh because "I felt that I needed to come forward, you know, because I felt bad about what he had done and somebody needed to know." On cross-examination, Al Lowes questioned his real motivation.

> Q. Well, right after that, your bond went down from $50,000 cash to $3,000, and you got out on the ground, didn't you?
>
> A. Yes, I did because there was no evidence in my case.
>
> Q. Oh, I see. Well, now, you were charged with, you and another fellow, beating up and like to killing some poor citizen, weren't you?
>
> A. Yes, we were.
>
> Q. And the other boy stood trial, and he got 35 years, didn't he?

Hulshof objected to this question, and the judge sustained. Lowes tried another approach.

> Q. Well, in any event, you managed to work yourself a 10-year sentence, didn't you?
>
> A. Yes.
>
> Q. And you and Pony Boy were charged with the same crimes, weren't you?
>
> A. Yes.

Lowes took Grah through a list of his eight prior felony convictions, including for kidnapping and burglary, and showed that he could have been sentenced as a prior and persistent offender, with sentences for multiple felonies strung end to end before he was eligible for parole.

Lowes worked to bring out discrepancies in Grah's testimony. He confronted Grah with the fact that the first few times he talked to investigators about Josh, he failed to mention anything about the confession he was now claiming Josh made. Asked to put a date on Josh's confession, Grah said it was "sometime in the middle of January, the end of January, the beginning of February," but he thought more likely it was the middle of January. Then, he admitted, as he had testified in his deposition, that it was in late January or early February, a date he remembered because "it was a couple of days after you got married and your wife had a baby two days after you got married, right?" Later in the trial, Lowes would introduce evidence that Stacy Reed was evicted from the place on Morgan Oak during the first week in January.

★ ★ ★

Samuel Wade Howard was the third snitch witness to testify. Kenny Hulshof took him through an account of the confession he claimed Josh had made while they were locked up together. "Well, we was in there, and he asked me, you know, about how did I feel about my case, about what happened, you know, and I told him that I felt pretty bad about it. He said, 'Yeah, I know what you mean.' I said, 'What do you mean by that?' you know, and he told me that he felt bad about shooting and killing Mischelle Lawless."

Hulshof asked Howard questions on direct examination intended to defuse Lowes's anticipated cross-examination. Hulshof introduced the re-cantation statement Howard had given to Rosener.

> Q. Did you tell Mr. Rosener that Joshua Kezer had confessed or admitted to you that he had shot and killed Angela Mischelle Lawless?
>
> A. Yes, sir, I did.
>
> Q. And how many times do you think that you told the defense counsel that while he was talking to you?
>
> A. To Mr. Rosener?
>
> Q. Yes.
>
> A. Probably several times, several.

Howard explained the recantation by claiming Rosener "wrote down things I didn't say." He claimed, "I told him about it, and he told me to put my initials in the margin next to each one. He said he would fix it, but I guess he didn't."

Howard insisted he wasn't promised anything in exchange for his testimony, but he did admit that the prosecution "come at me with a plea," which reduced the charge from first- to second-degree murder. He denied he told Rosener, when Rosener approached him at the Scott County Jail, that he wouldn't talk to him because he didn't yet have his deal.

On cross-examination, Howard did acknowledge, however, that he talked to Rosener just a few weeks after his plea and sentencing. Then, Lowes asked about the details of the statement he eventually gave Rosener.

> Q. Now, isn't it a fact that you talked to Rosener and you wrote out and on page two you signed it, "When I talked with Josh Kezer, during the summer of 1993, Josh repeatedly told me and the other inmates that he didn't kill the Lawless girl and that he was way up in Kankakee, Illinois, on the night that she got killed?
>
> A. No, sir, that is incorrect.

Hulshof objected that Rosener wrote the statement Lowes read and that it wasn't what he had said.

> Q. Well, he wrote it down and you signed the page, didn't you?
>
> A. Yes, sir, but he told me to initial the one for the mistakes.

Lowes jumped on the fact that there were no initials next to the statement that Howard claimed was incorrect.

> Q. Well, are there any initials about any mistakes?
>
> A. I would assume that there was initials on the outside of it.
>
> Q. You assume there were initials on the outside?
>
> A. Yes, sir.
>
> Q. Outside of what, the back side?
>
> A. No, showing the mistakes.

Howard acknowledged that he failed to mention these mistakes to anyone until Luther Van Godsey interviewed him shortly before the trial began.

* * *

Amanda Drury described her relationship with Josh. They met in June 1992, when she was 16. She and her best friend, Christy Naile, gave Josh and Kelly Church a ride when they were cruising Broadway in Cape Girardeau. She went out with Josh for a few months after that, usually driving around the way they had done the day she met him. "Christy usually drove us, but I saw Josh drive it once." She said, "Christy kept a spare key hidden in the wheel well in case she locked her keys inside. I was with Christy a couple of times when she used the spare, and I think Josh maybe saw her do it." She broke up with Josh in August, and she only saw him twice after that, in late August and early September, when he came to the Baptist church and to her grandparents' house.

On cross-examination, Amanda said she had never seen Josh with a gun and, as far as she knew, he didn't know Mischelle Lawless. She acknowledged a statement she had given the defense: "When I was interviewed by the police, it seemed like they, namely, Brenda Schiwitz and Bill Ferrell, just wanted me to say that Josh Kezer killed Mischelle. I was enticed by them by the possibility of receiving the $10,000 reward, but I didn't tell them that Josh killed her because I had no reason to believe that Josh did it."

* * *

Testimony of the key investigators, Brenda Schiwitz, Don Windham, and Bill Ferrell rounded out the prosecution's presentation of its case, and their testimony gave Al Lowes another chance to undercut the credibility of Mark Abbott and the three snitch witnesses.

Brenda Schiwitz said Abbott came to see her at the sheriff's office the afternoon of the day he reported finding Mischelle's body. Lowes tried to cast Abbott as a likely suspect that investigators overlooked. He asked Schiwitz, "Why is it he was never vampired so his blood could be compared to blood at the crime scene?" She said that was Sheriff Ferrell's decision, but she also insisted that Abbott "wasn't a suspect in the killing, not at any time."

Schiwitz said Abbott told her about his encounter at the Cut-Mart with the young man driving a small white car. Confronted with the fact that Abbott had called Josh dark complected in contemporaneous police reports, she had to agree that "He is light complected now," and she added that "with black hair, naturally you will look a little darker complected." Asked to comment on the fact that Abbott had described the man in the white car as possibly Hispanic, she had to agree with Lowes's argument that "He does not speak or have anything that sounds like Spanish."

Corporal Windham was next. Mangus told Windham and Deputy Schiwitz that Josh took him aside while they were in Stacy Reed's apartment and said he had killed the girl in Benton. Two weeks before the beginning of the trial, Windham flew down to Louisiana on a State airplane with Luther Van Godsey to ask Mangus why he had recanted. Windham said Mangus told them that "the reason that he retracted his statement was because Mr. Rosener had told him that Kezer was making threatening phone calls, or phone calls to dangerous people that were inside gangs, and other dangerous people in the county and that his life was in danger." Then, according to Mangus, Rosener said he would not have such problems if he retracted his statement.

Windham described Mark Abbott's selection of Josh from the six-picture photo lineup that he and Deputy Schiwitz showed him. Abbott didn't stop to read the lineup instructions but immediately said, "This is him: he was wearing a black leather jacket." Windham was concerned that Abbott had answered too quickly and told him he had to be sure, but Abbott just repeated, "That is him." Windham said that Josh was wearing a black leather jacket when they picked him up in Kankakee. On cross-examination, Windham acknowledged that Abbott originally said the man was wearing a long-sleeved sweater.

Sheriff Ferrell's testimony was short and limited to just a few topics. His direct testimony was entirely about the written statement that Wade Howard gave him—how Howard said Josh admitted to him that he had killed Mischelle. Al Lowes's cross-examination also was limited. The sheriff acknowledged that investigators found no evidence that Mischelle Lawless knew Josh.[2] He also acknowledged that they hadn't found the murder weapon or any physical evidence linking Josh to the murder.

At the end of Ferrell's testimony, the State rested. After some discussion of admission of exhibits, the judge and the lawyers adjourned to chambers to discuss the fact that a new witness had suddenly come forward. Mischelle's friend, Chantelle Crider, had been watching the trial since it began. Hulshof informed the judge she had just told Luther Van Godsey that she recognized the defendant from a Halloween party she had attended with Mischelle a week before Mischelle was murdered.[3] The judge ordered that Chantelle be made available for her deposition before she would be called as a witness in rebuttal. Then, he came back on the bench, and the trial resumed with the presentation of the case for the defense.

★ ★ ★

Testimony of defense witnesses took up the rest of Wednesday, June 15, and most of the following day. Al Lowes relied primarily on four kinds of evidence. Five Kankakee area residents testified that Josh was there at or around the time of the murder. Chuck Weissinger testified that Mangus's account of Josh's tearful confession had all been a lie. Several law enforcement witnesses further undercut Mark Abbott's credibility regarding what he saw at the crime scene that night. Finally, two witnesses from the state crime lab testified regarding the lack of physical evidence linking Josh to the murder. With all that going for the defense, Lowes felt good about his chances of getting a verdict of acquittal.

★ ★ ★

Brenda Garduno was 39 years old. At the time of the trial, she lived in Metropolis, Illinois, in the far southern part of the state, across the Ohio River from Kentucky. In 1992, she was living in Bradley, near Kankakee. "I met Josh for the first time in July or the beginning of August 1992, shortly after I moved up to Kankakee. He came to my house to see his cousin, Michael Whisker, who was living at my house with my daughter, Christina. Pretty soon, Josh was spending a lot of time at my house." Garduno said, "I saw him at my house on the night of November 7." Lowes asked if there was some reason that she remembered that particular date. "It was the same night my daughter Christina, Josh's cousin Michael, and one of my sons were in a car wreck."

Garduno said her mother died in Metropolis on November 3, and she went there for the funeral. She was just crossing the bridge coming back into Bradley on November 7 when she heard the sirens of the emergency vehicles racing to the accident scene. "When I heard the sirens, I looked at my watch, and it was around a quarter to 7:00." She said, "Around 8:30, while I was visiting at my father's house, my daughter and Michael showed up. They were driving my father's car and needed to tell him about the wreck." She continued, "I was worried about both of them, but especially my daughter because she was three months pregnant. I was relieved when they told me they already were examined at the hospital. They were shaken up, but they weren't badly hurt."

Garduno said she spent some time trying to contact the salvage yard to find out what had happened to the wreck. They all went home after a late dinner at McDonald's. Her husband went to bed right away, and Christina and Michael did the same a little later.

> I stayed up watching television with my youngest son and my oldest daughter. I was watching television when Josh came to the door with Jeremy Daniels and another boy. It was about 11:30. Josh was upset, and he wanted to talk to his cousin to make sure he was all right. I told him that Michael had a headache. I said I didn't want to wake him, but I said I would check if he was asleep. I went to the bedroom door, and Christina told me Michael was asleep. Josh was satisfied to hear that, and he left.

If the jury believed Josh was in northern Illinois at 11:30 p.m. on November 7, they would have to conclude that he couldn't have murdered Mischelle less than two hours later, 350 miles away.

During cross-examination, Hulshof questioned Garduno's ability to remember the exact date Josh came to visit his cousin when she had trouble remembering other dates, like the date Rosener visited to take her statement in the case. She repeated that November 7 was memorable because it was the day she returned from Metropolis after burying her mother and the day of her pregnant daughter's car wreck. Al Lowes called an officer from the Kankakee Police Department as a witness later that day who identified a police report of an accident involving Michael Whisker on November 7, 1992, at 6:44 p.m.

Josh's maternal aunt, Kathryn Faye Smith, his mother's older sister, testified that she talked to Josh from work by telephone twice between 4:00 and 6:00 the evening of November 7, 1992. "I called home after my dinner break around 4:00 or 4:30, and Josh answered. I talked to him again when he called me to give me the message that my brother, Hank, called about returning a costume he borrowed the week before for a Halloween party. I'm sure these calls happened on November 7 because it was the day that one of my nephews, Michael Whisker, was in a car accident."

Theresa Mae Griffey was 35 years old when she testified. "Josh moved in with us soon after [they met], and he stayed until the beginning of December." She said Josh was at her home on November 7.

> I remember that day because he was upset that his cousin was in a car accident. I tried to calm him down. We talked for a while, and then he left to go over to his cousin's house to check on him. When he came back a little later, he still was upset. He had an argument with Kim, who was staying with us. I finally got him to calm down about 3:00 in the

morning, and we all went to bed. I got up in the morning and fixed breakfast for everyone, and Josh was there.

Then, Lowes said he wanted "to get the times pinned down on the seventh."

Q. What time, approximately, would he have left your house and went to see about his cousin?

A. If I am not mistaken, it was around 12:00 in the afternoon.

Lowes was taken aback but continued as best he could, without seeming like he was trying to impeach his own witness.

Q. Twelve in the afternoon, right?

A. Right.

Q. And about how long was he gone or about when did he come back?

A. He was gone about an hour, or two hours at the most, and then he came back.

Q. Okay. Did the accident happen at night or in the daytime?

A. I believe that it happened during the day.

Unable to induce a correction, Lowes shifted to trying to demonstrate that Josh was at the Griffeys' home the rest of that day and night.

Q. Okay. In any event, you think that he came back after an hour or so?

A. Yes.

Q. And some time that night, midnight or after, while around there, he and some other young ones got in a little argument and you had to make peace with the kids, huh?

A. Yeah.

Hulshof began his cross-examination by questioning Griffey's certainty about events on November 7, saying her memory for a lot of dates wasn't so good but for the day "Rosener wanted her to remember," her memory had gotten better. She said he was making her nervous and tried to explain that she had trouble remembering exactly when she met Josh in GED class because she had been taking GED classes since 1986. She dug in deeper with her insistence that Josh left to see his cousin around noon. When Hulshof told Griffey that Brenda Garduno remembered "the time the defendant may have been there . . . was that it was at midnight because she was upset and her husband was upset that the defendant had woken them up," she said, "he left on two occasions," once with her son and the second time by himself.

★ ★ ★

Kenny Hulshof proposed to have Chantelle Crider testify that she and Mischelle Lawless encountered Josh at a party they attended together on Halloween night, a week before Mischelle's murder, to rebut testimony that Josh didn't know Mischelle and to provide a motive for the murder. He proposed to have Doug Brantley testify that Josh threatened him with a gun that same night outside the Billiards Center in Cape Girardeau, to rebut testimony of witnesses who said they had never seen Josh with a gun. Al Lowes tried to counter this anticipated rebuttal testimony with evidence Josh was in Kankakee for Halloween.

Josh's Aunt Kathy said she had bought some candy for her youngest son, James, and Josh to pass out to trick-or-treaters on Halloween in 1992, but she discovered when she got home from work at 5:00 p.m. that evening that the two boys had eaten most of the candy already. When she left around 9:00 or 10:00 p.m., Josh was in the garage with his cousin, James, playing very loud music.

Angela Marcotte said she was Christina Garduno's best friend and knew Josh from seeing him at Christina's house. She said she picked him up on Halloween in 1992 at the Griffeys' house just as it was getting dark and took him and others to Angie Graham's to go trick-or-treating.

David Griffey said he and Josh got together about 7:00 or 8:00 p.m. that evening and went trick-or-treating with five or six of their friends. He and Josh dressed up as ninjas. He believed Josh spent Halloween night at his house.

★ ★ ★

Chuck Weissinger was Al Lowes's answer to Mangus and Grah. He knew both of them and had been locked up with them in the Cape County Jail. Unlike Mangus, however, Weissinger stood by his recantation of that tale and testified for the defense.

Weissinger said he was 25 years old and lived in Cape Girardeau, working as a laborer at Cape Vault making caskets and burial vaults. Lowes knew Hulshof would use Weissinger's criminal record to attack his credibility. Hulshof even had direct knowledge of some of those facts. He had represented Weissinger as a public defender on one of the charges. In an attempt to lessen the impact, Lowes took Weissinger through his long string of felonies.

Weissinger said he was in the Cape Girardeau County Jail from about January 24, 1993, until sometime in May of that year, with Shawn Mangus, Steven Grah, and Isaac Johnson. He said Mangus and Johnson were the first to discuss the plan and that Grah joined in later. Mangus said they could get lighter sentences because "the Lawless murder was a big deal in Benton." Weissinger said Mangus supplied the details of the story they were to tell, weaving together truth and fiction. "It's true we all knew each other and spent time hanging out at Stacy Reed's apartment, with a lot of other people, at the end of 1992 and the beginning of 1993. Shawn told us all we had to do was claim we were there with Josh, in Stacy's bedroom, and Josh told us he killed the girl in Benton. Shawn also told us we could get a reward."

Weissinger told the jury that, in fact, Josh never "admitted he had anything to do with the death of Mischelle Lawless." His written statement to investigators—that he had seen Josh carrying a variety of handguns—"was a lie." Weissinger illustrated his dependence on the tale Mangus gave him to repeat by recounting how he first told the investigators that the murder happened in the Benton that was across the river in central Illinois. He described how investigators subtly coached him, using the written statement Mangus had given them, to identify the right Benton and to correct his testimony on other points.

★ ★ ★

Lowes called several law enforcement witnesses for various reasons. Roy Moore told the jury that the window on the driver's side of Mischelle's car "was down only five to seven inches when I arrived at the crime scene," too little, he thought, to allow Mark Abbott to reach in the window and pick up a body. He also testified he was certain the Hispanic man who stopped at the crime scene wasn't Josh, but on cross-examination, he said he didn't search the car, suggesting that Josh could have been hiding inside.

Deputy Beardslee told the jury about his interview with Mark Abbott, in which Abbott failed to mention anything about the Hispanic man in the small white car looking for "fuel." He also testified, somewhat reluctantly given his position as Ferrell's chief deputy, about the implausibility of Abbott's account of what he did when he found the body.

Q. You saw that car and where the window was, and it would have been pretty difficult to reach very far in, as big as the Abbott boy is, wouldn't it?

A. I don't believe I could have done it, but I just don't know.

When Beardslee said Abbott described the window as only "partially" or "halfway" down, Lowes referred him to the transcript of his interview, where he agreed that Abbott had told him the window was all the way down. Beardslee said the transcript of the tape would have the definitive answer.

Then there was the issue of Mischelle's rings, which according to Deputy Schiwitz's inventory, were sitting in the center console of Mischelle's car but that Abbott claimed he saw on Mischelle's hands.

Q. Tom Beardslee didn't see any rings on the little girl's fingers, did he?

A. I don't recall any; no, sir.

Beardslee said that Abbott wasn't a suspect and that they did take his fingerprints for comparison with those at the crime scene.

Q. Do you know why Abbott, neither one of the Abbott boys, was not vampired in this investigation?

A. What?

Q. Vampired, blood drawn?

A. Blood samples?

Beardslee said he didn't know.

★ ★ ★

Al Lowes called two witnesses from the state's crime lab to emphasize the fact that there was no forensic evidence connecting Josh to the crime.

Dr. Robert Briner, the director of the state crime lab, testified that Josh's blood type is A, which eliminated him as the source of the B antigen under Mischelle's fingernails. In connection with the luminol reactions on Josh's jacket and in Christy Naile's car, he explained that luminol detects only the "possible presence of blood." Other substances show the same luminescence. The FBI Lab couldn't do anything with the Scott County samples. It couldn't even tell if the specks were blood.

Andy Wagner was a firearms and tool marks examiner at the state crime lab. Over the course of the investigation, he test fired about a dozen guns, all .380s, including one that was provided by the Kankakee Police Department. None of them matched the bullets that killed Mischelle, and none had a connection with Josh.

At this point, the defense rested, and the prosecution spent the rest of the day presenting its two rebuttal witnesses.

★ ★ ★

Defense counsel had an opportunity to interview Chantelle Crider the previous night and confirmed that her account of the Halloween party would provide a link between Josh and Mischelle and a motive for the murder. Al Lowes objected to Chantelle's testimony, arguing that her description of Josh's attempt to kiss her was inadmissible evidence of another crime—"Sexual assault, probably in the second or third degree." Judge Murphy overruled the objection and allowed her to testify.

Chantelle said she lived in Sikeston and despite being a year and a half younger, was "best friends" with Mischelle Lawless. "I went to a party at John Worley's trailer with Mischelle and Lelicia O'Dell. We got ready at Lelicia's house and left there about 7:00 or 7:30. We got to the party about 8:30. There were about eight girls at the party, I think, and the rest were guys. Everyone was standing around a bonfire in the back and drinking."

Chantelle said that at one point in the evening, she and Mischelle went inside the trailer to use the bathroom. As they were walking out, a boy she didn't know but identified as Josh came up to her and asked her out. "He tried to kiss me, and I told him no." She was "pretty sure" he was drunk. Then, he asked Mischelle out, and she said no. He got mad and called Mischelle a "stupid bitch."

Chantelle said they left the party fairly early, around midnight at the latest. Lelicia was driving, Chantelle was on the passenger side, and Mischelle was in the middle, and the windows were down. "As we were leaving, [the young man she identified as Josh] came up to the car and asked if he could come with us, and we said no. He grabbed the door handle and yelled at us to stay, but we took off with him holding the handle." That was the last time she saw him until the trial.

On cross-examination, Chantelle acknowledged that she said nothing about the incident at the Halloween party when she was interviewed by Don Windham shortly after the murder. She explained that she looked at Josh's face at the trial, and it started coming back to her who he was.

Doug Brantley lived in Cape Girardeau. On Halloween night in 1992, he was at the Billiards Center with his wife, his sister-in-law, and two of his brothers-in-law. They were playing pool at a table near the door. "About an hour before closing, I noticed three young men standing near the door talking. One of them had a cup of something, I think it was beer, in his hand, and he was spilling it on himself. He was wearing eyeliner and had an upside-down cross painted on his head."

Brantley and his little group left the Billiards Center around 1:00 a.m., as the place was closing. The three young men who were standing by the door were still there when Brantley walked out. They followed Brantley down the street and crossed toward a mid-70s three-quarter ton pickup with Illinois plates. "The boy who spilled beer on himself yelled at us, 'Are these the head-giving whores?' I asked him, 'What did you say?' and he repeated the question. The other two boys were getting in the truck, and I told the one yelling to get in with them and leave. He yelled back to me, 'Fat boy, I'll kill you.' He had a handgun. It was black, with a rectangular barrel; it was the kind of gun that loads bullets in a clip." Then, Brantley pointed to Josh and identified him as the drunk who had threatened him. After Brantley testified, Hulshof announced that he had nothing further, and the trial ended for the day.

★ ★ ★

On Friday, June 17, the proceedings continued with a brief "surrebuttal" witness. Al Lowes wanted to call Corporal Windham to testify about his interview with Lelicia O'Dell, given shortly after the murder, in which she said it was a boy named Todd Mayberry who was kissing Mischelle at the Halloween party. In a conference outside the hearing of the jury, Lowes explained to the judge that he wanted to show it was someone other than Josh who had harassed Mischelle. Hulshof objected to this proposed testimony as hearsay, and Judge Murphy sustained the objection.[4]

Lowes called Windham as a witness anyway. Windham testified that Chantelle Crider hadn't mentioned anything about Mischelle being harassed at a Halloween party when he interviewed her soon after the murder—that she mentioned it for the first time when he interviewed her during the trial. Lowes couldn't, and didn't, ask him about Lelicia O'Dell or Todd Mayberry.

At that point, the trial testimony concluded. Al Lowes renewed his motion for a directed verdict of acquittal, in his own peculiar fashion. "I guess, Judge, we are going to give the Court another chance to make another mistake. Just as before, obviously, we don't think that the case has been made on the first count, and the second count tags along."

The judge quickly overruled the motion and went on to reading the instructions that would govern the jury's deliberations. Closing arguments began after that.

★ ★ ★

After Al Lowes made his closing argument, Kenny Hulshof had the last word, and he used it to send the jury to deliberations primed to convict Josh. He portrayed Josh as a gun-flashing hothead, capable of murderous rage when spurned by a girl he liked, tying together testimony of Steve Grah that Josh proudly displayed a .380 Beretta, of Corporal Windham that he bragged he could get a gun any time he needed one, and of Chantelle Crider that he fought with Mischelle at a Halloween party when she rejected him. He asked the jury to "imagine with me the last minutes of Mischelle's life" as "she fought with [Josh] for her life down the embankment next to the highway exit and how [Josh] pointed his prized Beretta through the open car window and fired into her head." Then, he turned to filling holes in the prosecution's case.

Hulshof recounted that Mangus stuck to his story the first few times Rosener visited him. But then, Josh's lawyer says:

> You know some people, some phone calls are being made out there. You are a sitting duck in here. You are going to have some problems. You are going to be labeled a snitch. . . . I think that you all can use your common sense to decide that once you are labeled a snitch, you know, life ain't pretty from that point on as long as you are in the prison. As long as you are within this little city within a city or this group of people. "All of your problems have gone away," says Josh's lawyer. "All you got to do is sign on the dotted line," and he did it.

For Hulshof, Rosener was behind Wade Howard's recantation too.

> And did you see Mr. Howard on the stand, did you watch him? That man was telling the truth. "I told him that they didn't intimidate me, but he was writing it down before I even said it and I told him that it wasn't right," and he said, "Just put your initials on it and I will correct it." So Mr. Howard unfortunately trusted defense counsel to do the right thing, and then suddenly they try to jam that statement down his throat.

But what about Josh's alibi witnesses? For Hulshof, David Rosener was the explanation again. "There were inconsistencies from their own witnesses. Is it just coincidence that David Rosener went up to Kankakee, and because of his confrontation with Mr. Brantley on Halloween, he was there and said that we needed to alibi him for Halloween, and these witnesses say, 'Sure.'"

His voice dripping with sarcasm, Hulshof continued:

One witness, Ms. Smith, said, "Josh and my son were handing out candy to trick-or-treaters." Remember, she said that she got home and she was upset because all of the candy was gone and then they were out in the garage playing this loud music. That is what she said happened on Halloween. Then we got another guy that comes in and says that they were dressed up like ninjas.

Hulshof had a little more to work with when he got to the alibi witnesses for the night of the murder. Brenda Garduno had testified that Josh came to her house not long before midnight to check on his cousin. Theresa Griffey had testified that Josh left the house to check on his cousin at noon. Hulshof pounced on this discrepancy.

Let's move ahead to the other date that Rosener wants them to alibi his client for, and that is of course the murder. We don't dispute the traffic records. In fact, unfortunately this fellow up there had this car wreck; we don't dispute that fact. But we have got one lady who says that "He showed up at midnight banging on my door, and my husband was upset because I had to get up and let him in." Then, we have got another one of their witnesses who says that he left at noon. I submit to you that the time of 12:00 was suggested to them. Only one of them thought that they were supposed to say 12 midnight, and the other one said 12 noon.

If Rosener was the sort of lawyer who threatened and tricked prisoners into recanting, he certainly was capable of persuading Josh's friends to lie to protect his client. And Rosener couldn't respond because Lowes promised he would not be a witness.

Another weakness in the prosecution's case was the lack of physical evidence linking Josh to the crime. Hulshof made a few tiny luminol spots on Josh's leather jacket and the armrest of Christy Naile's car seem like the scientific link the prosecution needed, and he bolstered Mark Abbott's credibility in the process.

It was Mark Abbott who was there, who saw him. And is it coincidence, ladies and gentlemen, when he is shown the photospread he says, "That is him and he was wearing a black jacket?" Is it a coincidence, ladies and gentlemen, that they spray luminol on the sleeve of the jacket, on the right sleeve, they find the presence of blood? Is it a coincidence, ladies and gentlemen, that he picks Christy Naile's car out, never knowing that she has got a connection to the defendant and that they spray her car with luminol and it glows like a Christmas tree? Is that a coincidence?

Did the jury remember the expert testimony that luminol reacts with a number of substances other than blood and that there wasn't enough of the substance on the jacket or in the car to determine that it was blood, let alone the blood of anyone connected to the case?

★ ★ ★

The jury went out at 1:46 p.m. and came back at 5:15 p.m. The verdict was guilty on both counts—second-degree murder and armed criminal action. As the *Southeast Missourian* reported the next day, "As the jury exited the room, Josh—listening to the muffled sobbing of his mother sitting nearby—began to cry. Josh's tears turned to audible sobs as bailiffs began to lead him from the courtroom. His mother, who was being helped along by family members, moved forward to embrace her son. 'No, I didn't do this,' Josh wailed. 'I didn't kill her. Why didn't they believe that?'" Then, the room closed in on him, and everything went black. The next thing he remembered was lying with his head in his Aunt Kathy's lap.

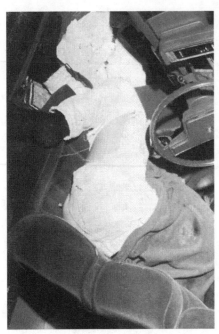

Crime Scene Photograph. *Source: This image is used with permission of the Lawless family.*

Obviously a Mugshot

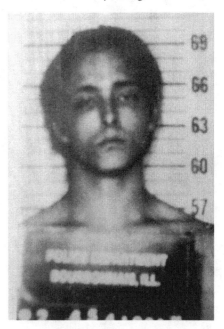

SOUTHEAST MISSOURIAN

VOL. 90...No. 252 Copyright © 1994 Southeast Missourian   SATURDAY, JUNE 18, 1994   50 CENT

Fleeing Simpson captured

■ The arrest shortly before 11 p.m. CST culminated an incredible drama that unfolded on live national TV.

By Michael Fleeman
The Associated Press

LOS ANGELES — O.J. Simpson was hunted down and captured in his driveway Friday night after running from charges of murdering his ex-wife and her male friend and leading police along 60 miles of freeway and city streets.

"I can't express the fear I had that this matter would not end the way it did," said Simpson's attorney, Robert Shapiro, who had been worried the former football great would kill himself.

Outside the walls of Simpson's estate, members of Simpson's family hugged each other and cried after word of the arrest came out. A cheer came up from the crowd

of 200 spectators.

The arrest shortly before 11 p.m. CST culminated an incredible drama that unfolded on live national TV in which police first announced charges against the for-

O.J. Simpson and his former wife, Nicole Brown Simpson, together in October 1993. Charges were filed Friday against Simpson in the slaying of his ex-wife.

mer football great, then said he had disappeared and finally followed him along the highways for more than an hour.

See SIMPSON, Page 4

Thomas Melzer

Fed official defends interest rate hikes

■ Thomas Melzer addresses about 500 people attending Southeast Missouri State

Jury rules that Kezer is guilty on two counts

■ The Ste. Genevieve County jury recommended a prison sentence of 30 years on each count for the death of Angela Mischelle Lawless.

By Cathryn Maya
Staff Writer

STE. GENEVIEVE — It took a Ste. Genevieve County jury less than four hours to return a verdict of guilt against Joshua C. Kezer, accused of the Nov. 8, 1992, shooting death of Angela Mischelle Lawless.

Kezer, 20, sat stone-faced when Circuit Judge Stan Murphy read the jury's decision at the close of the five-day trial Friday night. The jury found him guilty of second-degree murder and armed crimi-

nal action, and recommended he be sentenced to a prison term of 30 years for each count.

As the jury exited the room, Kezer — listening to the verdict sobbing of his mother sitting nearby — began to cry.

Kezer's tears turned to audible sobs as bailiffs began to lead him from the courtroom. His mother, who was being helped along by family members, moved forward to embrace her son.

"No, I didn't do this," Kezer wailed. "I didn't kill her. Why didn't they believe that?"

The body of 19-year-old Lawless was found slumped over the front seat of her car at about 1:25 a.m. Sunday, Nov. 8, 1992, at the end of the northbound Interstate 55 exit ramp to Benton. She had been

See KEZER, Page 4

Josh Conviction Shares Headlines with O. J Capture. *Source: This image is used with the permission of its copyright holder, the Concord Publishing House and the Cape Giradeau Southeast Missourian.*

Josh and His Father on the Kankakee River

Josh and His Mother through the Years

Joshua Kezer was led out of the Ste. Genevieve County Courthouse with his mother Joan after he was sentenced to 60 years in prison Tuesday for killing Angela Mischelle Lawless.

Kezer: Man sentenced to 60 years for Lawless' killing

Josh's Mother Following Him Back to Prison. *Source: This image is used with the permission of its copyright holder, the Concord Publishing House and the Cape Girardeau Southeast Missourian.*

Angela Mischelle Lawless August 2, 1973–November 8, 1992

Josh
in Thailand

Josh and Judge Callahan Making a Presentation

Josh
and
Titan

PART III

BEHIND THE WALLS

"The vilest deeds like poison weeds
Bloom well in prison-air:
It is only what is good in Man
That wastes and withers there:
Pale Anguish keeps the heavy gate,
And the Warder is Despair."

—Oscar Wilde, "The Ballad of Reading Gaol"

10

POSTTRIAL PROCEEDINGS

Josh was taken to the Ste. Genevieve County Jail to await sentencing. "I don't remember the drive from the courthouse to the county jail. When they escorted me into the jail, I stood cuffed and in shackles, in tears." The Ste. Genevieve County Sheriff, Bob McKlin, attended Josh's trial. He knew something wasn't right with Josh's conviction. He told Josh, "Look at me. You're going to be OK." McKlin and his jailers walked Josh back to his cell. They asked him, "You're not going to kill yourself, are you?" Josh said, "No, no, that's not in me." They believed Josh was innocent. Following his conviction, Josh's cellies had been watching television and following the NBA and NHL finals when news of O. J. Simpson's chase in the infamous white Bronco broke. They switched to watch the chase. Josh laid in his bunk in the fetal position and cried. Later that night, a preacher visited Josh. "He'd seen how crushed I was, but knew I needed tough love." He said, "This shouldn't have happened, but it has. You're going to prison. Your tears aren't going to help. It's time to man up." The next day, Josh saw that his conviction shared the front page with Simpson.

The newspapers around Southeast Missouri carried the story of Josh's conviction on the weekend after the end of the trial. One of those papers was the *Scott County Signal*. A 19-year-old Benton girl named Lacey Warren read the story in the Sunday, June 19, edition. She knew Mischelle Lawless from Kelly High and had been following the case in the news. She had seen pictures of Josh in the newspaper and on television and was startled to read that Chantelle Crider testified he was at a Halloween party in Benton a week before the murder. According to the *Signal*, Chantelle said, "I remember his face. There's no doubt in my mind that was him at the party." Lacey was at the party, too, with her friend, Dawn Worley, who also went to Kelly High and knew Mischelle. In fact, Dawn lived in the trailer where the party was held, on a dirt road just off Highway 77 a mile east of the intersection with Interstate 55, the place where Mischelle was murdered.

Lacey went over to Dawn's house the following day. She showed Dawn a copy of the *Signal* with the article about the trial and Chantelle Crider's testimony. "I'm not going to say anything. Just read this article and tell me what you think." When Dawn read the part about Chantelle's testimony, she immediately said, "That was either a downright lie, or she was grossly mistaken."

Both girls agreed. They were sure that Josh wasn't at the party. They knew every boy and every girl who came except for a few who came with their boyfriends and the two who came with Mischelle Lawless—Chantelle Crider and Lelicia O'Dell. Later, at home, Lacey asked her father, "What should I do? That boy wasn't there." He told her, "Get in touch with his lawyer; he'll know what to do." Both girls went to see Al Lowes. By the end of the week, both had signed affidavits swearing that Josh wasn't at the party.

Dawn Worley told Lowes, "I was the host of the party, and my boyfriend, Richard Pierce." She said, "My cousin John was the one who rounded up everybody. He knows a lot of people around Benton." Some of those interviewed in the investigation assumed it was John Worley's party. According to Dawn's affidavit, "There was a bonfire in the backyard, and everybody was near it. Most of the kids were drinking, and we were on the third keg before the party was over. Mischelle showed up about 8:00 and parked near the bonfire. She came with two girls I didn't know. One was a blonde, and the other was a short brunette."

These descriptions fit Chantelle and Lelicia. They came in Mischelle's car, which Dawn described as maroon in color. Mischelle moved around the party, talking to everyone and having a great time. According to Dawn's affidavit, "After Mischelle had been there about an hour or so, she started kissing and making out with Todd Mayberry. I've known Todd for many, many years, and everyone at the party was really surprised that Mischelle and Todd had gotten together that night. They were kissing and smooching for quite some time and seemed to be getting along just fine."

Then, around 10:30 or 11:00, Mischelle and her two girlfriends got into a black Ford Bronco driven by a boy Dawn knew as Mark, whose last name, she was sure, began with a B. "Mark used to work at Raben Tire in Sikeston with my boyfriend and my brother. Mischelle sat in front with Mark, and her two friends sat in back." Mark and the three girls returned before midnight but didn't stay long. Around 12:00 or 12:30, Mischelle and her two friends left in Mischelle's car. "I didn't notice anything eventful happen as they left," Dawn said. "And I didn't notice anything out of the ordinary the two or three times I talked to Mischelle."

Dawn concluded her affidavit by saying she "knew for sure that Chantelle didn't see Josh Kezer at the Halloween party." For good measure, she attached a list of 45 names of those who were there. She explained that she "would not want Josh Kezer or anyone to be blamed for something that they just didn't do."

Lacey's affidavit was similar. She heard about the murder around noon on Sunday while she was at the home of her boyfriend's grandmother. In her affidavit, she said, "I saw [Mischelle] again at Dawn Worley's Halloween party. My boyfriend and I were among the first to arrive, before it was fully dark. Except for a short trip into Benton around 10:00 p.m. to buy cigarettes and a soda, my boyfriend and I spent the whole evening at the party until we left a little before 1:00 a.m."

Lacey remembered Mischelle arriving at the party with two girls she didn't know. She noticed their arrival because most of the vehicles were parked in the front yard, but Mischelle pulled around into the backyard and parked near the fire. Lacey said, "I saw pictures of Josh Kezer in newspapers and on TV and other pictures that Mr. Lowes showed me. I'm absolutely positive I didn't see him at the Halloween party." She said, "I know Todd Mayberry, and I listed him as one of the people I remembered being at the party. But I didn't see a drunk boy harassing Mischelle or hanging on her car as she left the party."

★ ★ ★

On July 8, 1994, the defense team filed a Motion for Judgment of Acquittal or in the Alternative for a New Trial that asserted 60 points of error.

Number 38 was based on Judge Murphy's allowing Chantelle Crider to testify. The first part of the argument regarding Crider was an objection to allowing a surprise witness who hadn't been deposed by the defense to testify, especially after she sat through the trial, unlike other witnesses who were sequestered prior to testifying. The second part was a presentation of the posttrial affidavits of Dawn Worley and Lacey Warren refuting the Crider testimony. Numbers 56, 58, and 59 related to Kenny Hulshof's attack on Josh's alibi witnesses—that it was an error to let Hulshof accuse David Rosener of coaching these witnesses to lie. The rest of the legal arguments were longshots, with little chance of success.

The sentencing hearing was held on August 2, 1994, which would have been Mischelle's 21st birthday. Judge Murphy heard oral arguments on Lowes's motion. He said, "There were aspects of the case that concerned me, but those concerns are not sufficient to discount the decision of the jury." Then, he sentenced Josh to 30 years on the second-degree murder count and 30 years on the armed criminal action count, with the two sentences to run back-to-back (60 years). Josh was 19. Even if granted parole, he would be well past middle age before he was released, and there was no guarantee he would ever be paroled.

According to newspaper accounts, Marvin Lawless "thought the sentence was too lenient." Josh's mother felt otherwise. Joan Kezer wrote a letter to the editors of local newspapers.

> My name is Joan Kezer. My only child, Joshua C. Kezer (19), was recently convicted of 2nd degree murder and armed criminal action. He's been sentenced to 60 years in prison. But I am absolutely positive that my son is innocent. Aside from the fact that Joshua is a fair and kind young man, who once had me stop the car so that he could move a turtle to safety, we have concrete evidence proving that he was over 300 miles from Scott County at the time of this crime. He was in no way connected to or even acquainted with the victim.

Josh's grandmother wrote her own letter to the editor. She mentioned the changing stories of jailhouse snitches who were looking for a deal in their own cases and the witnesses who placed her grandson in Kankakee at the time of the murder. She concluded with the comment, "We know [Josh] is innocent, and there is a killer somewhere loose, walking around."

Two days after the sentencing, Morley Swingle dropped the unlawful use of a weapon charge against Josh, which was based on the incident outside a Cape Girardeau billiards parlor on Halloween in 1992. Brantley's testimony at Josh's trial had served its purpose. Scott County pursued the Randy Eskew charge against Josh, but it was dismissed during a preliminary hearing for lack of evidence months before Josh's trial.

Josh's family was out of money to pay Al Lowes to pursue an appeal. As Lowes put it in a letter responding to the Ste. Genevieve County Clerk's attempt to collect $5,781.02 of court costs charged to Josh, "I am returning the cost bill that you sent for the court costs regarding Joshua Kezer. First of all, we no longer represent him. Second of all, he is broke flat as can be and is in the pen."

Lowes wrote the Office of Appellate Public Defender and enclosed copies of his Motion to Withdraw as Counsel of Record, which had been signed by Judge Murphy; a Notice of Appeal; and the posttrial motion he filed on Josh's behalf. Referring to his 60 points of error, he said, "The good would-be congressman, 'Cool Breeze,' let everything hang out, as you can see, in our motion for new trial, and the judge reined him in some but not enough."

11

THE APPEAL

At the beginning of their time in a Missouri prison, inmates are tested and classified at a diagnostic facility into one of five levels of security for assignment to facilities ranging from honor camps to maximum security institutions. Josh served that phase of his incarceration at the facility in Fulton. Processing at Fulton was humiliating. "They took my clothes, gave me a towel the size of a hand towel, and locked me in a room filled with others. One at a time, they brought us out; they had us lift our ball sack and bend over and spread our ass, throwing a hand full of bug powder on each of us. Those of us in the room could see each man suffer this indignity and shower. Then, we were given jumpsuits, photographed, and processed."[1] Most male prisoners convicted of murder are assigned to one of the facilities with the highest security classification, at least to start, regardless of other factors that might be considered. Josh's fellow inmates at Fulton were counting on that. It wasn't long before Josh overheard some of them "taking bets on how long I would last before I was killed or raped." Another inmate Josh had been in a fight with in the Ste. Genevieve County Jail heard it too. He told Josh, "You'll be OK. You hit hard. If anyone here tries you, just punch him like you punched me."

The State Office of Appellate Public Defender sent Josh the forms he needed to fill out to get free appellate representation. Gary Brotherton, an assistant public defender, was assigned to handle Josh's appeal and entered his appearance as counsel of record in the Eastern District Court of Appeals on August 23, 1994. Brotherton wrote Josh the same day to introduce himself and explain what the appeal would entail. "The Court of Appeals will only review what happened at your trial. We cannot present any new evidence, and you will not be able to appear personally before the court."[1]

Brotherton explained that Josh could challenge his conviction under Missouri Rule of Criminal Procedure 29.15 if he had any complaint about the way his trial counsel represented him or any claim about the constitutionality of his sentence but that he would have to file the motion himself, before a strictly enforced deadline, and ask for counsel to be appointed.

Josh sent the public defender's office a letter expressing his fear of harm from fellow inmates.

> I wrote a letter to my case worker, I believe that my life is in serious danger here in Mo. corrections and I believe that I would at least have a chance in Ill., that's where my family is too (north) but I'll take what I can get. I'm only 19 and someday I want another chance, put it this way I believe that I'll be killed (without a shadow of a doubt in my mind) in Mo. corrections so please get me to Ill. <u>PLEASE</u>!!!!!!!!!!!!!!!!!!!! one for each year of my life please get me to Ill. so I can have more! Please come down and talk to me as fast as possible.

Brotherton answered Josh's letter on August 29.

> Unfortunately, there is nothing specifically that I can do to help you get transferred to the Department of Corrections in Illinois. You have taken the correct first step in contacting your caseworker regarding a transfer. Generally, a transfer is not made unless the receiving state also has an inmate which is seeking transfer to Missouri. I understand your concerns, and hope that you are successful in getting your transfer. Please keep me advised.

Brotherton also told Josh that his grandmother had called his office and offered the family's help with the appeal. He warned Josh that anything he, Brotherton, told Josh's family regarding the merits of his case would not be subject to the attorney–client privilege.

Josh's grandmother wrote Brotherton on September 5 that the family "were very much devastated by this awful trial & conviction" and mentioned in particular Chantelle Crider (the "surprise witness") and the fact that "two girls who were at the Halloween party came forward to say Josh wasn't there." In a September 16 letter reporting on the status of the appeal, Brotherton told Josh about the letter he had received from Josh's grandmother and repeated his warning that discussing the case with Josh's family could result in loss of the attorney–client privilege.

Al Lowes wrote a letter to Brotherton, dated September 14, offering his legal research and other files as help with the appeal. "We would sure like this matter reversed and remanded for another trial. Maybe the next one would not have Kenny Hulshof, a/k/a Cool Breeze, so anxious to put someone away so he can run for Congress."

Josh's relationship with Brotherton was driven by a naive optimism. He wrote Brotherton, "I couldn't understand how anyone would believe I killed Mischelle Lawless. I was 350 miles away in Kankakee at the time. I thought my witnesses proved that at my trial. With the new evidence from the two girls who said I wasn't at the Halloween party, I was even more certain I would be released soon." Josh continued his letter to Brotherton: "I am asking you to please think of this case as being special. If you know of any other organization who could give me special help, then please write them or give me the address."

On September 19, Josh wrote Brotherton in a panic. He had spoken to someone in the prison law library who told him the courts would throw out his Rule 29.15 motion if he waited too long to file it. Completely confused, he wrote: "Is a Form 40 and a 29-15 the same thing? What do you mean by saying whatever I say in my pro se motion? Oct. 31 is that the day I get the transcript? or do I have to have the pro se motion by that time? What date should I set to file my motion to courts? Please help me—your my attorney and I need your help bad so please help me."

In a letter mailed on October 7, Josh wrote Brotherton again and told him, "I'm getting an out of state transfer to one of these places (subject to change)." And then he listed three states: Iowa, Nebraska, and Kansas. Missouri and Illinois, he told Brotherton, didn't have a "compact" governing prisoner transfer. Josh wanted to know if Brotherton would continue to represent him on his appeal if he transferred to a prison in another state. "The superintendent tells me I'll probly be here another 4 to 6 months (here at F.R.D.C.) so maybe we can get on ball an get this appeal won before I even leave state. So far you seem like a decent lawyer so if you can and want to stay on my case after I leave state I would be happy to have you (all I ask you is kick the case into overtime)."

Finally, Josh addressed the attorney–client privilege issue. Apparently thinking Brotherton was concerned his family would reveal confidential information about his case to someone else, he scolded him: "About this not telling my Gramma anything stuff—I want that to stop . . . I trust them with my life to the full extent." He closed with a "Thank You" and a request to "please write me back on the matters I explained and ASAP?!"

In a letter dated October 13, Brotherton assured Josh that he would continue as his lawyer if he managed to get transferred to a prison in another state and that there was no reason to worry about missing the deadline for filing a Rule 29.15 motion. "Your letter indicates that you plan on reiterating the sixty points alleged in your motion for new trial in your Rule 29.15 motion. You should note that the Rule 29.15 is not designed to remedy purely trial error. Rule 29.15 is designed to remedy situations such as ineffective assistance of counsel."

Brotherton also explained that the appeal process would not move as quickly as Josh seemed to believe. He told Josh it would take 9 to 12 months, unless he filed a Rule 29.15 motion, which would put the appeal on hold and double the amount of time for the entire process. Brotherton finished by repeating what he had said about conversations with Josh's family. "I understand your desire to have your family involved in your case. However, I will not discuss the merits of your case or my advice to you with any member of your family."

On October 28, Brotherton wrote Josh again. He warned him not to talk about his case with reporters, would-be authors, or anyone else investigating his case, no matter how good their intentions might be. "Nothing you tell them can possibly help you in this matter." He also told Josh it was too soon to ask the governor for a pardon. The appeal process was only beginning, and a pardon assumes acknowledgment of guilt, something Josh wasn't about to do, and some evidence of rehabilitation in prison, something Josh didn't think he needed because he was innocent.

When Josh learned that Brotherton had filed a request for more time to file his appellate brief, he tried to reach Brotherton by telephone and ended up talking to his secretary. Brotherton wrote Josh on November 1.

> Apparently you are unhappy with my services and expressed a desire to "fire" me in your phone conversation with my secretary yesterday. Your case will not be reassigned, and I will remain your attorney as long as you continue with your request for Public Defender services. You have two options: 1) you may represent yourself in this appeal, or 2) you may employ a private attorney to represent you.

Brotherton finished by scolding Josh about the way he treated his secretary. He explained that his research often took him away from his office and that his secretary answers in his absence. He told Josh to stop calling and to direct any further communication to him in writing. According to Josh, "I was frustrated, angry, and in prison for a murder I didn't commit. I shouldn't have popped off at his secretary, but I needed to speak with Gary, not his secretary, and he never made the time to speak with me. It felt as if I didn't matter to him. How should a 19-year-old boy that's been stomped on by the system speak to a secretary or lawyer when he's fighting for his life and feeling ignored?"

Josh was chastened somewhat by this letter and wrote back as soon as he received it.

> I don't wish to fire you, but if I can get a attorney who will even go as far as walk in a courtroom instead of just filing and leaving it at that, then I will do so (It would be only wise). Until then I am sorry (I'm just upset about being in here for something I didn't do) and will be honored to have you as council. I'm 19 years old and I'm scared I'll die while I'm in here, and that's a shame cause I'm innocent.

Josh also agreed he would not talk to the reporter who contacted him if Brotherton thought that was best, and he asked Brotherton to telephone the reporter for him with that message.

On November 9, Brotherton wrote Josh that he was "glad to hear that you have decided to continue with my representation." He told Josh he would write the reporter to tell him he should not contact Josh about his case any further. But he also laid down a set of ground rules for the relationship as it continued. He said his office didn't have funds to pay for routine collect calls from clients. He would arrange for occasional collect calls when necessary, limited to 15 minutes. For those calls, Josh should have his questions and concerns planned in advance so the time could be spent productively. According to Josh, "Despite writing this to me, Brotherton never once spoke to me over the phone." Finally, Brotherton told Josh that he should direct any questions or concerns to him, not his trial attorneys, who no longer represented him.

Josh wrote Brotherton on January 2, 1995, to ask for copies of trial exhibits and a telephone call to discuss his case. He also told Brotherton he "would really appreciate a visit from you to discuss the matter of how your gonna go about winning this case for me."

David Rosener wrote Josh on January 5 about Josh's recent request that he contact reporters who were interested in his case. "Josh, as I have told you all along, the first rule when you are criminally charged is to keep your mouth shut about your case." He told Josh that he believed there was a good chance of getting a new trial in his appeal and that anything he said to anyone other than his lawyer could be taken out of context, misconstrued, and used against him. "You should be well aware, both Mr. Zellmer and Mr. Bell are journalists and, of course, journalists like to sell newspapers, books, etc." He told Josh he had tried to cooperate with Bell and Zellmer, as Josh had requested, "but only by telling them to read the court files, which were public record."

On February 3, Brotherton received a note from his secretary that Josh had called twice, collect, asking for someone to hand carry his transcript to him and saying Josh wanted to know "What points are being brought up in brief (he has 60 pts)." Brotherton responded to Josh's phone messages in a February 6 letter. He mentioned his secretary had told Josh on the phone that they would not be able to hand carry the transcript but would send it marked "Legal Mail." He said he would not know what points would be included in the appellate brief until he had a chance to review the transcript and the legal file but assured him he would raise every issue he could argue in good faith. He also raised the subject of a Rule 29.15 motion again, emphasizing that it would be Josh's only opportunity to challenge his trial attorney's performance and explaining how this motion would put the filing of his appellate brief, which would otherwise be due in mid-April, on hold.

On February 8, Brotherton sent Josh the transcript and legal file in his case, told him he had filed both with the Court of Appeals that day, and reminded him that a Rule 29.15 motion would be due within 30 days, on March 10. "While the decision whether or not to file such a motion is entirely your own," he said, "it is probably in your best interest to file it." He reiterated his advice that filing this motion was particularly important if he had any complaint about the performance of his trial counsel. Josh didn't think he could file because of what Judge Murphy had told him.

On February 22, Josh wrote Brotherton to inform him he had decided he would not file a Rule 29.15 motion: "We have 60 points of err, a new powerful statement, and we have Jesus (believe me when I say, I'm praying—1 Thess. 5:17). With that much, I'm not staying in for another year if I don't have to, we should be able to do something great." Brotherton responded in a March 6 letter, telling Josh that his brief would be due on April 10 because Josh wasn't filing a Rule 29.15 motion.[2]

On March 8, Josh wrote Brotherton to tell him a girl who was writing to him (a "girlfriend" who had become an "ex-girlfriend") knew a girl named Crystal whose brother, Christopher Daniel Durham, knew who killed Mischelle Lawless. According to Durham, who was serving time in the California prison system, it was "Mischelle's boyfriend." Brotherton answered on March 14. He reminded Josh that the Court of Appeals won't consider new evidence. Then he said, "If you are granted a new trial, the information regarding Christopher Daniel Durham may be investigated."

David Rosener and Gary Brotherton had an uneasy relationship. Rosener offered his help with the appeal. Rosener desperately wanted to help the innocent boy he believed he and Lowes had failed. But Brotherton believed he needed to take a fresh look at the case, unencumbered by the views of the trial team. On March 24, Rosener wrote a letter to Lew Kollias, the director of the Office of State Public Defender. He had three issues with Brotherton's handling of the case: the rejection of Rosener's offers of assistance, the rejection of an offer from the National Association of Criminal Defense Counsel to file an "amicus" brief (also known as friend of the court), and the complaints of Josh and his family about a lack of communication with his client. Regarding a possible amicus brief, he said that "Essentially, Brotherton told the NACDL *Amicus Curiae* Committee to go to hell and that he didn't need any help."

Brotherton had a different view of these issues. He responded to Rosener's letter in an email to Steve Harris, his immediate supervisor. He admitted he had been trying to keep Josh's trial counsel out of the appeal. He resented the fact that Rosener, a 1993 law school graduate, wanted to tell him, a veteran of more than 150 appeals, what arguments he should raise. He also believed that it was in Josh's best interest to challenge his trial team's performance in a Rule 29.15 motion and was concerned that Josh would not file one if they were telling him he had a good chance of reversing the conviction on appeal. He believed Josh's decision to pass on the motion had validated that concern already.

Brotherton said he didn't understand that Lawrence Fleming, the lawyer in St. Louis who Rosener contacted about an amicus brief, was connected with the NACDL until he saw mention of that in Rosener's March 24 letter. And even if Brotherton had known of the NACDL connection, he said, he wouldn't have asked for the NACDL's assistance. He doubted that an amicus was appropriate anyway because of the prerequisite of showing that an important issue "is not being adequately presented to the court by the parties."

The whole issue was a muddle of misunderstanding. On March 8, Al Lowes answered a letter from Fleming to Rosener. On letterhead that showed Rosener's name crossed through by hand, Lowes first informed Fleming that Rosener "has gone off to practice law on his own." He told Fleming "the people who were paying us [Josh's grandparents] ran out of money, hence Mr. Brotherton sort of 'heired' this case." He closed by saying, "Now I bet Mr. Brotherton would not be bothered a bit if you fellows wanted to help out a little bit or maybe a whole lot."

Lowes copied Brotherton on the letter, and Brotherton wrote Josh on March 10: "It appears that you are trying to retain Mr. Fleming on your appeal. If you are able to retain Mr. Fleming as your attorney, please let me know as soon as possible." Josh called Brotherton on March 20 and left a message with his secretary. He said he didn't hire Fleming and hadn't talked to him but knew he was "doing another appeal" for him.

Brotherton wrote Fleming the same day. He told him that he had investigated and determined that Josh hadn't retained him for the appeal but admonished that "I will not act as co-counsel in this matter." He finished by telling Fleming, "If you wish to handle this appeal, you need to enter your appearance in the Eastern District, and I will withdraw. However, until you have entered your appearance, I will move to strike any filing you attempt to make in this case. You should make no effort to contact Mr. Kezer while I am representing him."

Fleming replied on March 23. He said, "I have no idea what you're talking about, have no intent to enter an appearance on behalf of Joseph [*sic*] Kezer and no intent to file any pleadings or briefs." He explained that his only interest in the matter, on the recommendation of David Rosener, was as the chairman of the NACDL Amicus Curiae Committee. He said the NACDL was considering filing an amicus brief but would not do so over the objection of the attorney of record.

Lew Kollias provided the official response to Rosener's letter complaining about Brotherton that followed Brotherton's explanation of events closely but was a bit more diplomatic. He assured Rosener that Brotherton would act in Josh's interest but "does not feel having amicus here is going to further the case." He asserted, "It is his case to handle, and he will do it well." On April 10, Steve Harris wrote a follow-up to the Kollias letter. He took issue with Rosener's claim that Brotherton had rejected the NACDL's offers of assistance: "To date we have had no direct communication from NACDL." Then he turned to Josh's decision not to file a Rule 29.15 motion. He acknowledged that some convicted felons do not file under this rule but noted:

> However, in cases of the magnitude of Mr. Kezer's where such blatant injustices have occurred, as you believe, it is unusual. I would hate to discover that Mr. Kezer's failure to file was in any way influenced by your actions. He had an absolute right to file a Rule 29.15 case and have conflict-free counsel independently review the criminal case, which could disclose claims of ineffective assistance of counsel. I believe it would be inappropriate for trial counsel to do anything to interfere with an individual exercising their rights under the rule.

The most glaring example of this ineffective assistance was Al Lowes's agreement that Rosener would not testify. The judge had specifically told

Josh that he could never raise the issue of ineffective assistance of counsel if he agreed to keep Lowes & Drusch as his lawyers. He also told Josh that a public defender could call Rosener to testify against the snitch witnesses and certainly would have postponed the trial to allow a public defender to prepare. Josh didn't understand all the implications of Hulshof's maneuver, which might be grounds for overcoming the judge's warning. But Al Lowes certainly did, as his statement indicated that the defense had other ways to deal with the claims of the snitches.

Harris wrote to Rosener again on April 19, responding to Rosener's request for a meeting with Harris and Brotherton to discuss the appeal. He told Rosener that they had no intention of meeting with him but would withdraw from the case if Rosener intended to enter an appearance.

By this time, Brotherton's relationship with Josh's family had deteriorated too. Josh's mother called Brotherton on April 17. According to Brotherton, she became rude when his secretary asked to take a message. Josh was not surprised by this news. He told me, "You're damn right she was rude and abusive. She was my mother. She had had enough of being dismissed and ignored and playing nice. I've no doubt my mother used foul language to communicate her foul mood." Brotherton told Joni Kezer in a letter, "Rude, abusive language is unacceptable. Please do not telephone the office again. You are not my client, your son is. In order to preserve the attorney/client privilege, my practice is not to discuss cases with family members." He finished with an overview of the appeal process, including the current briefing schedule and potential delays.

On April 21, Brotherton discovered he hadn't received transcripts of two key pretrial hearings on certain motions. He contacted the court reporter and discovered they hadn't been transcribed. They would not be ready in time for him to incorporate in Josh's initial brief, which at the time was due May 10. He received an extension from the Court of Appeals and then another when the court reporter informed him the transcripts still weren't finished. He finally filed the brief on July 14.

Under the rules governing appeals, an appellate court generally must assume that all the evidence against the convicted defendant was true and can't hear new evidence. Brotherton had to frame his arguments within the confines of those rules. Brotherton chose to argue what he considered the strongest points. Even with his focus on the strongest points, instead of the 60 in trial counsels' posttrial motion, the brief was 98 pages long, just short of the 100-page limit.

Brotherton led with the argument that the jury was prejudiced against Josh and his trial team by the trial court's decision to allow Josh's attorneys to represent him. He was doing his best to disguise the fact that he was arguing what amounted to ineffective assistance of counsel, a situation Al Lowes had created by promising that Rosener wouldn't testify. Judge Murphy had protected himself by explaining the alternatives to Josh and having Josh choose Lowes instead.

The case was set for oral argument, at Brotherton's request, and argued on November 9, 1995, before a three-judge panel. The Eastern District Court of Appeals denied Josh's appeal on February 6, 1996. Not surprisingly, the opinion concluded Brotherton's first argument, that the trial court should not have allowed Lowes to try the case, was an argument involving ineffective assistance of counsel, which Josh had waived by failing to file a Rule 29.15 motion. The opinion rejected the other arguments.

Brotherton mailed Josh a copy of the Court of Appeals opinion on February 7, 1996. Brotherton told Josh he disagreed with the opinion and would request a rehearing by the full Eastern District and then appeal to the Missouri Supreme Court. He filed such a motion on February 20 and sent Josh a copy the following day. He argued only the conflict of interest issue.

On February 29, Josh sent Brotherton a letter requesting certain documents and information. At the end of the letter, he posed two questions: "1. Please explain to me why you didn't accept extra help from Flemming in my case when I wanted it from him. 2. How come you never came to see me?" That last sentence of the letter put it all in a nutshell. Josh had concluded, rightly or wrongly, that Brotherton didn't care about him because he never came to visit.

In the same letter, Brotherton told Josh he already had filed a motion for rehearing or transfer on the conflict of interest issue and would file a motion for transfer to the Missouri Supreme Court at the proper time.

The Court of Appeals denied the motion for rehearing or transfer on March 11, and Brotherton filed an application for transfer in the Missouri Supreme Court on March 25. The issue was the same, the conflict of interest inherent in David Rosener's status as a witness and as counsel for Josh. The application was denied. Brotherton informed Josh in a May 7 letter that there was nothing more he could do for him and that he was closing the file.

12

INTO THE LION'S DEN

Nothing ever came of Josh's request for a transfer to a prison in another state. He was sent from Fulton to the prison in Jefferson City, which at the time, provided the best odds for the other convicts at Fulton who had been betting against him. It was the original Missouri State Penitentiary, known as "The Walls." When Josh arrived, it was the oldest prison west of the Mississippi still in use—a hellhole populated by violent and notorious criminals, where he was expected to spend what could be the rest of his life. It looked like a fortress, sitting on the banks of the Missouri River on 47 acres at the edge of the central core in the state capital of Jefferson City. With 40-foot-high limestone walls intersected by 15 guard towers, it was a terrifying sight to any new inmate approaching in a prison transportation van, let alone a teenager like Josh, who knew that the hardened and stronger inmates would try to take advantage of him.

The Walls was described as "the bloodiest 47 acres in America" in a 1967 *Time* magazine article. It was home to some infamous inmates, such as Charles Ray Hatcher, a serial killer who murdered 16 victims within a 12-year span. James Earl Ray was serving a 20-year sentence there for a 1959 grocery store robbery when he escaped in April 1967. On April 4, 1968, he killed the Reverend Dr. Martin Luther King Jr. in Memphis.

Josh was surrounded by some of the most violent men on the planet. "I kept to myself as much as I could and finished my GED. I tried to carry myself as someone not to be messed with. I wasn't a nice person in those days." But he was too kindhearted to be truly violent. "I wasn't even much of a Latin King. I was a poor kid from a broken home. I joined a gang to feel like I belonged. I guess I just wanted respect." His attempts to impress others with his toughness had come back to haunt him. Kenny Hulshof used them to convince the jury that he was something he wasn't.

After one night in a prep cell in Housing Unit 1, Josh was assigned to a cell in Housing Unit 3A, one of the original stone buildings. The damp cell measured about 6 by 10 feet. In addition to the two-man bunk, the bare stone walls enclosed a sink and a toilet. His cellmate's first name was Moses, a career criminal who was serving a sentence for murder. "I didn't like Moses. He was arrogant and bossy, and I tried to stay out of his way." Fortunately, they didn't have to spend much time together. Moses was transferred to a lower security unit. Josh said, "I snapped. A real murderer was considered less of a threat than a kid like me who was innocent. I yelled at my caseworker and complained to the guards that it just wasn't fair."

Jefferson City is about 250 miles from Chaffee and Cape Girardeau, where his mother and grandparents lived. His father lived even farther away in Illinois. "I realized it would be difficult for them to visit me regularly. I felt isolated and alone. I was haunted by the thought that I was convicted of killing a girl I never met." Yet he also was well aware that most of the rest of the world saw him as a heartless killer, the man who murdered Mischelle Lawless because she spurned him at a Halloween party. To know you are confined to a maximum security prison for a murder you didn't commit is the worst form of mental torture. "I couldn't understand how the justice system was so screwed up. I just couldn't believe I was convicted on such flimsy evidence."

Josh realized he would have to change, both physically and morally, if he wanted to survive. "I was going to have to toughen up. When I first got to prison, I was skinny, so I lifted weights. I gained pounds of muscle, and became visibly powerful." Joni Kezer told her son, "You do whatever you have to do. Become whatever it is you have to become to survive. All I ask is don't change with me. Please don't change with me." Josh knew fear would get him killed, and he knew he couldn't fight every battle. So he progressively denied his fear, letting himself "slowly die" internally. He hardened, and he did his best to "navigate hell without becoming hellish." He appeared as monstrous to others as he thought necessary. He stayed to himself, went to school, read, lifted weights, and went to church.

Josh also realized he would have to stay away from the worst aspects of prison culture, the gang rivalries and racial divisions that created a constant threat of sudden violence. Josh told me he called "someone" before he was convicted to say he left the Latin Kings. In prison, members of the Latin Kings saw his tattoo. When he told them he had left the Kings, they told him you can't do that. He said they could make something of it if they wanted. They didn't.

Josh had been "raised in the Church," as he later would describe it, mostly through the influence of his maternal grandparents, who were practicing Christians. But he had strayed far from those beginnings. "Before I went to prison, I was living off friends and acquaintances and on the street. I didn't just stay away from church. I got casual sex where I could find it. I drank a lot on a regular basis, and I took all kinds of drugs, marijuana, LSD, even crack cocaine once, but thankfully never heroin."

Josh got involved with the prison ministry. As time passed, he got more deeply involved, not just going to Sunday services, but joining Bible-study groups and participating actively in prison religious projects. "Something took hold of me, and my faith became the focus and center of my life. It gave me hope for the future, and it helped me handle the nightmare that was the present. Somehow, it was all part of a plan Jesus had for me." As he told the *Southeast Missourian* years later, "I lived every day like I was going to get out the next. I read the word of God. I was on my knees. I had to resign myself to the fate that either God was going to give me a miracle or I was going to die in prison."

In 1998, Missouri opened a new prison, Crossroads Correctional Center, located in the town of Cameron in the northwest corner of the state. The Department of Corrections populated Crossroads with inmates drawn from other prisons around Missouri. Josh was one of the first. "One day not long after I got to Crossroads, two inmates came up to me in the yard. The bigger of the two put on a pair of jersey gloves as they got near me, and I knew what they had in mind. As the littler one began to talk, I said I wasn't interested and turned to walk away. I felt a thud against my face almost immediately, and then I felt a second and a third."

Josh's knees buckled, but he managed not to lose consciousness. He charged and began to punch the bigger guy. "I hit him again and again and again. I drove him backward until he had his back against a fence. I kept punching him as he slid down the fence, and I punched him repeatedly in the head when he slid down below my level. At some point, the little guy began punching me in the kidneys."

Josh was so absorbed in the fight, he was only dimly aware of the pain in his lower back. When the little guy's kidney punches didn't work, he began yelling "police is coming" repeatedly. "That was the prison warning that guards were near. I heard later that there were guards near, but no guards came. The trick worked. I stopped punching and walked away."

The plan for Josh was to make him the little guy's boy, to be used for sex and traded for cigarettes and other favors. He wasn't supposed to fight back. The two who tried to implement the plan didn't abandon it.

Josh had embarrassed them, especially the bigger one, and he would have to be taught a lesson. First, they had someone pass Josh a letter that said, "Even Jesus knows what you are. You're a bitch. Do what we want, and we won't make you wear panties and makeup in the yard. Don't, and it'll be like that." A few days later, Josh had a visit in his cell from a messenger. "The man looked at me and asked, 'What's it gonna be?'" Josh said, "I guess it'll be like that." The man asked, "Are you sure?" Josh nodded, and the man left.

Josh knew what was coming. He didn't want to be caught inside his cell, so he went outside, locked his door behind him, and waited. "Four men approached, coming at me from all sides. I tried to fight them off, but there were too many of them." They beat him until he lost consciousness. And then one of them dragged him under a stairwell and left him. When he awoke, bloodied and bruised, he staggered to his cell and washed his face. When he discovered he couldn't breathe through his nose, he was forced to say something to a guard. "I spent a week and a half in the prison infirmary. My face was such a mess the doctors thought my cheekbones were broken. That turned out to be wrong, but I did have a large hematoma inside my nose that had to be surgically removed."

The guards asked who had done this to him. "I said nothing. You're supposed to stand on your own, not run to the guards. If you wanted revenge, you took care of it yourself." The prison put him in "ad seg." The inmates called it the "hole," a cell without blankets or bed sheets. He had what he needed to write his mother about what happened to him and to let her know he was alright. But he wrote on the outside of the envelope not to open it without having a friend present.

But Josh wasn't alright. "I kept thinking to myself, 'How fucking dare they think they could make me their bitch?!'" Then, the guards told Josh he would be released into the same general population cell block where he had been attacked. Anger swelled up in him, and he started thinking about how he could make weapons to kill or maim those who had attacked him. "I wanted to let everyone know I wasn't to be fucked with ever again. And then I remembered my mother, and I hit my knees in tears and cried out to God. I didn't want to become what I was wrongly sent to prison for, and I didn't want to disappoint my mother. On my knees, alone in a dark and damp cell, I cried, and gave my rage to God."

When the guards came to take Josh to general population, Josh said he wanted to go to protective custody. When he was with the caseworker, he said he had changed his mind. He never intended to go to protective custody. But he knew the prison couldn't force him into protective custody, and it couldn't keep him in the hole indefinitely. The guards were angry with him and said, "Ok, Mike Tyson," and they decided to put him back in the hole. He had successfully manipulated the system and removed himself from the temptation to seek vengeance. A few months later, he was transferred back to Jefferson City.

When Josh returned to Jefferson City, word had gotten out about his fight and his refusal to snitch on the men who attacked him. He was gaining respect. Years after Josh was transferred back to Jefferson City, two familiar faces were themselves transferred to Jefferson City and individually approached him.

Afraid of how Josh might react if he randomly came across him, Chuck Weissinger approached Josh.

> He came to me like a man and apologized. He didn't attempt to defend his actions. He just wanted to apologize. I accepted, and I went a step further. Had it gotten out that he had been one of the original snitches responsible for framing me, he might have been stabbed, beaten with a pillow case and a can of chili or a padlock, burnt with boiling baby oil, or raped or even killed. I kept it to myself.

Jeff Rogers had found out somehow that Josh attended church with some men in his housing unit. He had those men tell Josh he wanted to talk.

> Rogers begged me to believe he never wanted to testify against me. "Josh, the investigators lied. I'm telling you they lied." I conceded that it was possible he was telling some form of truth, but from what I knew of his interactions with my attorneys, Lowes and Rosener, I knew he was lying. I told Rogers I wasn't prepared to believe him, but following prayer and wrestling with God, I forgave him. It wouldn't have taken much to have him killed in prison for what he had done to me. He was a child molester. A whisper here, a few boxes of cigarettes there. But I kept it to myself. I was locked up with Rogers for the rest of my time in prison, but I didn't throw him to the wolves.

Josh wanted to forgive Shawn Mangus. He was prepared to after he received the note Mangus passed to him in the jail and even after he was convicted. "I forgave him decades ago, but I never got the opportunity to let him know. It saddens me when I think of him overdosing, and dying with the burden of knowing what he had done to me and my family."

On September 10, 2001, Josh facilitated the second of three days of an Alternatives to Violence workshop. Alternatives to Violence workshops in the old Jefferson City prison consisted of three days of group activities meant to teach inmates alternatives to what were considered culturally acceptable acts of violence in prison. On the morning of 9/11, Josh watched the attacks on New York and the Pentagon. On his way to the group, he stopped and asked a prison lieutenant to put the flag in the prison yard at half-staff. Josh changed the curriculum that day. In the direct aftermath of 9/11, Josh facilitated a discussion on the attacks, and the group processed their emotions together.

In 2008, in the newer Jefferson City prison, Josh was playing in a two-man team pinochle tournament, and the bigger guy from the first attack in Crossroads sat down to play across from him. Josh had bulked up from years of weightlifting. The man turned pale when he recognized him. Josh watched him closely but said nothing about the fight. When the game ended, the man got up to leave without saying anything. Josh blocked the man's way with his arm and motioned for him to lean down close to his face. "It's over as far as I'm concerned," Josh told him, "if it's over for you." The man relaxed. "It's over for me too," he said, and he walked away.

In 2005, Josh was placed in the hole again. "I didn't get along with my cellie, and the cellie wanted to make a change. Instead of just talking to me or requesting a cell transfer, he planted a razor near my bunk. I never saw it and only heard about it from the guards. Then, he reported me on an anonymous hotline, claiming I had dangerous contraband." The man's plan didn't work. "Both of us got sent to the hole." His cellie said it was Josh's razor, but "we both had to go because it was in our cell." The guards who knew Josh told him they believed his version of events but said there was nothing they could do. Mentally, being in the hole wasn't a pleasant experience. Josh remembers that he was sent to the hole on the night his home state Illini played in the NCAA men's national championship, which he had been looking forward to watching.

> I lost my job. I couldn't attend church. I lost my right to watch TV. Everywhere I went, I was in handcuffs. I had to be walked to the shower in the middle of the night with a dog leash. I had to do my exercises in my cell or during certain times of the day locked in a cage in a row of cages. Once I heard my former cellie telling other men in those cages that I was the one who set him up. He didn't realize I was there. I spoke up, and he shut up.

Josh and his father had a strained relationship before his incarceration. Charlie Kezer only came to see his son twice because knowing Josh was innocent, it hurt him too badly to see him in that hellhole. Josh's father suffered a major heart attack in 2005 shortly after Josh had been placed in the hole over the razor blade incident.

> I remember being called out of the cell, and speaking with him over the phone just before he went into surgery. I was told that due to his diabetes and dialysis he might not live through the surgery. More than anything, I remember crying with him and praying. When they brought me back to my cell, I punched the concrete wall and steel bunk several times. I remember hitting my knees and crying out to God, like a little boy, "PLEASE LET MY DADDY LIVE!"

His father did survive.

Josh learned something that disturbed him while he was in the hole for the razor blade incident. One day, while Josh was in the cages, Gordon Evans, a man serving two life sentences for the 1994 murder of 17-year-old Amy Sue Morningstar, in the cage nearest to Josh told Josh his brother had visited him in the Scott County Jail in the 1990s and told him Bill Ferrell had offered to pay Gordon $1,000 to stab Josh in prison. Evans later gave Josh a typewritten and signed statement dated February 23, 2006. Evans has since denied telling Josh this. Josh has shared what he was told and the statement he was given with Scott County Prosecutor Amanda Oesch, Prosecutor-Elect Don Cobb, and Assistant Attorney General Kevin Zoellner. He's been told it's under investigation. Evans is currently paroled in Scott County and lives in Sikeston.

Despite his deepening faith, there were times when Josh weakened and fell into despair. One of those occasions was when he was sent to the hole for the razor blade incident. He prayed, "Lord, I don't want to wake up another day in prison. I'm tired, and I've had enough." He said he woke up disappointed. He wasn't losing hope, but he was tired of waking up every day to the same life. But then he believed God told him, "I've gotten you this far. What makes you think I can't get you to where I want you? Five years from now, none of this will matter."

The man who accused Josh went back to the general population before Josh. Josh had to stay because he was on the man's enemies list and the man wouldn't sign a waiver to remove him. "The guy was a white Muslim. A lot of the Muslims knew me by reputation and didn't believe what my cellie was claiming. They persuaded him to sign the waiver, but I had to promise I wouldn't hurt him first. I didn't mind doing that. As long as I could get out of the hole and he agreed to avoid me, I was satisfied."

13

THE CASE AGAINST JOSH
BEGINS TO FALL APART

The seeds of Josh's deliverance were planted in 1996 when a 42-year-old social worker from nearby Columbia who was involved in a prison ministry noticed him. Jane Williams grew up in Platte City, Missouri, a small town of about 5,000 people located approximately 20 miles north of downtown Kansas City. She attended the University of Missouri in Columbia as an undergraduate and in 1977 earned a master's degree in social studies. Shortly after graduation, she married Scott Williams, an associate pastor at Christian Fellowship Church in Columbia, and took a job as a medical social worker at Ellis Fischel Cancer Hospital in Columbia, eventually advancing to director of social work. After working at Ellis Fischel for a number of years, she left that job to stay home and raise the couple's two children. In the late 1990s, she went back to work at Boone County Hospital. She cofounded three charities: Granny's House (a Christian-centered after-school haven for children in public housing); Columbia Center for Women's Ministries (a peer counseling center for women in need of guidance or support); and Love Columbia (an organization that facilitates networking among churches to provide relief services and support to persons in need).

Jane also wrote devotionals that were distributed to inmates in Missouri prisons. The Walls had a program that allowed outside speakers to visit once a year and make presentations to the prisoners. In 1996, Jane was invited as part of this program to make a presentation of her devotionals in the prison chapel. On her first visit, Jane saw a young inmate in a ponytail, kneeling alone in the chapel, away from the other prisoners who had gathered to hear her speak. John and Joy Long, who were members of her church, were there for her presentation. Joy was the one who told Jane that

Josh was innocent. Josh doesn't know why Joy said he was innocent. He assumes Joy noticed something different about him

She thinks she may have said hello to Josh on that occasion, but nothing more. The image of one inmate on his knees and those words—"He's innocent"—kept coming back to her over the next several years. But she remembered thinking, "If he's innocent, why isn't someone helping him?" For the next five years, each time she made her annual visit, Josh was in attendance. "I never engaged him in discussion about his background or his conviction, and he didn't volunteer any information about himself." In 2002, because the prison was changing its rules, she was making her final visitation. "It was my last chance to talk to Josh about what Joy Long had told me six years earlier." She told him, "I'd like to know more about your personal story; will you write to me?" Josh said he would.

Josh had shared the details about his innocence with others, and those others had disappointed him. Josh wasn't sure he wanted to take a chance on another disappointment with Jane. Surrounded by men, what Josh really wanted was a woman to discuss the Bible with to get a woman's perspective. Josh wrote occasionally, and Jane responded. Jane asked him about his innocence, but at first, Josh didn't want to talk about it. It took some time before he was willing to share any details of his case. Missouri opened a new prison on the outskirts of Jefferson City, the current Jefferson City Correctional Center, in 2004. The Walls was closed, and its inmates, including Josh, were transferred to JCCC.

Early one morning in 2004, Jane was praying for guidance, asking God what she should do about Josh. Around 6:30 a.m., the phone rang. "It was a woman I had helped previously calling to tell me a man who was very close to her had just been released from prison." He was serving time for rape, and his accuser had come forward to admit that the accusation was false. "I was struck by the coincidence. While I was asking God whether I should help one man prove his claim of innocence, a woman called to tell me about another man's exoneration. I took the call as a sign."

About the same time, Josh sent Jane interview reports written in 1997 by Jim Sullins, the private detective working for Josh's mother. As she read these reports, she became more and more interested in the case. Jane Williams learned that Josh's maternal grandmother, Jane James, had copies of partial transcripts of the trial and newspaper articles about the case. In May 2006, she asked Mrs. James to get the complete file from Al Lowes. Jane and her husband drove down to the James home in Chaffee to pick up the files. She started digging through them. Jane spent countless hours on the phone discussing the case with Josh. They knew the details were important, but to capture someone's attention, they had to highlight Josh's humanity. She outlined the main points that she extracted from the transcript and wrote a six-page, single-spaced memorandum summarizing the trial, pointing out along the way, the problems with the trial and the evidence. She sent the memorandum to Josh to review and approve.

★ ★ ★

On July 31, 1995, a man telephoned Al Lowes about the Kezer case. Lowes wasn't available, and the man talked to his secretary, who memorialized the conversation. The man said, "I won't give you my name, but I'll give it to Al Lowes when I call back. Kevin Williams, Mark Abbott's friend, is a big drug dealer around Southeast Missouri. He's the one who killed Mischelle Lawless." According to the caller, "She was killed because she was mixed up with crank. Mark prob'ly knows something about the murder too. Kevin threatened me. He told me he already killed one person, meaning Mischelle, I guess, and he'd get me too." According to the caller, "Kevin has the gun he used at his body shop in Commerce. It's the same gun, I think, that he used to kill Randy Martindale." The man didn't call again.

On July 16, 1999, a woman called Lowes's office anonymously and talked to a secretary, who memorialized the message in a memo. "Kevin Williams shot Mischelle over drugs. He told her he wanted his money or he wanted her to give back his drugs. Mark Abbott was supposed to shoot Mischelle but chickened out. Kevin Williams would shoot you in a minute over nothing." Lowes sent a copy of the memo to Cristy Baker-Neel and suggested she give it to the sheriff to have someone look into the allegations.

A woman named Cathy Fowler called Lowes on January 15, 2002, with a story about Kevin Williams boasting in 1996 that Mark Abbott killed Mischelle. The same day, Lowes dictated a letter to Sheriff Ferrell conveying Fowler's message. "It all happened when I was married to Jimmy Joe Fowler. Jimmy Joe hung around with Kevin Williams and Mark Abbott. He was kind of involved in their drug business." According to Lowes's letter, Williams was visiting the Fowlers when he said, "That Kezer boy is innocent; Mark Abbott killed Mischelle Lawless."

★ ★ ★

Jim Sullins contributed significantly to our work, even if he did have a tendency to be a bit quick to believe wild and implausible stories about the murder. He'd met Joni Kezer in 1997. He was working in Fruitland, just north of Cape Girardeau, and saw her waiting tables at a diner where he was eating. He could see she was bothered by something and asked her, "What's wrong?"

"My son was convicted of murder," she said, "but he's innocent." She told him about the lack of physical evidence against her son, the snitches who kept changing their testimony, the inconsistencies in Mark Abbott's account of the man at the gas station, Chantelle Crider's last-minute identification of her son at the Halloween party that Lacey Warren and Dawn Worley refuted almost immediately after Josh's conviction, and the failed posttrial motions and appeal in which those facts didn't matter.

Sullins looked and acted like the movie stereotype of a private investigator, a bit rumpled in a sport coat and loosely knotted tie but with a sure sense of fairness and justice. Before he left the diner, he followed Joan into the kitchen to give her his card and said, "Call me if you want to talk." She called, and he told her, "I'll poke around a bit and see what I can find out." She said, "I can't afford to pay you," and he told her, "Don't worry about that."

Sullins found quite a few people around Cape Girardeau and Benton besides Josh's mother who thought Josh was innocent and thought they knew who really killed Mischelle Lawless. Most of these people were linked together loosely as part of a circle of friends and acquaintances that had Mark Abbott, Kevin Williams, and methamphetamine at its center—drug users and dealers and their girlfriends, wives, ex-girlfriends, and ex-wives. One of the girls in the group, in a phone call with me, referred to it as "the White Trash Mafia." With a few exceptions, these people did not know Mischelle, even casually, and none of them had even heard of Josh until he was arrested for Mischelle's murder.

Dewayne Kluesner was an example. He sold drugs with the Abbott twins and Kevin Williams in the early 1990s. Sullins interviewed him in 1997, and Kluesner told him, "Mark Abbott and Kevin Williams claim they know who really killed Mischelle because they were there when it happened." Kluesner told Sullins, "Mischelle was beaten and raped and her throat was cut." Mischelle had been beaten. She may have been raped, but there wasn't any evidence of it. Her throat wasn't cut. Abbott and Williams apparently didn't do anything to discourage the stories about their involvement in the murder and made statements implying the stories were true.

Several of these accounts of Mark Abbott's and Kevin Williams's involvement in Mischelle's murder included something happening in one of the empty trailers at the Ferrell Mobile Home Sales lot across the field from the spot at the Interstate 55 exit where Mischelle's body was found. Marvin Glyn Ferrell owned the business. He was not related to Bill Ferrell.

Jim Sullins interviewed an employee there, Dwight Buckner. Buckner said, "I found blood in one of the trailers when I came into work the Monday morning after the murder."

Helen Natvig was distantly linked to Josh by marriage. Her sister was married to Josh's grandmother, Jane James's, nephew. Word had gotten back to Jim Sullins that she and her husband had some helpful information on the Lawless murder, which they had obtained from Kevin Williams. Jim Sullins and his partner interviewed both Natvigs twice. Helen told Jim and his partner, "I know Kevin Williams. He told me and my husband that Kezer is innocent, and he said he knows that because he was there when she was killed. Mark is the one who shot her—because she knew too much about their drug operations and was threatening to turn them in."

Paula Cornell told Sullins, "Donna Sue Robinson claimed she knew Mischelle. Mischelle told Donna Sue that she was dating Mark Abbott and told him she was pregnant with his baby, but it really was a black man's baby." Donna Sue's theory was that Abbott found out about the pregnancy and killed Mischelle over it—because she was pregnant and the baby wasn't his or because the baby's father was black. Robinson couldn't verify any of that for Sullins. Sadly, she was found dead on the side of a highway with a balloon of meth down her throat, her body apparently dumped from a boyfriend's 18-wheeler.

Glyn Ferrell spent some time in prison for income tax evasion, and there were rumors that drugs were shipped to Scott County hidden in trailers delivered to his lot for sale. In addition, Kevin Williams and his wife and mother had worked at Ferrell's lot at one time.

Jim Sullins interviewed Glyn Ferrell in 1997, right after he had gotten out of prison. He told Sullins, "I know who killed Mischelle and I'll tell you who it was if you give me the initials of who you think did it." Sullins called him on the telephone a week later and gave him the initials M. A. and K.W. Ferrell hung up. A week later, Sullins received a letter from Ferrell's attorney warning him not to contact Ferrell again.

Sullins wrote a report based on his 1997 findings and gave it to various local politicians. Nothing came of the effort, and Sullins moved on to other cases until he began working again nine years later at the request of Jane Williams.

On August 4, 2006, Sullins spoke to Edward Downs, a man who had been in prison in Marion, Illinois, with Glyn Ferrell. Downs told Sullins, "Glyn knows who really killed that girl. He felt real bad that the Kezer boy was convicted, but he didn't tell me who it was." Downs knew Josh. They had been in the Ste. Genevieve County Jail together. Another inmate attempted to bully Downs, and Josh protected him. The other inmates left him alone after that.

Matt Moore was another acquaintance of Abbott and Williams in the drug trade. He told Jim Sullins, "Mark Abbott claimed he was involved in the murder of Randy Martindale. The gun was supposed to be the same one that shot the Lawless girl. Mark said he paid Mancillas to throw the gun in the Mississippi." Branden Caid, a Scott County sheriff's deputy, tracked Mancillas down. He denied disposing of a gun for Mark Abbott. He said he was just a kid at the time, in junior high school, and asked the same question I had asked myself, why Abbott wouldn't just throw the gun into the river himself.

Margie Fowler was married to Jerry Fowler. She knew a lot of the local drug characters, including Mark Abbott and Kevin Williams, and had drug problems herself. Jim Sullins interviewed her for the first time on August 19, 2006. She was familiar with the stories about Abbott and Williams killing Mischelle. "Me and my good friend, Melissa Randol, called a local TV station. We told the person on the phone that the Abbotts and Kevin were the real killers, but he thought it was a prank and hung up." Margie Fowler also was friends with Ricky Clay. "I think Mark and Kevin killed Randy Martindale too. Not Ricky." Fowler also told Sullins, "The Abbott twins and Kevin killed a man over drugs and fed his body to the hogs."

Melissa Randol had her own set of stories for Sullins. "My boyfriend, Brian Conklin, got a call from Mark Abbott, and we picked Mark up at the truck stop and drove him to his car in Sikeston the night Mischelle was murdered. And Mark Abbott showed up at our house all muddy the morning after Randy Martindale was murdered, like he spent the night hiding in the swamp, and had Brian and me drive him down to New Madrid to pick up his truck."

I could see there were problems with these stories about Abbott and Williams claiming to be the real killers. If the stories accurately reflected what Abbott and Williams actually said, the details of these accounts were improbable or just plain wrong. The autopsy proved that Mischelle wasn't pregnant and her throat wasn't cut. There wasn't even any evidence at the time of our investigation that Mischelle knew Abbott or Williams, let alone knew about their drug business or was pregnant by one of them. And the timeline seemed all wrong. If Mischelle left Leon Lamb around 1:00 a.m. or even a little earlier, I didn't believe there would have been enough time for an argument leading to murder at Glyn Ferrell's mobile home lot. And the trail of blood and trampled grass to and from Mischelle's car parked on the interstate exit ramp didn't extend anywhere near that lot.

Abbott and Williams might very well have been telling these implausible stories to scare or impress the listeners or for some other perverse reason. Or maybe there was a grain of truth in what they said, which they wrapped in falsehoods.

14

THE BEGINNINGS OF JOSH'S EXONERATION

Rick Walter always knew he wanted to have a career in law enforcement. But he was making good money working at Penzel Construction as a superintendent and later as a project coordinator.

> I had a family that had gotten used to the money, and I didn't think I could afford the big pay cut so I kept on after 1992 as a volunteer Scott County reserve officer. Then, in 1996, I started thinking my chances for a law enforcement career were slipping away, so I became a full-time deputy. After a year, Penzel made me an offer to come back at a higher salary and with hours flexible enough I could continue full-time in the sheriff's department, working late shifts after my days at Penzel as a project coordinator. That arrangement lasted about a year. Having two full-time jobs was too much for me and my family, so I went back to being a part-time deputy.

At some point in the mid-1990s, he isn't sure exactly when, Walter decided for certain that he eventually wanted to run for sheriff. "In 2000, I decided it was time. By then, Bill Ferrell was sheriff for 20 years, and I thought maybe Democrats in Scott County would be ready for a younger candidate." Walter was 39, with an attractive family: his pretty wife, Lisa, and three children, Natalie, 14; Trent, 12; and Seth, 9. "I went into the sheriff's office to tell Bill in person, as a courtesy, that I would be running against him. There already was a lot of tension and suspicion in our relationship, so I thought I better record our conversation on a little tape recorder I had in my pocket. Good thing too. I asked the receptionist to see Ferrell, but she told me he wasn't in." Not wanting to leave a message that he was running for sheriff, Walter said he would come back later. "That afternoon, I was at a basketball game and three other deputies called me on my cell phone. They all asked something like, 'Have you lost your mind?' Ferrell held a meeting of deputies to order my arrest. He claimed I yelled and cursed and threatened him when I came to see him earlier that day. I told them it wasn't true and let them know where they could find me." Walter knew he had the recording to prove Ferrell wrong. "For some reason, I wasn't arrested, and Ferrell called me later to ask what I wanted to see him about. I still didn't want to tell him over the phone, but he insisted." Finally, Walter gave in and told Ferrell what he was planning. "Bill said 'I would make a good sheriff' but then said, 'You would be making a big mistake to run.' I asked what he meant by that, and he said, 'You don't have enough money, and your family isn't influential in the county.'" Walter didn't take Ferrell's advice.

As had been the case for generations in Scott County, winning the Democratic primary in August was virtually a guarantee of victory in November. Publicly at least, there was no mudslinging by the candidates. Walter emphasized that he was a lifelong resident of Scott County and talked in terms of fresh leadership in the sheriff's department. Ferrell emphasized his experience and accomplishments as sheriff. When the ballots were counted, Walter had lost by only 200 votes.

Encouraged by the small margin of his loss, Walter didn't give up on the idea of running for sheriff. He didn't want to spend the next four years outside law enforcement. A job as full-time deputy in Scott County under Bill Ferrell wasn't an option, so he ended his career in the construction industry and became a federal customs agent. "There aren't any jobs for customs agents in Southeast Missouri, so I ended up commuting between home and Chicago for about eight months. But being a weekend father and commuting just wore me down. And the Hatch Act prohibited federal employees from running for public office for a year after leaving federal employment." For those reasons, he left the Customs Service and joined the police department in the nearby city of Charleston in Mississippi County.

In 2004, Bill Ferrell decided not to run for a seventh term. At the time, he was the longest-serving sheriff in Missouri. He was 64 and said he wanted to spend more time with his wife, his four children, and his five grandchildren. In October, he told the *Southeast Missourian* he was most proud of the Kezer case. "We got a conviction almost entirely on circumstantial evidence. I'm really proud of the effort that went into that case and brought it to a conclusion." Brenda Schiwitz said, "We'll miss him terribly. I don't know if I can work for another sheriff. I'm kind of used to him."

Ferrell's retirement opened the way for Walter. In the August Democratic primary, Walter defeated Jerry Bledsoe, a captain in the sheriff's department. In the November general election, he faced Wes Drury, who was running as a Republican. At the time, Walter was a police sergeant in Charleston, and Drury was an investigator for the Scott County prosecutor. Walter won with 9,246 votes to Drury's 8,054. A good man who was law abiding had just been elected sheriff.

After he was elected, Walter made some changes in how the sheriff's department was run. Ferrell supplemented his income by providing food for prisoners in the county jail. This was the practice the Missouri state auditor had criticized in 1992. Walter abolished the long-standing practice and drew a straight salary.

Walter was never comfortable with the jury's guilty verdict in the Kezer case. He didn't attend the trial other than to testify briefly about finding Mischelle's body, and he knew about the prosecutor's evidence only from what he had read in the newspapers. "There were serious unanswered questions. How did Josh get from Kankakee to Benton to be able to use Amanda Drury's car? Why would he have wanted to kill Mischelle in the first place? Being rejected by a girl at a party seemed an unlikely motive to travel 350 miles to hunt her down and kill her a week later. I thought that at the least, others had to be involved."

Walter said he kept hearing rumors about the murder over the years as he talked to people in Scott County about other crimes. These were the same rumors Jim Sullins had heard. It was speculation, without any solid facts behind it, but the important point was that the drug users, drug dealers, drunks, and petty criminals of the county all seemed to think Josh was innocent.

Not long after his election, Walter started looking through the sheriff's department files from the Kezer case. With all the duties of a sheriff, including some that were related as much to politics as to law enforcement, he had little time to work on a closed case. He knew exactly the person he wanted for the job. Branden Caid was a native of Scott City. Fresh out of the Marines, he spent a little less than a year as a jailer with the Scott County Sheriff's Office. Then he joined the Mississippi County Sheriff's Department as a road deputy. Caid came into contact with Rick Walter when he became a public housing officer with the Charleston Department of Public Safety.

In November 2006, Walter received budget authorization from the County Commission to hire Caid as a full-time deputy with duties as department investigator, working primarily on the Lawless murder. Walter told me, "I wanted Branden to take a fresh look at the case."

Caid pored over the cardboard boxes of documents and other evidence in the case file. "My first impression after a quick review was that the case against Josh was pretty solid. There were those reported confessions and the eyewitness identifications by Mark Abbott and Chantelle Crider." But as he dug deeper into the files, the various threads of the case began to unravel.

Walter didn't want word to get out that he had reopened the investigation, and that fact wasn't widely known beyond Walter and Caid even in the sheriff's department. But not long after Caid started reviewing the files, Kevin Williams stopped by the sheriff's office and asked to speak to Walter. "Bill Ferrell told me you opened up the investigation of the Lawless murder and I'm the number one suspect. I had nothing to do with that murder." Walter was shocked. He told Williams, "I hadn't even heard of you until you came to see me today." Walter assumed Ferrell had told Williams he was the number one suspect.

Williams told Walter, "Bill Ferrell came up to me when I was tearing down a building in Miner. He told me about your investigation. We been talking a lot since then, but I guess you know about that from the phone taps." Walter assumed Ferrell had told Williams about the phone taps too. What was going on? Before he left, Williams called his wife, Terri, and had her tell Walter she was with her husband at a party at his boss's house the night of the murder.

★ ★ ★

By 2005, Jane Williams realized she needed to find a lawyer to take Josh's case. "The first three lawyers I approached turned me down. Then a friend, Warren Mayer, suggested I contact his brother-in-law, Ken Parsighian." Parsighian was a Boston lawyer who already had gotten one man out of prison and, at the time, was working on freeing another. "I sent Ken a copy of my summary of the case. He read it and called me a couple of times with follow-up questions. He said the case looked like it had merit but he was very busy and didn't think he could give it the attention it deserved." Parsighian told her a lawyer in Missouri would be in a better position to help and offered to ask Missouri members of an organization to which he belonged, the American College of Trial Lawyers.

Parsighian contacted James Wyrsch, a well-known criminal defense lawyer in Kansas City, who at the time was the Missouri State Chair of the American College of Trial Lawyers. Wyrsch had devoted many hours to pro bono legal services himself and was sympathetic. He listened to Parsighian, and they agreed the undertaking could be too much for a solo practitioner or small firm to handle. The complexity of the case called for the resources of a large firm, so Wyrsch contacted Charlie Weiss at the St. Louis office of Bryan Cave LLP, the largest law firm in the state. He knew Weiss as a member of the Missouri State Committee of the American College of Trial Lawyers.

Weiss agreed to look into Josh's case. He contacted Jane Williams to get more information and circulated an email within the Bryan Cave St. Louis office soliciting help from any other lawyers who might be interested. Two lawyers joined the team and stayed with the case to the end. I was one of them. The other was Jim Wyrsch, not the one in Kansas City who contacted Weiss, but coincidentally, a younger cousin.

Bryan Cave's paying clients are mainly corporations that need assistance with commercial transactions or commercial litigation. Except for some defense of white-collar corporate crimes and cases of indigents occasionally taken on by individual lawyers, there was little about the practice of the firm that could be characterized as criminal law. As a young lawyer at Bryan Cave, Charlie Weiss volunteered to take pro bono criminal appointments the partners were assigned but didn't want to handle. He took one to the US Supreme Court and won. I was appointed to handle a federal parole violation case in the early 1980s when I first joined the federal bar, but that was the last appointment I received. Jim Wyrsch was the only one of us who had any real experience as a criminal trial lawyer. He spent a short time as a public defender before joining Bryan Cave.

On September 12, 2006, the Bryan Cave team met with a group of Josh's supporters at the Bryan Cave office in a conference room looking out on the Mississippi River. To prepare for the meeting, we read Jane Williams's summary of the arguments for Josh's innocence and some of the underlying documents. Her friend, Melanie Brown, was there too. So were Jim Sullins and his partner. It had been arranged that Josh would call from prison at a specified time. While we waited for the call, the lawyers discussed their initial impression of the case. Perhaps somewhat naively, we expressed our amazement that Josh had been convicted on such flimsy evidence and that the statements of Dawn Worley and Lacey Warren hadn't been sufficient to get him a new trial.

Then, we received the call from Josh and interviewed him on the speakerphone. After listening to him, we were convinced that he was innocent. Over the next several weeks, the Bryan Cave lawyers started working on the case in earnest. The first task was for everyone to get a deeper understanding of the mountain of facts and then to bring some kind of organization to them. There were several boxes of documents to review: the three-volume trial transcript, transcripts of dozens of depositions, trial exhibits, hundreds of pages of sheriff's department and highway patrol investigation reports, and photographs of the crime scene and from the autopsy, Mischelle's journal, and photographs of some of the key witnesses in the case.

PART IV

NEVER TOO LATE

"[I]t is never too late for courts in habeas corpus proceedings to look straight through procedural screens in order to prevent forfeiture of life or liberty in flagrant defiance of the Constitution."

—Justice Harry Blackmun, US Supreme Court, *Sawyer v. Whitley*, 505 US 333, 357 (1992)

15

THE HABEAS CORPUS
INVESTIGATION

The most significant evidence against Josh fell into three categories: the jailhouse snitches' accounts of his supposed confessions, Mark Abbott's identification of him as the man in the white car looking for gas, and Chantelle Crider's story of his confrontation with Mischelle at Dawn Worley's Halloween party. Even though no one on the legal team had much experience with postconviction remedies, we had a general understanding that we needed new evidence of Josh's innocence.

Since testifying against Josh, Mark Abbott had been convicted of selling meth, along with his brother Matt, Kevin Williams, and others whose names kept surfacing in connection with Mischelle's murder. These loosely affiliated groups, more collections of criminal entrepreneurs than gangs, made the meth themselves or bought it in California from Mexican drug cartels and hauled it back to Southeast Missouri hidden in with regular cargo in tractor trailers.

The risks were great. If you didn't get maimed or killed in a meth lab explosion, there was the constant threat of arrest. Mark Abbott's career as a drug dealer was relatively short. He was arrested in late 1996 as part of a sweep by the Southeast Missouri Drug Task Force. He was sentenced to 20 years in federal prison, twice what his twin brother and Kevin Williams received, in large part because he cut off his ankle bracelet and fled the area while awaiting sentencing. Authorities caught up with him later in the woods on the other side of the state, cooking meth. By 2006, Mark Abbott had served a little more than half of his sentence and was living in the Federal Correctional Institution in Oxford, Wisconsin. By then, Matt Abbott and Kevin Williams were out and had moved on with their lives. The fact that the Abbott twins and Kevin Williams had been imprisoned after Josh's conviction was new evidence, but it did not affect their credibility enough to make a difference to a jury decision.

The new evidence we had at the beginning mostly related to the accounts of various people that Mark Abbott and Kevin Williams had confessed in the years after the trial that they were responsible for Mischelle's death and that the wrong person had been convicted. To counter Chantelle Crider's trial testimony, we had the two girls who came forward in 1994, right after the trial, to say that Josh wasn't at the Halloween party. Technically, that was new evidence in the sense that it was not presented at Josh's trial even though it had been presented in Al Lowes's motion for a new trial. As to the snitches who claimed Josh admitted to the murder, we planned to have David Rosener testify that he hadn't threatened Shawn Mangus or tricked Wade Howard, but we had nothing else that was new.

We would have to file a state habeas corpus case to free Josh. Courts in the United States are extremely reluctant to overturn a jury verdict that a judge has declined to overturn on a motion for new trial. Thus, the burden of proving a right to habeas corpus relief is extraordinarily high. In effect, although a defendant is presumed innocent until proven guilty, the presumption is reversed when the defendant is convicted.

We would have been in a much better position if we had some way to prove that Josh hadn't gotten a fair trial. One common way to do that is to show that the prosecution withheld exculpatory evidence, evidence tending to prove the person is innocent. This often is referred to as "*Brady* evidence," named after the US Supreme Court case of *Brady v. Maryland*. It is a violation of a defendant's right to due process under the 14th Amendment of the United States Constitution to withhold material exculpatory evidence, either intentionally or inadvertently. Unfortunately for Josh, we weren't aware at the beginning of any *Brady* evidence.

In the 2003 case of *State ex rel. Amrine v. Roper*, Missouri became a state that recognizes what has been called a "stand-alone" claim of actual innocence, in which proof of actual innocence alone can lead to the inmate's release. Under *Amrine*, the constitutional violation is in the conviction of an innocent person itself, rather than in any particular procedural defect. In effect, this means that the inmate must present new evidence that is sufficient to refute essentially all of the evidence indicating guilt and prove conclusively that the inmate is actually innocent. That meant we would have to demonstrate to a high standard of proof ("clear and convincing evidence") that no reasonable juror would have found Josh guilty beyond a reasonable doubt knowing of the new evidence on which the proceeding is based.

* * *

Mark Abbott was a key witness. When he testified, Abbott had no doubt that Josh was the menacing man at the Cut-Mart who told him he was going to have to ride with him to get gas. The jury didn't seem to be bothered by the inconsistencies demonstrated by cross-examination at trial. To us, Abbott's uncanny powers of perception and memory were just one more reason to be suspicious of him. Eyewitness identification of a stranger is notoriously untrustworthy, even coming from a well-intentioned witness, especially when the exposure to the witness is brief and in poor lighting. Hundreds of studies have demonstrated that most people can't reliably identify someone under those circumstances, yet juries typically find eyewitness identification among the most persuasive types of evidence. The fact that Abbott could give only a vague description of a man with a dark complexion right after the crime was consistent with that research. The fact that Abbott five months later could identify Josh indicated that Abbott relied on hints built into the two photo lineups and perhaps on hints, conscious or unconscious, from those who showed the pictures. In addition, we knew that Abbott was trying to divert suspicion from himself.

The police department sign across Josh's chest in the photo lineup was a clear giveaway, but it wasn't new evidence. Al Lowes tried to have the lineup excluded and then cross-examined Abbott about the way the picture stood out from the rest. The selection of the picture of Christy Naile's car wasn't so easy to explain. There was nothing about the pictures themselves that suggested one in particular. Three of the eight had louvers on the back window, and five didn't. But the three louvered cars were very similar. Ultimately, to me, the most convincing argument that Abbott didn't see Christy Naile's car at the Cut-Mart that night was the fact that he picked it out of the photo array.

It's an open secret in law enforcement that investigators give hints during photo identifications, sometimes consciously but more often unconsciously. Don Windham and Brenda Schiwitz had testified that they conducted the photo identifications properly, without suggesting answers, and that Abbott went straight to the "correct" picture of the car without any help. But they knew which photo was the "correct" one. Without even realizing what was happening, one of them could have put special emphasis on the picture Abbott selected, lingering on it or moving it around.

* * *

Bryan Cave hired Jim Sullins[1] to continue investigating on Josh's behalf. He had interviewed Dewayne Kluesner in 1997, when he was working for Josh's mother. He and Mary Hickman interviewed Kluesner for us in Benton on September 25, 2006. Kluesner had someone with him at the interview whom he introduced as his brother. He was nervous about meeting with them, not knowing for sure "which side they were on." The brother, in fact, was Scott County Detective Branden Caid. Kluesner told Sullins the same story he had told him in 1997 about Mischelle being beaten and raped and her throat being cut.

Kluesner asked Sullins, "Have you talked to Rick Walter yet about the case?" When Sullins said he hadn't, Kluesner suggested, "You should arrange to interview me at the Scott County Sheriff's Office, with Rick Walter there too. I got some threats. I'm not sure I can trust you and those mystery people behind you, whoever they are." We had decided soon after we took Josh's case that we needed to talk to the sheriff anyway. We wanted to see if we could get his cooperation or at least convince him not to interfere in our investigation, and this seemed like a good opportunity to establish that sort of relationship.

Sullins called Walter on September 27 to tell him he was working on the Lawless murder and to arrange for the meeting with Kluesner. Walter was busy the coming weekend. He had to be at the Cotton Carnival in Sikeston early on Saturday and had personal commitments the rest of the weekend. Both parties to the phone conversation were being cautious. The sheriff asked Sullins, "Who is it that hired you?" Sullins, being unnecessarily mysterious, would only say, "There are some people from St. Louis I want you to meet." The sheriff said, "I'm not real comfortable with that whole thing, the way it was set up, the way it happened. In fact, I have part of the file sitting right here next to me on my desk. I welcome your help, as long as you're going in the right direction. I don't care what you end up proving."

At the same time, Walter cautioned Sullins about relying too much on Kluesner. "His recollection of events is likely to be a bit fuzzy. He has a history of drug and alcohol abuse, and a few of his brain cells have probably been burned out." He also told Sullins that Kluesner was scared of retaliation if he helped exonerate Josh. "He'll be a nervous wreck at the meeting, and he probably won't tell us anything, anyway."

Charlie Weiss and Jim Wyrsch drove down to Benton on October 2 for the meeting with Rick Walter and Dewayne Kluesner. Walter had put on weight over the years, and his handsome face had filled out a bit. He spoke with a drawl like most of those in that part of the state. Branden Caid was there, as himself this time. He was short but muscular and wore glasses. So were Tom Beardslee and Roy Moore. Beardslee was Walter's chief deputy, as he had been, in name at least, for Bill Ferrell, and Roy Moore had gone from part-time Benton policeman to full-time Scott County deputy. Kluesner didn't show up, which wasn't too surprising in light of what Walter had told Jim Sullins. Sullins introduced the Bryan Cave lawyers as part of the legal team in St. Louis who had agreed to take Josh's case.

The sheriff asked, "Do you mind showing some ID to prove who you are?" He told us much later, with some embarrassment, that he had the driver's licenses run to confirm the lawyers' identity. "I reopened the investigation. But you need to be aware I'll follow the trail wherever it leads," he told them. "I don't think the evidence against that boy adds up. But if any evidence points to your guy, I'll follow that evidence too." The two sides agreed, in principle at least, to work together and to exchange what evidence they had found.

Tom Beardslee visited the Bryan Cave office in St. Louis on October 10. He was middle aged and rather nondescript looking and all business without any small talk.

> Bill Ferrell lost interest in all the other suspects and focused on Kezer as soon as Shawn Mangus and the other jailhouse informants came forward. I thought that was unwise, but I had little to say about the course of the investigation. I never considered Mark Abbott's ID of Kezer was credible. Abbott was my leading suspect. I think Kezer probably did tell Mangus he killed Mischelle, but he did it to impress him, not because it was true. In Beardslee's opinion, "The boy was convicted because Al Lowes's courtroom style antagonized the jury. Some of them made comments like that."

When we started on Josh's case, we had the benefit of the prior work of Jim Sullins. When a witness's story held some promise, we followed up to try to get a sworn statement. Sullins interviewed Cathy Fowler on September 10, 2006. She confirmed the story she had told Al Lowes four years before, that Kevin Williams told her Mark Abbott killed Mischelle Lawless. Fowler told Sullins she believed Abbott and Williams also were involved in the 1994 murder of Randy Martindale. "The same gun was used in both murders. Kevin gave my husband the gun to set him up for the two murders. I made him give the gun back."

★ ★ ★

On the afternoon of December 13, 2006, Branden Caid called and left a message that Rick Walter wanted to visit Josh in prison. By the time we returned the call early the next afternoon, Walter, Caid, and Moore were at the Jefferson City Correctional Center.

The guards pulled Josh out of the general visiting area—a large, open room where friends and family of inmates can sit at tables, snacking on items purchased from the vending machines—where he was visiting with Jane Williams and Melanie Brown. The guards told him he had other visitors and ushered him into a private meeting room. Josh was frustrated when he realized what was happening. Rick Walter tried to put him at ease, saying the sheriff's office was taking a fresh look at the Lawless murder. According to Josh, "He told me he thought I might be innocent but because of the conviction, I was still his number one suspect. He said there were a few others he was looking at but if he could eliminate me, he would do what he could to get me out."

Josh just sat and listened to Walter. When the interview was over and the officers rose to leave, Rick Walter tried to shake Josh's hand, but Josh pulled back. He asked Walter, "See that badge on your sleeve? What's it say? Scott County?" Walter answered, "Yes, sir." Josh said, "I've had experience with the Scott County Sheriff Department before. I don't believe a damn word coming out of your mouth. If you do what you say you'll do, I'll shake your hand, but not yet." To his credit, Walter said he understood.

We were upset that the sheriff had interviewed Josh without giving us an opportunity to have one of the legal team present. Josh prepared a written summary of the discussion for us. Toward the end of the summary, he described what he had learned from the incident. "Some of it is pleasing. Some of it is disappointing. Some of it is confusing. By the goodness of God, all of it will come together for good in the end. I have to believe this. My relationship with Jesus is what gives me my sanity and the faith I have for the future."

Josh described the tumult of "overwhelming" emotions he experienced during the interview, and fear for the negative impact a bungled interview could have on his chance for a release. "Looking into the eye of this storm was more than I could handle yesterday. Like Peter, I found myself crying out for Christ when the storm revealed his . . . my weakness in the moment. I have grown through this. Last night, I went to church and was given Psalms 94:11–23 by the pastor."[2]

The real danger from being so candid in the interview was losing the support of the sheriff's office. If Rick Walter had decided Josh was guilty after all, he might have shut down his investigation and left us on our own. But as it happened, the interview had the opposite effect. All three officers were impressed by Josh's candor and left Jefferson City all the more convinced they were on the right track.

★ ★ ★

Going through the boxes of documents in the case file, Branden Caid found a three-page interview report by a police lieutenant in Scott City named Bobby Wooten. The person interviewed was Mark Abbott, and the report was dated November 18, 1992.

Branden Caid called the Bryan Cave lawyers on the telephone and told us, "It's attached with a paper clip to one of Deputy Schiwitz's investigation notebooks; it's a 5-by-7 steno pad." After vague descriptions in interview reports the first day after the murder of a possibly Hispanic man with a dark complexion, Mark Abbott suddenly knew exactly who the man was. "Abbott told me in the interview that he didn't want to give the information to the sheriff's department because Deputy Beardslee thinks I'm the murderer and the sheriff wants me to take a polygraph. The people at the sheriff's department are a bunch of assholes." The report continued:

> Abbott asked me if I know someone named Ray Ring. I told him I didn't. He said he met Ring recently at a party. I understood the party was the night of the murder. Then, Abbott said he saw Ring again, right after he found the Lawless girl's body. Ring was across the interstate driving a white car and looking for gas. Abbott said Ring sent word through his friends, Kevin and Terri Williams, that he wanted to talk to Abbott—presumably to try to find out what Abbott saw that night.

Ring was Lyle Day's half African American friend who had provided Day with an alibi, being with Day and Gene Haynes at a party in the town of Matthews the night of the murder.

According to the report, as soon as the interview was over, Wooten called Ferrell and Deputy Chambers to tell them what Abbott had said. He had his account of the interview typed at the Scott City police station, and he put it in Ferrell's inbox so he would have it when he came to the office the next day. Ferrell's interview of Ray Ring early on November 19, treating Ring as a suspect and reading him his rights, suddenly made perfect sense.

The Wooten report was important but not because it was evidence Ray Ring was involved in the murder. As it turned out, being with Lyle Day and Gene Haynes gave Ring a fairly good alibi. It was important because it undercut Abbott's credibility.

Caid asked if we had seen the report. It wasn't among the documents produced by the prosecution in Al Lowes's files. It wasn't a trial exhibit, and it wasn't mentioned anywhere in the 1994 trial transcript or in any of the pretrial depositions. Suddenly, we had a *Brady* case.

Jim Sullins found Bobby Wooten. He was out of law enforcement and operating a bail bond business from his home. He remembered talking to Mark Abbott about Ray Ring and signed an affidavit to that effect.

The notebooks to which the Wooten report was attached contained more *Brady* material. This was particularly telling in light of the fact that Al Lowes had asked Deputy Schiwitz in a deposition before Josh's 1994 trial if she had any investigation notes and she said she took notes of what she was doing but hadn't kept them after she typed up her formal report.

It was clear from the notebooks that Mark Abbott was a suspect from the beginning, something that Deputy Schiwitz had denied. She recorded discussions at a meeting of the investigative team on November 11, just three days after the murder. That was the meeting at which Deputy Beardslee nominated "Mark Abbott—Matt Abbott" and Sheriff Ferrell suggested giving him a polygraph. Deputy Schiwitz wrote on November 19, the day after Wooten's interview of Abbott and the day Ferrell interviewed Ray Ring, "Abbott went back to accident scene after he left S.O.!" On November 23, she wrote, "Take polygraph—Why telling several stories—tell [Abbott] haven't talked w/ Ray Ring" and "Mark Abbott—ask him if he knew Mischelle—<u>don't</u> mention Ray Ring—ask about guy @ phone? see if he gives name."

The description of the man at the Cut-Mart that Abbott gave in his November 23 interview was even more unlike Josh in the Schiwitz notes than the descriptions in the official written summaries that Schiwitz and Windham prepared. In her notes, the man was under 20 years of age and was "not <u>white</u>—Mexican or Negro." He had a "mustache—maybe" and perhaps was a "light/Black male w/ mustache—hair longer around sides & down on neck somewhat." According to Schiwitz's official report, however, "the driver was not a Negro, but could have been Hispanic or Mexican as he had a dark complexion."

In an entry on May 2, 1994, the month before Josh's trial, the notes revealed something relevant to the credibility of the snitches that wasn't even hinted at anywhere else. Sheriff Ferrell and Deputy Schiwitz had traveled to the state prison in Farmington to interview Joseph Flores, who had been in the same cell with Josh, Wade Howard, and Jeff Rogers the previous year during the time when Howard and Rogers offered to testify about Josh's purported confession. Flores wasn't happy to see them and cut the interview short. According to the Schiwitz notes, he told them that Josh said the authorities had "confused him with someone else," that he was "in another state" when Mischelle was murdered.

★ ★ ★

During a telephone conversation with Bryan Cave lawyers on March 2, 2007, Branden Caid said he was at Cape Girardeau police headquarters on another matter and happened to tell one of the detectives he was working on the reopened investigation of the Lawless murder and Mark Abbott's role in the case. The detective told him he should talk to Bill Bohnert because Bohnert had gotten some information from Mark Abbott about the Lawless murder during a drug roundup about 10 years earlier.

William J. Bohnert had been a Cape Girardeau police officer since 1983. In the mid-1990s, he was a detective in the Narcotics Division, assigned to the Southeast Missouri Drug Task Force. He knew the Abbott twins and Kevin Williams and had arrested all three of them on various drug and weapons charges. Mark Abbott also had served as his confidential informant for a period of time. Mark Abbott was in the custody of the US Marshals Service in the Perry County Jail. Herman Hogue, a DEA agent in the task force, called Bohnert and told him Mark Abbott wanted to see him because he had information about the Lawless murder.

Bohnert tried to find some documentation of the conversation he had with Mark Abbott, but he couldn't find anything in the archived files. His recall of the event was vivid, so he prepared a written summary for Caid from memory. According to the summary, Abbott told Bohnert, "I know I'm going to prison. I want a deal for a lesser sentence if I testify about what I know." He claimed, "Kevin Williams killed the Lawless girl because she was pregnant with his baby and was going to tell his wife."

We reasoned, whether Abbott was or wasn't lying about Williams killing Mischelle, his credibility as a witness against Josh was seriously undermined by yet another conflicting story.

★ ★ ★

Rick Walter received a call one night from a friend he knew from his days in the construction business. The friend had just received a disturbing call from Kevin Williams. Rumors about Walter's investigation zeroing in on Abbott and Williams apparently had gotten back to Williams. He first asked the friend if he was Walter's friend. When the man said he was, Williams told him, "If Rick Walter's house blows up, I hope his family is in it with him."

★ ★ ★

Jim Sullins found Chantelle Crider and starting on November 11, 2006, talked to her at least nine times by telephone over the next six months. By then, she was 31 and had four children and a new last name, Carlisle. Divorced a second time, she and her children were living with her mother in Sikeston. Both Chantelle and her mother were frightened at first by the very idea that Mischelle's murder was being brought up again. They were frightened of the Abbotts, whom as it turned out, Chantelle had come to know. Her husband at the time of Josh's trial, David Franklin, had drawn her into the same drug world the Abbotts and Kevin Williams inhabited. Franklin was one of their subsidiary dealers, and he and Chantelle became users themselves.

Chantelle was wary of Sullins. She wasn't even sure at first that he wasn't working for the Abbotts. Chantelle insisted the first in-person interview be conducted in a public place. Jim and Mary met Chantelle in a Sikeston park, and she brought her mother. They sat around a picnic table, and the interview was videotaped. The result was chaotic. Chantelle had trouble following through on a thought. Jim and his partner jumped back and forth asking questions, and Chantelle's mother kept interjecting. Chantelle wasn't all that sure anymore that the boy who supposedly harassed her and Mischelle at the Halloween party was Josh.

Chantelle agreed to give a sworn statement in a more formal setting, one we could file in support of a habeas petition. On February 7, 2007, Charlie Weiss questioned her under oath before a court reporter, and I observed. She was short and a bit overweight but cute in a vacant sort of way. She looked at a photograph of Josh as he looked at the time of the murder, a little unkempt, with longish hair piled higher on top and hanging down in the back. "I'm a hundred percent positive the person in that picture is not the boy who harassed me and Mischelle at the Halloween party. That boy was clean cut and had short, light brown hair." She insisted, "I made an honest mistake."

But there was more. "Mark and Matt Abbott were at the party too. They had on black and white face paint. I didn't know them then, but after I saw Mark at the trial, I realized he was at the party." Chantelle married David Franklin the month before Josh's trial. The marriage lasted about six months. In the transcribed interview, Chantelle said, "One night not long after Josh's trial, I was out riding with David, and he told me he had to stop to see a friend. He took me to one of the Abbotts' businesses in Scott City. Mark was there. I recognized him from the trial." She saw Abbott frequently over the next year, at the business and at hotel parties in the Hatfield Inn. "He forced me to snort amphetamine once, and I saw a lot of the drug dealing that went on."

Chantelle said she wasn't aware that Mischelle knew Mark Abbott, but she did overhear comments by him and others in the group that suggested Mischelle knew something about his drug dealing. "I heard them talk about how she'd never talk again and that they wanted to do me the same way because they didn't want me talking. . . . They, you know, were afraid I was going to expose it because I found out by overhearing and what I just happened to come upon and see." Not surprisingly, with experiences like this, she was afraid of Mark Abbott, and he seemed to delight in scaring her, taking her for unexplained rides at night on dark country roads to mysterious meetings. "He came by my house once and wanted to take me for one of those rides, but I made some excuse and didn't go."

Chantelle also said she came to know Todd Mayberry in the years after Josh's trial, not just as the drunk at the Halloween party, but as himself. "I was afraid of Todd too. I was riding in a car with Lelicia O'Dell and Dwight Buckner. Lelicia liked Dwight at the time." This was the same Dwight Buckner who worked at Glyn Ferrell's trailer lot. After cruising for a while, Dwight dropped Lelicia off at her car. "Instead of taking me home, Dwight and Todd took me for a ride on the back roads. I was frightened. I pulled on the wheel and crashed the car into a tree." As she saw it, she only managed to escape being harmed because another car stopped to help them.

We didn't get a chance to find out what Todd Mayberry had to say about that night. On January 27, 2008, the *Southeast Missourian* reported that Mayberry had died two days before, at the age of 37, in Orange County, Texas. There was no explanation of the circumstances of his death in the obituary, only a brief outline of his life.

★ ★ ★

We had a good feeling about the new evidence we had accumulated by mid-2007. There was no predicting what crazy claims Chantelle might make in a hearing, but combined with the testimony of Dawn Worley and Lacy Warren, her recantation about Josh should be enough to remove any doubt about Josh's presence at the Halloween party. The report of Bobby Wooten's interview with Mark Abbott went a long way toward destroying Mark Abbott's already shaky credibility, and the suppression of that report and Brenda Schiwitz's notebooks gave us a *Brady* case. Proof that the prosecution withheld material exculpatory evidence from the defense might be enough to get Josh a new trial, but that approach wasn't guaranteed.

Rather than rush to file a habeas corpus petition in the middle of 2007, we continued to try to find more exculpatory evidence. Josh was frustrated, but he understood this strategy. "I don't want to be released with a cloud hanging over my head. I want to be found actually innocent. I don't want anyone to be able to say I was released on a technicality."

The members of the legal team visited Josh in prison at the beginning and occasionally over the period we represented him. We couldn't make the trip to Jefferson City regularly. These few visits didn't add much to our preparation of his case, but they helped build a relationship of trust that was important in more intangible ways.

We did talk on the telephone frequently. Josh started calling one or the other of us about once a week, sometimes more frequently during the last year leading up to the hearing. We talked about progress in the case—especially any promising new developments like the discovery of the Wooten interview. We were getting more and more confident as the case fell into place, and so was Josh. He told me, "I need to start thinking about what I want to do when I get out." I responded, "You should think about going to college." I encouraged his optimism, but I tried not to let him take anything for granted.

Occasionally during these conversations, his understandably bad feelings against those who got him convicted emerged. On one of those occasions, I told him, "Don't let these feelings fester. I know you don't want to hate the people, like Bill Ferrell, who put you away. It's not consistent with your faith." But sitting in prison all those years knowing he was innocent, he would have had to have been some kind of saint not to carry a grudge. Most of the time, instead of feeding him platitudes, I tried to emphasize the practical benefit of forgiveness. "Hatred will eat away at you and feed on itself until it overwhelms you. It won't have any impact on the people you hate. You'll be happier if you can let it go."

★ ★ ★

The testimony of Shawn Mangus, Steve Grah, and Wade Howard, the jailhouse informants who claimed Josh confessed, was our weak point. We had no new evidence to address that issue other than what David Rosener would say and Deputy Schiwitz's notes of the interview with Joseph Flores. The obvious place to start looking for more was the snitches themselves. Maybe we could get another recantation. Before long, we discovered that Branden Caid was on the same trail.

Caid learned from Shawn Mangus's mother that he died in Seattle of a drug overdose in 1997, but he was reluctant to take her word for it. The obituary of Mangus's father, Mackie Gromer, in the July 24, 2006, edition of the Sikeston *Standard Democrat* said Gromer was predeceased by his son, Shawn Mangus.

Steve Grah was living in Millersville, Missouri, with his mother. In the middle of May 2007, Caid left his card at Grah's home. Grah called Caid twice on the telephone. These two conversations didn't yield much that was useful, but we could have Caid testify about those conversations at the hearing.

Branden Caid interviewed Wade Howard at the state prison in Moberly. Like Grah, Howard was not cooperative and provided nothing we could use at the habeas hearing. A year later, as the hearing approached, we considered contacting him to at least confirm our suspicion he would not help. By then, he was out of prison, and we had lost track of him.

Then, there was the snitch who didn't testify at all, Jeff Rogers. Born in 1959, he was considerably older than Josh and the other snitches. He was arraigned with Josh on the same day in 1993 and was imprisoned with him in Jefferson City. Convicted of incest and statutory sodomy, he was serving six life sentences—three running back-to-back and three at the same time. In prison, Rogers told Josh on one of those occasions that Sheriff Ferrell had pressured him into signing a false statement that Josh confessed.

On April 14, 2007, after hearing this from Josh, Branden Caid visited Rogers in prison and made a tape recording of the interview, which he shared with us. Rogers said, "Kezer never admitted killing the Lawless girl; he always claimed he didn't do it." He described how Sheriff Ferrell, with a combination of threats and promises, had gotten him to sign a statement saying otherwise. He also explained, "I wouldn't testify at my deposition because I didn't want to commit perjury." When Wade Howard recanted in 1993, he told a similar story about Sheriff Ferrell pressuring him to testify that Josh confessed. Rogers's testimony in a habeas proceeding would cast doubt indirectly on Howard's testimony regarding Josh's confession.

*   *   *

Early in 2007, Jim Sullins suggested we talk to Ricky Clay about the Lawless murder.[1] Cathy Fowler and others told Sullins they had heard Abbott and Williams were involved in the 1994 murder of Randy Martindale and they believed the same .380 was used to kill Martindale and Mischelle Lawless. The two murders also were potentially linked by the fact that Abbott, Williams, and Clay had been friends or at least associates in the drug trade. Some of our informants believed Clay was innocent and had been blamed for something Abbott and Williams did. In some ways Clay did seem like an unlikely murderer. He had been prom king at Kelly High and joined the Marines shortly after graduating. Like Josh, he had always maintained his innocence.

Randy Martindale lived in New Madrid County. His estranged wife, Stacy, had a long-running affair with a man named Chuck Sanders, who also was supplying her with drugs. She offered Sanders money to kill her husband. He turned her down, but she allegedly got his friend, Ricky Clay, to do it. On May 19, 1994, Stacy talked her husband into spending the night after he returned their two young sons from an outing to a baseball game in St. Louis. Clay supposedly hid in the bedroom closet and came out shooting. Police chased Stacy Martindale's red Camaro, which she said Clay took when he fled her house. Clay was caught the next morning hiding in the swamp near the Mississippi, not far from the abandoned car, when he lifted his head out of the murky water to breathe. Clay insisted that before Randy Martindale was killed, he and Sanders left the Martindale house in the car Stacy let them use. He ran when police chased the car because he was carrying drugs. There was no physical evidence linking Clay to the murder, such as gunshot residue, and Stacy had gunshot residue on her hands. Clay was convicted almost entirely on Sanders's testimony against Clay and Stacy. Clay was condemned to death, but his execution had been delayed repeatedly by appeals.

When Sullins first suggested we talk to Clay, there was a moratorium on all executions in Missouri because of a constitutional challenge to the particular method of lethal injection then in use. I was skeptical about the speculation there was a link between the two murders, and even if there were, I doubted that Clay would help us. Tying Abbott and Williams to the two murders would not help Clay unless it also showed that he wasn't involved in either. Fortunately, we decided to follow Sullins's suggestion anyway.

I worked through Jennifer Herndon, Clay's appointed death penalty lawyer. She would have to decide there was no harm in letting him talk to us, and then Clay had to be willing to do it. It was a slow process, spread over several months that spring. Herndon was busy trying to find new ways to save Clay's life, and Josh Kezer wasn't a particularly high priority for either of them. On June 11, Sullins sent an email informing us he had heard on the news over the weekend that Jay Nixon, still the Missouri Attorney General, was pushing for certain long-delayed executions to be scheduled, Ricky Clay's among them. That gave a new urgency to our efforts. Eventually, after more letters and phone calls, Clay consented to a telephone interview, and we talked to him on July 18, 2007.

Clay was extremely helpful but in a way we hadn't imagined. Not surprisingly, he said, "I don't know nothing about the Lawless girl's murder. I don't know if Mark Abbott or Kevin Williams was involved." But he did know something else. Clay said he was out drinking with Mark Abbott when Abbott told him it was a carload of Mexicans in the white car at the Cut-Mart.

Like Bobby Wooten's report of his interview with Mark Abbott, Clay's account was contemporaneous with the murder. It was another version of Abbott's story about the man in the white car, which was inconsistent with his subsequent testimony that the man was Josh, and Abbott told it to Clay about the same time he told Bobby Wooten the man in the white car was Ray Ring. We arranged for Clay to provide us with an affidavit describing what Abbott had told him.

16

HABEAS CORPUS
PRELIMINARY PROCEEDINGS

There was nothing left to do but file the habeas petition, nominally against David Dormire, the superintendent of the Jefferson City Correctional Center, where Josh was being held. We did some last-minute polishing and on April 1, 2008, filed the petition, the supporting brief, and three volumes of sworn statements, documents, and the trial transcript. Josh found it amusing that his case began on April Fools' Day.

The Jefferson City Correctional Center is located in Cole County, the 19th Judicial Circuit, with its seat in the state capital of Jefferson City. With the Jefferson City Correctional Center and the Algoa Correctional Center within its boundaries, Cole County saw more than its share of prisoner suits. In addition, suits against the State of Missouri, whether directed at an action of an agency or department of state government or of the governor himself, generally must be brought in Cole County. As a result, the judges in that circuit got the most politically sensitive cases and weren't strangers to controversy. We felt fortunate to be able to file the case there. Outside the St. Louis and Kansas City metropolitan areas, trial judges are elected, and releasing a convicted murderer wasn't likely to be a popular move for a judge who would have to stand for reelection. The same was true of Cole County, but at least those judges were used to the pressure.

The 19th is not a large circuit in terms of the volume of cases filed or the number of judges available to hear them. Josh's case would be assigned to one of three circuit judges. We were hoping we would draw Richard Callahan, and we did. Judge Callahan was born in St. Louis in 1947. He earned a degree from Georgetown University in three years, graduating in 1968 in the same class as Bill Clinton. He stayed at Georgetown for law school, graduating in 1972.

Callahan was elected circuit judge in 2002. He had spent most of his career before that as a prosecutor. He started as an assistant in the circuit attorney's office in St. Louis in 1972. In 1979, he moved on to the office of prosecuting attorney for Cole County and served there as an assistant prosecutor from 1979 to 1986 and as the elected prosecuting attorney from 1987 to 2002. Like Kenny Hulshof, he also was a special assistant in the Missouri Attorney General's office for a time. He served on the Missouri Prosecutors Association Board of Directors from 1987 to 2002 and as president in 1990. He also served on the National District Attorneys Association Board of Directors from 1994 to 2002 and as vice president from 1996 to 2000.

As a prosecutor in Cole County and for the attorney general's office, Callahan went after politicians and politically connected individuals from both parties. He prosecuted a brother-in-law of Congressman Ike Skelton, Missouri Secretary of State Judith Moriarty (for an election offense involving her son) when his own daughter was an intern in her office, and State Senator Jet Banks from St. Louis. As he once told *The St. Louis American* in an interview, "In Jefferson City, if I didn't investigate or got a special prosecutor every time I had a connection to somebody in the office I was dealing with, I would have been on vacation six months a year."

We hoped that as an experienced prosecutor, Judge Callahan would quickly recognize the flaws in the original case and the merit in our new evidence, especially the evidence that had been withheld from the defense. We also believed that Callahan's credibility as a prosecutor would insulate him from any political or public pressures he might encounter if he saw the case as we did.

In addition, although cases are supposed to be assigned randomly, as a judge, Callahan seemed to get most of the political hot potatoes that were filed in Cole County, and he wasn't afraid to rule decisively, against the government where necessary, without regard to party or political philosophy. This was a trait we saw as essential in a case attacking the work of two men who were in the process of running against each other for governor.

★ ★ ★

Shortly after we filed the petition, Judge Callahan issued an order requiring the State to "show cause" why the request for a writ of habeas corpus freeing Josh should not be granted. In doing so, he wasn't sending a signal how he viewed the case. It was the standard procedure under the Rule of Civil Procedure governing habeas cases. He also set the case for an initial status conference on June 9, 2008. Michael J. Spillane was assigned by the attorney general's office to represent the State of Missouri. Mike was a longtime assistant who, among other things, had handled many prisoner habeas cases. He is tall, with glasses and a neatly trimmed beard. His manner is formal in the extreme, addressing other lawyers, even those he has known for years and respects, as sir or by last name with Mr. in front of it. But he approaches cases with an open mind and doesn't twist facts to suit his purpose or engage in any of the trickery that characterizes some in the profession. When it comes to professional ethics, he is nothing like Kenny Hulshof.

It was Mark Abbott, not Spillane, who filed the first response to our petition. He sent a letter to the judge from prison, received on May 5, demanding that he be given a polygraph to prove he didn't kill Mischelle Lawless, which he labeled "Request for Motion to Grant a Polygraph Test." The court treated the letter as if it were a pleading and entered it on the docket but otherwise ignored the request. Abbott wasn't a party to the case and had no legal standing to intervene and become one.

Spillane filed the attorney general's response to the show-cause order on June 9, the day of the first hearing. The State argued that Bobby Wooten's report of his interview with Mark Abbott, in which Abbott said the person he saw at the Cut-Mart was Ray Ring, didn't appear to be authentic and that the information wasn't material in any event because Abbott said the person might have been Ring in an interview report that *was* disclosed.

Chris Pickering, an investigator in the attorney general's office, interviewed Wooten and claimed in an interview summary filed with the State's show-cause response that Wooten told him he didn't remember the interview and didn't believe the signature on the report was his. According to Pickering, Wooten would only say the document was in a form he had used and looked like a report he would have written. Pickering also talked to some of those who were mentioned in the report, and each of them contradicted what it said about them in some way. We were concerned that Pickering had spooked Wooten. We had only communicated with him through Jim Sullins and didn't have a very good feel for him as a witness. Maybe Pickering accurately portrayed what Wooten had told him, and Wooten would repudiate his affidavit and the interview report when it came time to testify.

The State's other argument was something we had anticipated. Mark Abbott did mention Ray Ring in an interview with Windham and Schiwitz on November 23, 1992. According to Windham's interview report, Abbott said Kevin and Terri Williams told him Ray Ring wanted to talk to him, and based on that, he thought the man who talked to him at the Cut-Mart "could have possibly been Ray Ring." It was one thing for Abbott to speculate that it might have been Ring at the Cut-Mart; it was something else entirely for him to tell Wooten it *was* Ring.

★ ★ ★

Jefferson City is situated on the south bank of the Missouri River in the middle of the state, about halfway between St. Louis and Kansas City. The Cole County Courthouse is "downtown" on High Street—as its name implies, the street that runs up and along the peak of the heights above the river—several blocks east of the supreme court building and the attorney general's office. The capitol building, state offices, and old penitentiary also are located in that area of the city. The county courthouse is an elegant white limestone building, with turrets and a red roof.

In the early afternoon of June 9, lawyers and others with business before Division 2 were gathered in the hall outside the locked courtroom waiting for the afternoon session to begin. Marvin Lawless was there, too, with his new wife. He was angry that we were trying to get Josh released and was following the progress of the case closely. When we approached and extended our hands, he said, "I'm not sure I want to shake hands with you," but he did it anyway.

A little before 1:30, we entered the courtroom and waited for the judge to appear. When our case was called, the lawyers approached. The room has the high ceilings common in old courthouses, and Judge Callahan was sitting on "the bench" in the back corner high above the floor. He was surrounded by a massive wooden desk with a raised step around the bottom, on which lawyers can stand to be nearer to the judge's level. Judge Callahan has a distinctive way of speaking, almost chewing on the words as they come out of his mouth but somehow speaking clearly and distinctly. He was usually very serious as befit the gravity of his office, but he could flash a wry smile when some irony or humor in the occasion called for it.

Spillane raised the so-called gateway issue, contending that the case we had presented in the habeas petition didn't even satisfy the minimum requirements for being granted a hearing. His arguments were the ones he presented in the State's show-cause response. In effect, he was asking that Josh's petition be summarily dismissed. The judge listened but didn't respond one way or the other. He noticed that Sheriff Walter was present and asked rhetorically, "Whose side is the sheriff on?" There was to be no ruling on anything that day, but we felt at least that we were starting to get the judge's attention and found his comment about Rick Walter's presence encouraging. He told the parties to prepare proposed orders on some discovery motions that we argued, took everything under advisement, and set another status conference for July 29.

★ ★ ★

The attack on the authenticity of Bobby Wooten's report of his interview with Mark Abbott made us nervous. We had heard about Chris Pickering's interview with Wooten several weeks before Spillane filed the show-cause response, in which it played such a crucial role. Sheriff Walter and Deputy Caid told us that Pickering had confronted them with Wooten's account of the interview when he came to Benton in mid-May to review the sheriff's case file. "The interview was like an interrogation," Walter told us. "It was like we were being investigated on suspicion of fabricating exculpatory evidence."

When I looked in our supporting exhibits and compared the signatures on the 1992 report and the signature on Wooten's affidavit authenticating the report, the difference was obvious—the two signatures didn't look the same. In our enthusiasm, we hadn't noticed what caused Spillane and Pickering to be suspicious.

We knew that signatures tend to change over time and be different in different circumstances. A proper comparison would be with interview reports of the same type that Wooten had signed in 1992. We asked the sheriff to see if he could get some examples of Wooten's signature from the Scott City Police Department records. Walter told us, "At first, they didn't think they kept records that far back, but they managed to find a few old reports that Wooten prepared and signed." Those signatures looked to us exactly like the one on the report of the interview with Abbott. We hired a handwriting expert, who confirmed our conclusion.

On June 11, Spillane filed his own discovery motion. He reiterated what he had said about the Wooten report in the show-cause response two days before and asked the judge to order Sheriff Walter to produce the original for analysis by a handwriting expert. The judge granted the motion the next day before we had a chance to respond. We asked the judge to modify the order to require a comparison with the contemporaneous examples of Wooten's signature that the sheriff had gotten from Scott City and provided copies of those documents to the court and to Spillane.

When we arrived at the courthouse on July 29 for the status conference, Marvin Lawless and his wife were there again, waiting for what they assumed would be a public hearing. This time, however, we were the only case on the docket, and the clerk announced that the lawyers were to meet privately with the judge in chambers. When Judge Callahan realized that

Mr. Lawless was present and apparently wanted to observe the proceedings, he told Spillane to tell him, "I want to talk to the lawyers for both sides, candidly and off the record, and I can't do that in open court. If Mr. Lawless waits, I'll come out after the conference and explain what's happening in the case."

★ ★ ★

Kenny Hulshof was earning a reputation as a tough prosecutor with the Kezer murder convictions and convictions in several other high-profile cases. In rural Missouri, there isn't much difference between elected Democrats and Republicans on law-and-order issues, and both parties like prosecutors as candidates for political office. Hulshof leaned Republican, and it was as a Republican that he chose to capitalize on his background as a prosecutor with the attorney general's office.

In June 1994, as he was winding up Josh's trial, he was a last-minute replacement as the Republican challenger to longtime incumbent Democratic Congressman Harold Volkmer, representing the Ninth Congressional District in the US House of Representatives. At the time, the Ninth encompassed much of the largely rural northeast quadrant of the state west of St. Louis, an area known as Little Dixie. Rick Hardy, a political science professor at the University of Missouri in Columbia, on the western edge of the district, withdrew shortly after winning the primary when he was hospitalized for what was described as exhaustion. Hulshof replaced Hardy. He lost that election but did surprisingly well considering his late start and status as a relative unknown. He likely was helped by the same national shift in attitudes at the midpoint of President Bill Clinton's first term that led to Republican control of the House for the first time in 40 years and the installation of Newt Gingrich as Speaker of the House. Despite their political differences, Jay Nixon, a Democrat, kept him as an assistant attorney general through the election and beyond.

Two years later, Hulshof won the Republican primary again. During the campaign leading up to the general election, Volkmer warned Ninth District voters that Hulshof would be a puppet of Newt Gingrich. Hulshof countered that Volkmer had voted 20 times to raise taxes in his 20 years in Congress. Hulshof's argument apparently prevailed. He won the election with 49.4 percent of the votes to Volkmer's 47.0 percent. Hulshof later would say he probably wouldn't have run again in 1996 if the 1994 election hadn't been close.

Hulshof was elected to the House five more times between 1998 and 2006, with comfortable margins, receiving between 59.3 percent and 68.2

percent of the votes. During his 12 years in the House, he had a generally conservative voting record. A strong supporter of the military, he joined a congressional band, known as the Second Amendments, as drummer and played for US troops stationed overseas during the Christmas holidays. He received a 0 percent favorable rating from the National Abortion Rights Action League and a 100 percent favorable rating from the National Right to Life Council on abortion and related issues. He voted in favor of military border patrols in 2001 after the 9/11 attacks, in support of constitutional amendments to allow school prayer in public schools, to ban desecration of the flag, to define marriage as between a man and a woman, and in support of a continued ban on travel to Cuba until political prisoners are released. On the other hand, he had a 39 percent favorable rating from the NAACP; voted against bailouts for General Motors and Chrysler; and cosponsored the Ticket to Work and Work Incentives Act, which President Clinton signed into law. The purpose of this legislation was to allow individuals with disabilities to keep Medicaid while they worked so they could lead independent and productive lives.

Hulshof could have continued indefinitely as the Ninth District representative, but he was thinking about moving up to a statewide office, either state or federal. He bided his time and passed on chances to try for the Republican nomination for Missouri governor in 2004 (an election won by 33-year-old Republican Matt Blunt, the son of US Senator Roy Blunt) and for the US Senate in 2006 (an election won by Democrat Claire McCaskill). In 2007, he was toying with the idea of getting out of politics and became a finalist in the search for a new president of the University of Missouri system. Three weeks into January 2008, Matt Blunt stunned Missouri Republicans by announcing he wouldn't run for a second term. Suddenly, there was a vacuum at the highest political level in the state. Hulshof watched Lieutenant Governor Peter Kinder announce his candidacy, then State Treasurer Sarah Steelman. Finally, Hulshof jumped into the race. Kinder withdrew, and the party establishment threw their support to Hulshof. He would be running against his old boss, Attorney General Jay Nixon.

★ ★ ★

In chambers, the judge started by asking us to describe our case. At the end of our summary of the weakness of the evidence against Josh at trial and the strength of the alibi evidence presented on his behalf, the judge asked, directed at no one in particular but with a challenge to Spillane, "How did Kenny get a conviction in the first place?" No one answered. We also summarized the new exculpatory evidence set forth in our April brief. Then, Spillane provided his version of the evidence that was presented in the 1994 trial and the new evidence in our habeas case. He included his analysis of the Wooten report: "It's of questionable validity and isn't material in any event because of the memo about Ray Ring that was produced." He put all of the evidence for and against Josh in the context of the extremely high standard of persuasion that must be met to prevail in a habeas case.

The judge then turned to the practical mechanics of a hearing—when it would occur, how long it would take, and so on. He asked us whom we would have as witnesses. We provided a fairly long list of potential witnesses—many of the key characters in the investigation, the trial, and the reopened investigation, including Sheriff Walter and Deputy Caid. Spillane mentioned only "the prosecutor" as a possible witness. The judge blurted out, "Kenny, what if he's the governor by then?"

The judge addressed the question of how testimony of prison inmates would be presented. "Inmate testimony has to be by deposition; I won't bring any inmate except Mr. Kezer to this courtroom to testify live." At least three of the potential witnesses were in federal prisons in other states and beyond the reach of the Cole County Circuit Court in any event.

Both parties estimated the hearing would last several days. The judge told us, "I don't have enough time on my calendar for a hearing that long until early December." We jumped at the earliest of those dates, which would put the hearing after the November election. We didn't want Hulshof to be compelled to defend his prosecution of Josh as he went around the state campaigning. Those dates also would give both sides enough time to take depositions for discovery and for presentation at trial. "Then I'll set the hearing for December second and third. That should be enough time, but I'll give you additional days if it becomes necessary."

The judge made another comment spontaneously as we were leaving. "I wouldn't use snitch witnesses when I was a prosecutor. They'll tell you the sun is shining outside even if it's a cloudy day." We took that as an encouraging hint of how he viewed that part of the State's original evidence against Josh.

★ ★ ★

Ben Poston was a student in the graduate program at the University of Missouri School of Journalism in Columbia when the Bryan Cave lawyers started work on Josh's case. Accounts of Jane Williams's efforts to free Josh were well known to those at the J-School who had an interest in innocence cases. Steve Weinberg, one of Ben's professors, offered the story to his magazine-writing class as a class project, and Ben jumped at the opportunity. Jane gave him a good start by providing him with the information she had gathered. He interviewed Bryan Cave lawyers and most of the key witnesses, including Sheriff Walter, Detective Caid, Detective Bohnert, Trooper (now Sergeant) Windham, and Josh. He even interviewed Mark Abbott, who spoke to him by telephone from prison. Eventually, he made the story his master's degree project.

During the summer of 2006, Ben had worked at the *St. Louis Post-Dispatch* as a reporter intern, and he arranged to submit a version of his work to that paper for publication as an article. Ben believed in Josh's innocence, and we were confident his article would be fair. The article appeared in the *Post-Dispatch* on Sunday, November 25, 2007, at the top of the front page, right under the masthead stating the paper was founded by Joseph Pulitzer in 1878. The headline was "CASE CLOSED—THEN REOPENED." The lead read, "Mischelle Lawless was found in her car in 1992, fatally shot. Joshua Kezer was convicted and sentenced to 60 years in prison. The officer who responded to the incident still has doubts."

Right below that statement was a picture of Rick Walter at the murder scene, standing next to a floral display to Mischelle's memory attached to a sign pole on the Benton exit ramp. The caption noted that the picture was taken on the 15th anniversary of Mischelle's death and that her father ties a new memorial to the pole every year. The article told the story of the murder and Josh's conviction and covered the key points of the case we had built so far. In particular, it covered the interviews Wooten and Bohnert had conducted with Mark Abbott, in which he pointed a finger at Ray Ring and Kevin Williams, and Chantelle Crider's admission she made a mistake in claiming Josh was at the Halloween party.

Abbott denied that he ever told Detective Bohnert that Kevin Williams killed Mischelle, and he merely repeated what he had told authorities about Josh 15 years earlier. Judge Murphy, now retired, and Congressman Hulshof, through a press secretary, declined to comment. Bill Ferrell said Ben should talk to the highway patrol because "it was their investigation." He did that, and Sergeant Windham was quoted as saying, "One of the big rules of thumb is to eliminate the first person who found the victim. . . . and it sounds like we didn't eliminate him. . . . I'll feel bad if it comes out that Kezer is not involved in this thing."

Sheriff Walter told Ben he had been skeptical about Josh's conviction almost from the beginning. He believed the crime scene evidence indicated there were at least two attackers, yet the investigation had always concentrated on finding a lone killer. He related that "people in the law enforcement community" and "regular people here" had told him for years that the wrong person was in jail. "I wake up most mornings and wonder, 'Why am I sheriff?' I think this is why—to find the truth on this case." He said some people might dismiss Josh as a "nobody" but "We owe him this—to find the truth, because he is somebody. If I don't stand up for these people, who will?"

★ ★ ★

Bridget DiCosmo was a young reporter for the *Southeast Missourian* when Rick Walter reopened the Lawless murder investigation. She wrote a series of articles, starting on June 8, 2008, covering the investigation and the habeas proceedings. The first article summarized the 1994 trial and the new evidence and the comments on it from Kenny Hulshof and others. Mark Abbott had written a letter to the *Southeast Missourian* admitting "I might have made a mistake" in identifying Josh as the man in the white car at the Cut-Mart. Nevertheless, Hulshof defended Abbott's testimony against Josh. He said he and his investigator "hadn't been able to shake Abbott's story" and that Abbott had "testified consistently and credibly at the trial." He dismissed Josh's evidence that he was in Kankakee at the time of the murder, calling it a "quasi-alibi." He said he is still convinced that Josh committed the murder.

★ ★ ★

Alan Zaiger was a reporter for the Associated Press based in Columbia. He joined the AP staff after a year as a professional-in-residence at the University of Missouri J-School and during 2008, was covering the Missouri gubernatorial election. On June 7, 2008, the AP released an article he wrote scrutinizing Kenny Hulshof's record as a prosecutor, which appeared in the *Columbia Missourian* and other papers in Missouri and around the country. The article focused on seven murder cases in which the guilty verdict had been overturned or called into question. The seventh conviction was Josh's.

Zaiger's June 7 article noted that Hulshof, while in the attorney general's office, had a reputation for taking over and winning the most difficult cases that small-town prosecutors felt they couldn't handle. As Hulshof explained to Zaiger, "If it was the proverbial shooting-fish-in-a-barrel case, we wouldn't get the call." Hulshof's critics interviewed for the article acknowledged his great skill but questioned his aggressiveness and apparent desire to win at all costs. Sean O'Brien, a University of Missouri–Kansas City law professor who represented two of the seven defendants featured in the article on appeal, said, "He's always very aggressive. He is extremely skilled. And he creates suspicion out of no evidence."

Hulshof viewed the same events differently. To him, justice is the decision of a jury that hears the facts of the case presented by aggressive adversaries for the prosecution and the defense. As for the criticisms of his conduct as the prosecution in each of the cases, he had a response, which Zaiger noted in his article—a document withheld from the defense that he hadn't seen himself until after the trial, "a trial tactic" he had learned at a national conference of prosecutors that the Missouri Supreme Court only later rejected as unfair, and so on. None of these excuses addressed the fact that he had convicted people who were innocent.

17

DEPOSITIONS FOR THE
HABEAS HEARING

Josh's habeas corpus hearing actually started in August 2008. Witnesses
who couldn't or might not come to Jefferson City in December would
testify by deposition. This was particularly true of the witnesses who were
inmates in federal and state prisons.

★ ★ ★

Ricky Clay was living on death row in the state prison near Potosi, a little
town in the Ozark foothills about 75 miles southwest of St. Louis in Washington County. I took his deposition, the first of those to be used at trial,
at the prison on August 7.

Potosi was founded by a Frenchman in the 18th century and named
for the city in Bolivia famous for its silver mines. The ore that was plentiful
around Potosi wasn't silver but lead, which although a baser metal, made a
number of early Missouri mining families wealthy. Lead mining continued
in Missouri over the next two centuries, but demand for the ore weakened
as more environmentally friendly products replaced it. Mines closed, and
the local economy suffered. As in other parts of the county suffering job
losses, the prison at Potosi is among the major employers in Washington
County.

The Potosi Correctional Center opened in 1989 as a maximum-
security institution, with 70 condemned inmates transferred from the old
Walls in Jefferson City and others convicted of serious crimes, who with a
few exceptions, were serving sentences of life or what, as a practical matter, amounted to it. The entrance to the Potosi Correctional Center is up
the hill from the parking lot, and the complex looms over visitors as they
approach from below. Security is particularly tight. Lawyers are allowed
to bring in nothing but the basic tools of their trade, paper and writing

instruments. Court reporters, by special arrangement, may bring in their stenographic equipment. Everyone has to empty their pockets of everything, even pocket change, except for the key to the locker where they store what they aren't allowed to keep with them.

When the lawyers and the court reporter had proven their identity and were checked off the approved list, we passed through metal detectors, down sealed corridors through the high prison walls topped with rolls of razor wire, past checkpoints where barely visible guards sitting in semi-darkness behind thick Plexiglas scrutinized our picture IDs held up to the window. Once inside, the atmosphere was more relaxed. As we were taken to the conference room where the deposition was to be held, we passed through an open area where inmates were meeting with family members. When we arrived at the conference room, an inmate was sitting on a chair in the hall outside, unshackled and alone in a prison jumpsuit and booties, staring at his hands. After explaining where we were, our escort stood silently, at stiff attention, just inside the door. While setting up for the deposition, the lawyers made conversation with the court reporter about other people in the business we knew and the peculiarities of prison depositions. After what seemed like five minutes of this, it occurred to me to ask the guard, "Is the inmate sitting on the chair outside Ricky Clay?" "I'm sorry," he said, "I didn't know you were ready for him."

Clay didn't look like a killer or like the frightening drug dealer whom some of our informants had described. He is only five feet nine inches tall and, on that day, appeared much thinner than the 195 pounds listed as his weight on the Department of Corrections website. Middle aged at 43, he still was handsome but was going bald and wore glasses. As he entered the room, he carried himself with deference to the guard and the legal visitors. He was soft spoken and exceedingly polite throughout the proceeding.

Clay grew up in Commerce, which he described as "a little town six or seven miles down the road from Benton on the west bank of the river." He was in a taekwondo class with Marvin Lawless. "I practiced with him at his house once, and we traveled to a meet together. I remember his daughter when she was a little girl, but I didn't see her for some years before her death." He also knew the Abbott twins. They were part of a group, which included him, Kevin Williams, Randy Dukes, and others who "hung out" together. Clay said Mark Abbott was involved with drugs already at the time of the murder, something Abbott denied. Clay said he knew that from associating with Abbott "because a lot of us was into methamphetamine at the time."

Everyone Clay knew was talking about Mischelle's murder for weeks after it happened. "Why would somebody do that? You know what I'm saying? That kind of talk." He had only one conversation about the murder with Mark Abbott that he remembered about a week or 10 days after the event. "We was together somewhere drinking, partying. I'm not sure exactly where it may have been, whose party it was. But we was having a conversation, and he said that—to the point that you know—I found the Lawless girl."

Clay told Abbott he had heard that and asked him what happened. Abbott told him about finding Mischelle's body in her car. He said he thought he heard her breathing and jumped into his truck to drive to a nearby gas station and store on the other side of I-55 to call for help. He said the store had a number of names, but he thought it was called "Robert's" at the time.

> And he said, while he was trying to use the phone, he said a carload of Mexicans pulled up and said something to the fact that you need to go with us and get some gas. And he said, "Fuck you. I ain't going nowhere with you." And he said, "And then I got in my truck and drove off." And I was like, "Well, how did you know they was Mexicans?" And he said, "Well, they looked like Mexicans. They sounded like Mexicans." And then we started laughing. And I said, "Well, yeah, it must be Mexicans." And we left it at that.

Then Clay said, referring to Josh, "And you know, then I hear they got this little boy arrested for it. I'd never heard of him, never seen him."

★ ★ ★

Chuck Weissinger was next, on September 11. He was an inmate at the Federal Correctional Center outside Greenville, Illinois, a medium security institution just off I-70 two counties east of St. Louis. Physically, FCC Greenville is every bit as formidable as the Potosi Correctional Center, with a double layer of fences topped with razor wire and an enclosed passage through metal detectors and checkpoints with guards also sitting in semi-darkness behind thick Plexiglas. Still, the atmosphere seemed more relaxed to me, perhaps because the shadow of death wasn't looming over the institution.

We needed to get Weissinger to reaffirm his trial testimony that he had made up the story about Josh's tearful confession. He was a nice-looking young man, well groomed and well spoken. I thought, because his hair was cut neatly at a normal length and he had no visible tattoos, he looked nothing like the stereotype of a prison inmate. Out of his prison garb, he could have passed for the manager of the local Walmart. He spoke calmly and matter of factly as he described his own life of crime and the plot that Shawn Mangus hatched with him in 1993 that was supposed to get them out of the Cape Girardeau County Jail.

Weissinger's testimony was consistent with his testimony at Josh's 1994 trial. "Josh never confessed to killing Mischelle Lawless. . . . Shawn came to me with that story. . . . Kelly Church was in on the lie too. . . . It was a way for us to get out of jail early." And it worked. Weissinger said, "I was looking at a 10-year sentence as a prior and persistent offender and ended up serving a year in the county jail." Weissinger continued, "Grah overheard what we were doing, and he decided to try to get in on it." Grah "was only supposed to say he saw Josh with a .380 in his waistband and heard from Josh about the gang he joined."

There wasn't much left for Mike Spillane to do but attack Weissinger's credibility. Spillane asked him how many felony convictions he had, and he started rattling them off. With a remarkable memory for dates and specifics of charges, Weissinger ran through more than 30 convictions for everything from burglary to drug possession, and he topped off the litany by mentioning "the time I stabbed my brother."

★ ★ ★

Jim Wyrsch took Jeff Rogers's deposition on September 22, at the Jefferson City Correctional Center. He confirmed on the record what he told Josh and Branden Caid. Sheriff Ferrell had him brought over from the jail in August 1993 and presented him with a statement that he heard Josh confess to killing Mischelle Lawless when he and Josh were cellmates in the Scott County Jail.

> He had me sit down, and there was a piece of paper on the desk. It was just me and him in there. And he wanted me to read over it, and I believe he wanted me to sign it or rewrite it. I can't remember. It was either typed up already or wrote down already by hand. I can't remember which it was because it's been so long ago. And he told me in very short words that I can either cooperate and play along with this, go along with this, or suffer the consequences. . . . He told me he would make sure I got fucked around real good.

On the other hand, Ferrell told him he would talk to the prosecutor and see what he could do for him if he signed. Rogers said that the statement he was asked to make was false. Josh "told me he was innocent, and that's all he ever said." Rogers stopped answering questions during his deposition because he didn't want to lie. He said he knew he was "going to get screwed around" whatever he said, so his attorney advised him to refuse to say anything.

★ ★ ★

We wanted to take depositions of Brenda Schiwitz and Don Windham for discovery purposes because as the lead investigators, they might be witnesses for the State, in which case it would be important to know in advance what they were going to say. In addition, if we happened to get testimony that was helpful, we could use it in our case.

Brenda Schiwitz, the "sandy-blonde" in Weissinger's description to Rosener, was an attractive woman in her 50s at the time of the deposition. I took her deposition in Cape Girardeau on November 7, and Charlie was there to observe. She was wary of the proceedings but cordial. She identified the steno pads found in the case file as her investigative notes for the Lawless murder. But she claimed, "I provided all of that material to Mr. Hulshof and his investigator." That claim, however, wasn't consistent with her testimony in Josh's criminal proceedings that she destroyed the notes after her formal statement was typed.

I went through each of the important entries in the notebooks where she wrote something that was different from the version in the official reports or that didn't appear in the official reports at all—Tom Beardslee's nomination of Mark Abbott as a suspect at an early meeting of the investigative team, her own comments about Abbott's suspicious behavior, Abbott's description of the man at the Cut-Mart as "Mexican or Negro but not white," and the interview she and Sheriff Ferrell did with Joseph Flores at the Farmington Correctional Center. For the most part, she acknowledged that the notes said what she wrote, but she resisted drawing any conclusions or agreeing with any observations that might help Josh. When pressed, she said, "I don't know" or "I don't remember."

Schiwitz seemed to bend over backwards to rationalize Abbott's identification of Josh as the same man he had told her about early in the investigation, as her recently discovered notes disclosed was "Mexican or Negro" but definitely "not white." Asked if this didn't make her suspicious of Abbott's selection, she used a version of the same argument she had made at trial. "Josh was not necessarily a white boy. He had coal black hair and dark complexion at times." She implied he had acquired a tan hanging out on the streets in Cape Girardeau the previous summer. But she admitted that "a tan probably would have faded by November anyway." She said,

"Some people back then said Kezer looked like he could be Mexican or a light-skinned Negro." Asked who said that, she replied, "Somebody told me, but I don't remember who. It wasn't in my notes, and I couldn't find it in any of the formal reports."

Then Schiwitz tried another angle. Josh had dyed his hair black at one time, and she said his hair was dark when he was arrested. She concluded from this fact that "with extremely dark hair, someone might presume he was not a white man." Perhaps because she was dissatisfied with the logic of what she had just said, she followed it immediately with the statement, "I don't have any opinion on that."

Schiwitz tried to dismiss the Flores interview that she described in her notebook as inconsequential because Flores was uncooperative. "He didn't want to talk to the sheriff, and he got up after five minutes and left." Confronted with what her notes indicated Flores said during those five minutes—that Josh never confessed, that he always insisted he was innocent, and that he said he was in another city when Mischelle was murdered—she could only say, "That's what he said."

Don Windham had risen to the rank of sergeant in the highway patrol by the middle of 2008 when we first contacted him to be a witness in Josh's habeas hearing. He was handsome enough that a female public defender who knew him seemed infatuated when I told her at a barbecue about his testimony. He was surprisingly open and cooperative from the start. He met with me in person in Cape Girardeau a week before his deposition to go over details of what he remembered from the investigation. He wasn't quite convinced of Josh's innocence, but he hadn't closed his mind to the possibility. He read about our new evidence in the newspapers and told me, "I still think Shawn Mangus was very credible when we interviewed him in 1993." He also gave considerable weight to Mark Abbott's ability to pick Josh and Christy Naile's car in the two photo lineups. "Abbott picked Kezer and the car without any hesitation, and we did those lineups by the book." Still, he wasn't at all defensive about his work on the case. In the interview, he surprised me by asking, "Do you think I did anything wrong?"

I took Windham's deposition in Cape Girardeau on November 14. He said, "I can tell you I felt that Shawn Mangus was truthful to me where I didn't know about the others." He described the relationship between Bill Ferrell's sheriff's department and the highway patrol. "In my experience, the Lawless murder was the first time the patrol got involved in an investigation in Scott County, and my impression was that Ferrell didn't want our help even then. Tom Beardslee told me the sheriff was upset that he invited the patrol to help." According to Windham, this set Scott County apart from the other 12 counties in his region.

Windham identified his report of the interview of Ray Ring that he conducted with Sheriff Ferrell the morning of November 19, 1992, the morning after Bobby Wooten's late-night interview with Mark Abbott, in which Abbott identified Ray Ring as the man at the Cut-Mart. Asked how he came to be involved in the Ring interview, he said, "I don't remember, but I'm sure somebody in the sheriff's office, probably Brenda Schiwitz, asked me to participate. I don't remember being told why Ray Ring suddenly became a suspect, but it's obvious to me now that I've seen Wooten's interview summary." This testimony provided crucial support for our position that Ferrell had Wooten's interview report, or at least Wooten's verbal account of the interview, early on November 19.

Windham confirmed that Detective Bohnert contacted him sometime around 1997 to tell him that Mark Abbott claimed to have information about who really killed Mischelle. Windham said, "We didn't get into the details because I basically brushed him off and didn't want the information." He explained that Jim Smith, another Cape Girardeau detective, had come to him a couple of years before Bohnert with a similar story that Mark Abbott told him. "I asked Abbott about it, but he denied telling Smith anything like that. I assumed the story Abbott told Bohnert was about as useful. I told Bohnert to talk to Bill Ferrell, but I wasn't going to go to him."

Windham had learned from past experience that you don't second-guess Bill Ferrell. Even the highway patrol asked Ferrell's permission before investigating a crime there. As he told me in his deposition, "I made the mistake once of going into Scott County without first contacting Ferrell. I went there to retrieve 20 Michelin tires from a man who bought them from an interstate theft ring without knowing they were stolen. I just picked them up, didn't arrest him, didn't do anything, just said I know you bought them, and you didn't believe [them] to be stolen." Ferrell complained to his sergeant and his captain "because we were in his county and didn't tell him what we were doing." Windham didn't want to go through that again over another one of Mark Abbott's crazy stories.

★ ★ ★

Bobby Wooten was dying of cancer. Because Josh's *Brady* case depended so heavily on Wooten's interview report and because the State was attacking the report's authenticity, we had to have him testify as a witness, under oath and exposed to cross-examination by the State. After we received a copy of

Chris Pickering's summary of his May interview with Wooten, we tried to contact Wooten to find out exactly what he would say when it came time to take his deposition. Jim Sullins couldn't find him. He didn't answer his phone or respond to voice messages, and he didn't appear to be living in his house in Scott County. There were rumors he was staying somewhere in St. Louis for cancer treatment. By the middle of the summer of 2008, hearing from Branden Caid and others that Wooten was terminally ill and might not live long enough to testify at a hearing, we increased our efforts to find him. Eventually, word came back that he had hired a lawyer. Apparently, he was concerned he might be accused of fabricating evidence in some sort of conspiracy with Rick Walter, and he didn't want to talk to us informally anymore. We would have to subpoena him and go in cold, not knowing for sure what he would say.

I took his deposition on November 7. Wooten was accompanied by his lawyer, Allen Moss, and Charlie Weiss was there to observe. Wooten said he had a small-cell cancer of the lung that had metastasized. He appeared to be in reasonably good health, but he said that he had been given six to eight months to live—if he underwent treatment—less if he didn't. He had just finished 15 days of radiation to his brain the previous week.

I asked Wooten about his written report of the Abbott interview. He testified that he didn't remember making the report but he did remember talking to Abbott about the Lawless murder and enough of the specifics of what Abbott told him to prove what we needed to prove. "I don't remember details like getting a radio call from Scott City Police Chief Elledge to go to Store 24 or meeting Dave Beck [the former Scott City police chief] there, but I do remember interviewing Mark Abbott in his trailer at the Woodlawn Trailer Court."

Wooten remembered, independent of what he read in his 1992 report of the interview, that Abbott "told me about finding the Lawless girl's body at the I-55 exit and about somebody named Ray Ring that I didn't know approaching Abbott while he was standing at the pay phone at a truck stop across the highway. I think it was called Mo's."

Wooten didn't specifically remember contacting Deputy Chambers or Sheriff Ferrell with the information or delivering the written report to Ferrell, as the report indicated he had done, but he testified that with information this important, he certainly would have called Ferrell right away and would have gotten a written report to him as quickly as possible. "A copy of this report would have went to Bill Ferrell. It was very simple. You didn't let Sheriff Ferrell get up the next morning and go to the coffee shop and not know about something."

The State's handwriting expert, comparing the report of the Abbott interview with contemporaneous Wooten reports, had acknowledged that the signatures were the same. Informed of that fact, Wooten explained, "I questioned the way the *W* in my last name was made and the way the loop went around over the *T*. The Wooten part just didn't look right to me." But he testified that "I never said it wasn't my signature."

We apologized for putting Wooten through the deposition, and he shook hands with everyone as he left. He lived longer than the six to eight months he said he had been given, but not by much. The *Southeast Missourian* reported that Bobby Glenn Wooten died at his home in Jackson on Tuesday, September 1, 2009, at the age of 54. He left behind a wife, two sons, three daughters, and five grandchildren.

★ ★ ★

We considered whether we should take Mark Abbott's deposition. He was in the medium-security Federal Correctional Center in the village of Oxford, Wisconsin. Unlike the other inmates on the potential witness list, he wasn't conveniently located a short drive from St. Louis. Oxford is in a rural part of the state, 60 miles north of Madison, and we questioned whether it would be worth the trip. No one expected Abbott to admit that he or Kevin Williams killed Mischelle, as they had been telling people around Scott County for years.

On the other hand, we did know Abbott wasn't as sure about his identification of Josh as he had claimed to be on the witness stand in 1994. He said as much in his letter to the *Southeast Missourian*. In addition, Branden Caid obtained recordings of Abbott's telephone calls from prison after the story of the reopening of the investigation broke, and he made the recording available to us. These conversations had a certain awkward artificiality in places that made them appear staged for the benefit of the law enforcement audience Abbott knew could someday listen.

Matt told his brother that Rick Walter had reopened the investigation of Mischelle's murder and that Mark's name was surfacing as a potential suspect. Mark sounded shocked. He mentioned his testimony against Josh and said that Josh "looked like the guy I saw in the white car" at the Cut-Mart but that "it was the car I really recognized." There was something in the phrasing and the tone of his voice that signaled he wasn't at all sure he had identified the right man.

Mike Spillane made the decision about deposing Abbott for us. He scheduled the deposition as his witness for November 12. Because so much might depend on seeing Abbott's face and hearing his voice as he testified, we tried to arrange for a video recording of the deposition, but the prison would not allow us to bring a videographer without a court order. Spillane may have wanted a video deposition, too, but he couldn't consent to a motion asking Judge Callahan to order one because the attorney general's office was currently engaged in a suit defending a similar policy of the Missouri Department of Corrections.

Charlie Weiss planned to do the cross-examination, and I planned to accompany him. We looked into airfares to Milwaukee and Madison, and both were high. In addition, we still would have to rent a car in Milwaukee or Madison to go the rest of the way to Oxford. To save money, we decided to rent a car in St. Louis and drive directly to the prison. I drove while Charlie worked on his preparation for the deposition. We arrived late at what probably was the only decent motel in Oxford, a town of 607 people, and tired and sore from the long drive, we went to bed.

The next morning, we drove the short distance to the prison. The lawyers and a court reporter (who drove up from Madison) gathered in a room that was designed for parole hearings. Because Congress abolished parole for federal inmates who committed their offense after November 1, 1987, it was rarely used for that purpose any more. Abbott entered the room dressed in a T-shirt and sweatpants. He was muscular and wore his hair very short, not shaved but cut at the same close depth all around his skull like an Army recruit in basic training. He still was good looking, but his features had hardened compared to pictures we had seen of him from the early 1990s. When he spoke, it was with a slightly gravelly voice. His speech alternated between staccato bursts, like a machine gun, and a slow, languid Southeast Missouri drawl. He said he was 39. About halfway through his second decade in federal prison, he appeared healthy and fit and in good spirits for someone in his circumstances.

Spillane went first with his questions. Abbott was born in Cape Girardeau in 1969 and went to grade school and high school there, graduating from Cape Central High in 1987. He said he didn't know Mischelle Lawless. After high school, he lived with an aunt in Cape Girardeau for a year and then in trailers his family owned. He was living in the trailer park his father co-owned near Scott City with his girlfriend, Melissa Williams, Kevin's sister, when Mischelle was killed. He had always worked in family businesses—at Store 24 for five years or so starting when he was 14, maintaining and renovating family rental property, and building trailers with an uncle in Dexter.

Abbott described his drinking and drug use and his 20-year sentence for trafficking in methamphetamine. He claimed he didn't start using meth until 1994. Spillane then asked Abbott to take us through his day on November 7, 1992, leading to his discovery of Mischelle's body.

> I worked all day on my rental property. Then I stopped by a party at Kevin Williams's boss's house with my girlfriend to get Kevin, but his wife wouldn't let him leave. After that I went to Country Nights and ran into Heather Pierce. I drank and danced with Heather until closing time. I told Heather I'll come by her house later, but I was feeling kinda tired and got off the interstate at Benton to take the back way home.

Spillane had Abbott describe the murder scene as he found it. Abbott said he reached in the window of the car and pulled Mischelle up by her left shoulder into a sitting position. "Her face was covered by her hair, and it was soaked in blood. I thought she was still alive because I heard a kind of a like, you know, a gurgling sound. I think the girl might have helped me by trying to get up as I pulled on her shoulder. Then I left her sitting that way and went in my truck to try to get help."

Abbott described how he stopped at the pay phone outside the Cut-Mart. While he stood outside his truck, a white car approached from the exit he had just left. There was enough light that he could tell there was at least one other person besides the driver in the vehicle. The driver said, "Hey, we're out of fuel. We're going to have to go with you." Asked to describe the man who spoke to him, he said:

> He had on something black. To me—to me, he was a darker-complected white guy, you know what I mean, at the time. He wasn't black, he wasn't Hispanic. He wasn't Chinese like them people say. He was a white guy. He just had a little bit of a complexion on him, a dark complexion, some dark hair. He had something up with his hands. I always—I tried to think back, you know, and it looked like he had kind of like the motorcycle gloves on, but I'm not a hundred percent sure. It's dark.

Some of the uncertainty that was apparent in the recording of Abbott's phone conversation with his brother came through in his response to Spillane's questions about the photo lineup, which he remembered as being conducted by Ferrell and Schiwitz, not Schiwitz and Windham.

Q. Why did you pick Mr. Kezer's picture?

A. Because it looked like the guy in the car.

Q. The picture of Mr. Kezer looked like the guy in the car?

A. Yeah.

Q. And did you say it was the guy in the car?

A. No.

Abbott hesitated, and Spillane invited him to continue. What he said next made sense of his last answer. "Oh, yeah. They laid down so many cars. They laid down so many pictures of people. And this is it: It looks like this car, and it looks like him, period. And Bill Ferrell and that lady about jumped through the roof of my house when I did that. Right then I thought, wow, that must be him."

Abbott seemed no more certain in his identification of the car. He claimed he was a truck man and knew little about makes and models of cars. He said it was the "fin" on the back that distinguished the car he picked. "For those six cars or eight cars, however many that picture of that car that I picked out was the closest to it of what I think I seen. . . . Is that the car? Well, man, it looks like it. And that's as far as I went with them."

Abbott didn't remember if any of the other cars had fins, but he claimed the car he picked had a "unique" fin. It was on the trunk, not on the back window. He said, if the other cars in the pictures had a fin, the one he picked had a very different fin. In fact, none of the eight cars had a fin. Three of them, including Christy Naile's car that he picked, had a back window full of louvers, and there wasn't anything unique about any of them.

Asked whether he had testified truthfully to the facts as he knew them at the time of the trial, Abbott digressed into a long monologue about various things he learned before and during the trial that made him think he had picked the right man—the reaction of Bill Ferrell and Brenda Schiwitz, the testimony of the jailhouse informants that Josh had confessed, Josh's supposed theft of Christy Naile's car, and Chantelle Crider's story about the argument at the Halloween party. But now some of that evidence that had given him so much comfort was starting to crumble. He mentioned something he must have read in a news story his brother sent him: "Now they find out that he probably wasn't at the party." In light of all that, "I'm thinking, man, this guy—could I be wrong? Am I not—is it possible that I'm wrong? Yeah, it's possible that I'm wrong." Still, when Spillane asked if anyone had given him a hint what pictures to select, he denied that anyone had, almost indignant that we could think he would be a party to such dishonesty.

Abbott addressed head-on the fact that two law enforcement officers, Bobby Wooten and Bill Bohnert, had claimed he told them someone other than Josh—Ray Ring and Kevin Williams—had killed Mischelle. They were lying.

Abbott said he had spoken to Bobby Wooten "a hundred times in my life, 200 times," but never about the Lawless murder. "And if he says something like he's probably—he was a—he was a—how would you say this? And this is bad to say. He was a crooked officer." Abbott said that he had his brother confront Wooten about the account of the interview and that Wooten had denied ever saying what was reported in the media. Abbott said he didn't know Ring back then and only knew the name because he heard from someone that Ring was looking for him. "But later on, I find out he's a dope head that sells dope and runs around crazy."

Abbott said he knew Bill Bohnert. They had gone to the same church for years, but he denied he had ever tried to get a lighter sentence by telling Bohnert that Kevin Williams had killed Mischelle. Abbott went straight to that point. "I'd like to get a polygraph test from him and me on that whole deal, him saying that I said this. Me and him never even talked about it."

Abbott was so afraid of prison that he cut off his ankle bracelet and hid at the other end of the state, making meth in the woods, but he wouldn't snitch on a friend, even one like Williams, who got his own sentence reduced to five years by offering to testify against Abbott. In a conversation with me, one of the girls in the White Trash Mafia referred to all the informing that was going on as "the Great Southeast Missouri Snitch-Off."

Abbott said he didn't remember telling Ricky Clay about the carload of Mexicans approaching him at the Cut-Mart, but he didn't deny that he did it. His approach with Clay was different. He said he hadn't spoken 100 words to Clay in his life. He was "one of them guys you just didn't hang around with much if you had a job or at least worked every day." He said, "I might have told him anything just to get away from him."

Abbott claimed he spent little time with Kevin Williams. He said his family didn't like it when he did "because they knew he was nothing but trouble." But the two were frequently linked in Abbott's testimony. Mark Abbott lived with Kevin's sister.[1] Williams seemed to be the closest thing to a friend Abbott had. Abbott showed up at the party Williams attended with his wife on November 7 and tried to get Williams to go out with him, but Williams's wife objected.

On cross-examination, Abbott clarified his account of the man in a hooded sweatshirt on the exit ramp who jumped out of his way. That actually occurred several miles before the Benton exit. Abbott also claimed he hadn't heard that Roy Moore talked to a man with a heavy Hispanic accent who drove a small white car and stopped at the crime scene asking where he could find an open gas station. Abbott seemed genuinely stunned by Deputy Moore's report of that incident, which Deputy Schiwitz had shown him in late 1992. He said wow twice and asked, "Did they have this at the trial?" He agreed that the man who approached Moore looking for gas could have been the same one who had approached him with a similar request not much earlier—the man he identified as Josh.

★ ★ ★

We were hesitant to depose Kevin Williams for the same reasons we were hesitant about Abbott. We assumed Williams would deny any involvement in Mischelle's murder and didn't expect him to testify that Abbott had killed her. He would either deny he had told Cathy Fowler and others what they claimed he had told them or he would admit he had said what they say he had said and claim that he was only kidding. Again, Spillane made the decision for us. He scheduled the depositions of Williams and his wife for November 14 at the attorney general's office in Cape Girardeau. Charlie Weiss did the cross-examination, and I was there to observe. The Williamses were aware of Abbott's accusations against Kevin from news accounts, and they were anxious to prove that Kevin hadn't killed Mischelle. In the process, they helped Josh's case in a way we hadn't anticipated.

The lawyers were set up and waiting in the conference room when the witnesses arrived. As soon as Kevin entered the room, he started to shout at the two Bryan Cave lawyers. Red with anger, he said, "I hope you rot in hell for what you're doing to me and my family. Everyone in the county is looking at me like I'm a murderer. My son was expelled from school because he was fighting with other kids who teased him about it." His wife tugged at him, trying to get him to stop. Spillane managed somehow to get him calmed enough that he agreed to leave the conference room. Spillane would depose Terri first while Kevin waited in another part of the office. Later that day, according to his wife, Kevin beat her for getting in his way.

Terri Williams was in her mid-30s, with a pretty face, suggesting a younger girl attractive enough to catch Kevin's eye. Spillane asked her general background questions first. She was born in Cape Girardeau in 1972. Her family moved to Benton in 1982, and she attended Kelly Middle School and Kelly High School. She had heard of Mischelle Lawless back then but didn't know her. They had attended the same schools, but Terri was a year older. She was 15 when she quit school and married Kevin Williams, and they had been married 20 years at the time of the deposition. She worked at Shoney's, but she didn't know Mischelle from there.

On the night Mischelle was murdered, Terri and Kevin went to a party at the home of Kevin's employer, Carl Howell. It was a party Howell had every year in the late fall for the employees in his construction and excavation business. "Me and Kevin went early, around 5:00 or 6:00, with our two-year-old son. . . . Mark got there later with Kevin's sister, Melissa. Mark wanted Kevin to go bar hopping with him in Sikeston." Terri wasn't included in the invitation, and she was angry. According to Terri, Mark left but Kevin stayed. "We left the party around midnight. Kevin was drinking all night, so I drove home. We went to bed for the night, and Kevin didn't leave the house." She was sure of it. "We slept together, and I would know if he got up and left."

Terri said she and Kevin were still in bed when Mark Abbott called on the telephone early the next morning. "He was all excited. He said he found a body in a car on the highway exit. . . . He came to our house later and talked more about finding the body and seeing somebody at the truck stop across the highway." She said she didn't remember exactly what Abbott said about seeing the man at the truck stop. Then Abbott left, and Kevin went with him. She wasn't sure where they went, but they were gone for a fairly long time.

★ ★ ★

Kevin was a large, muscular man in his early 40s, with reddish brown hair that was just starting to turn gray. He said he was born in Sikeston in 1967 and lived in East Prairie until he was six. Then his family moved near Commerce. Except for a brief time when he worked in New Orleans after Hurricane Katrina, he had lived in and around Commerce ever since. He went to grade school in Scott City and graduated from Kelly High School in Benton in 1985. He said he had never, to his knowledge, met Mischelle Lawless, who graduated from there six years later. He worked at Halter Seeds in Benton while in high school and for a short time after he graduated, at Glyn Ferrell's Mobile Home Sales. He went to work at Howell Construction in 1990 and was starting his own welding and repair shop, where he also built cotton trailers, around the time of Carl Howell's 1992 employee party. Howell helped him get started in business and was one of his first customers, hiring him to work on his construction and excavation equipment.

Williams said he started selling and using meth toward the end of 1994. Before that, he mainly drank alcohol. He tried marijuana but didn't like it. "I called Terri from jail to tell her someone would be coming by to get some tires that were stored under our house. When the tires came out, some bags of cash from the drugs fell out too. Terri was convinced I was involved in something dangerous. She asked Glyn Ferrell what she should do. He told her to report it. And she did."

Williams said he knew Jimmie Joe and Cathy Fowler "through the drugs." As he put it, "We were always high." But he didn't recall ever telling Fowler and his wife Mark Abbott killed Mischelle Lawless. He remembered the Natvigs, too, but did not remember pointing to the trailer sales lot and telling them that was where Mark Abbott killed Mischelle. As for Ray Ring, "I heard his name since the story came out about Bobby Wooten, but I don't remember him. I never told Mark that he wanted to talk to him." Williams knew Bill Bohnert was saying Abbott claimed that he, Kevin, killed Mischelle. "I confronted [Abbott] about it. He told me it wasn't true; he never said that to Bohnert." Williams admitted that he had gotten a reduced sentence for the meth conspiracy because he had given information against the other conspirators, but he claimed he hadn't testified against Abbott, who was indicted 17 months later. Williams said Abbott "was working with them and saying stuff about me at the same time, and his dad." According to Williams, Abbott was so frightened at the prospect of prison that he was offering to give evidence against his own father.

Williams gave an account of Carl Howell's party that was similar to his wife's. He said he was an alcoholic and as he was accustomed to do, drank a lot that night. He and Terri fought all evening. Abbott showed up with Williams's sister and Williams's girlfriend, Laura Conklin, and wanted him to come out with them. His wife objected, "Because my girlfriend was with my sister and Mark was seeing my sister at the time and I was seeing Laura Conklin at the time and we were all going to go do stuff together." But he stayed at the party only because Terri "threw a fit." When they left to go home, Terri drove. "I'm sure I didn't drive because I was drunk and our two-year-old son was with us. We went home, and I went right to sleep."

The next morning, Mark Abbott called on the telephone and told Williams what had happened after he left Howell's party with their girlfriends. "He said he got into a big fight with my sister and went alone to the bars in Sikeston. When he was coming home, he found a dead girl in a car on the side of the highway at the Benton exit. He reached into the car and tapped her or something, and she just rolled over." Williams said Abbott had told him that he had hopped in his truck and driven over to the truck stop across the interstate to phone the sheriff's department and a car had pulled up next to him as he was trying to call. He said Abbott "told me he didn't see who was in the car. He saw only kind of an image of some people in the car—more than one but he wasn't sure how many." When the driver spoke, "it wasn't an English accent; it was a different accent like Spanish or something." Perhaps more importantly, Abbott told Williams he couldn't even make out the face of the man he swore a year and a half later was Josh.

By the end of the deposition, Williams realized that we weren't necessarily interested in proving he had killed Mischelle, only that Abbott's identification of Josh wasn't credible. After that, his attitude changed dramatically. I followed Williams and his wife to the door. He paused at the exit and offered to help us if he could. I reminded him that "we aren't the reason you've been labeled a killer; that's your friend Mark Abbott who's done that." He said "You're right," shook my hand apologetically, and headed to the parking lot.

★ ★ ★

Kelly Church's 1993 statement to the sheriff's department about Josh's supposed confession at Stacy Reed's apartment was consistent with the first contemporaneous accounts of Mangus and Weissinger in almost every detail, except that Church claimed Josh said he was *going to kill* a girl from Benton at a time when Mischelle already was dead. In any event, he wasn't called to testify at Josh's 1994 trial. Church's testimony that the story of Josh's confession wasn't true, if we could get it, would fit nicely with the fact that Mangus and Weissinger both admitted to David Rosener in the summer of 1993 that it was a lie cooked up while the three were together in the Cape County Jail.

Jim Sullins found Church in late October and persuaded him to come to Cape Girardeau while we were in the area. On November 7, Jim Wyrsch and I interviewed him in depth at his home, a rented trailer in Scott City with a plywood door on a gravel road near the railroad tracks. He was living with a pretty woman who appeared to be about 16 and several very young children. He was thin and not bad looking, but he had teeth protruding slightly from his mouth, which gave him a kind of goofy appearance. Much of the time during the interview, Church looked at us with a puzzled grin, responding slowly and cautiously to every question like he thought we were trying to trap him into some admission that would get him in trouble with the law. Eventually, he relaxed and told us, "Shawn was the one who come up with the idea. He said we would all get less time if we told the cops Josh told us he did it." He said he deliberately changed the one detail of the story as a kind of compromise. On the one hand, unlike Mangus, he thought, "I was gonna get out soon anyway, and I kinda felt guilty about gettin' Josh in trouble." On the other hand, "I wanted to back the others in the tale they was gonna tell."

The next decision was whether to have Church testify live in Jefferson City or to use his deposition testimony. Informed of the hearing dates, he told us, "I don't know if I can make it then; I got this little legal problem. I gotta get permission from the Scott County Sheriff to leave the county. And I'd probably need a ride." Rick Walter would gladly give Church permission and might even give him a ride, but considering Church's somewhat scruffy appearance, we took no chances and arranged for his deposition in Cape Girardeau on the following Friday, November 14.

I started by asking Church background questions. He was 33 and working sporadically as a tree trimmer. He had dropped out of high school when he was about 15, after finishing 10th grade, and he met Josh around the same time. They hung out together in Cape Girardeau as part of a larger group of boys, mostly along Broadway. They spent their time drinking and taking drugs, moving from place to place, mooching off girls they met, and sometimes living on the street. "I just know that there was a bunch of us walking around and we stayed on Broadway and we were doing like the runaway thing. We were staying with this girl and [her] parents would catch us and kick us out and we would end up having to stay on the street until some other girl picked us up. We stayed in the Laundromat and hey, what you doing, you know, tell stories and hang out for a month."

Church was 17 when Mischelle Lawless was murdered. He didn't know about the murder at the time even though he was living in the Cape Girardeau area. He first heard about it from Shawn Mangus, when Mangus and Weissinger approached him in the Cape Girardeau County Jail with a plan to trade the story of Josh's confession for more lenient treatment on their charges. "Well, we were sitting in jail and Shawn and Chuck, and Shawn came to me and said, 'Man, we're getting out of here.' I was like, 'All right.' He was like, 'No, they're going to come and question you and all you've got to say is that Josh told you that he killed somebody.'"

Church said he was in the Cape Girardeau County Jail because he was with Mangus when Mangus sold a man some LSD and then threatened to kill the man when he took too much and went berserk. Church claimed he actually helped the man escape, which is why he expected to be let off easy. "[Mangus] was selling some acid and he said he knew a buyer, so we went up there and hung out at this dude's house and this guy was an older fellow and he was like oh, man, y'alls acid nowadays ain't nothing. [Mangus] was like no, whatever man. He told the dude to take half a hit or something like that. Well, he bought three hits and took [a] big portion."

They left for a while, to look for something to do. Mangus was carrying a gun. Church said they didn't want to be stopped by the police and "girls tended to freak out when they realized you were carrying a gun." So they returned to the acid customer's house and found him "wigging out."

> He said he was going to call the poison control and Shawn was like no, you're not. You're going to sit down and they had some Cheech and Chong movie or something, trying to keep him calm. Anyway, all I remember is the dude got up, went to his silverware drawer and started throwing the silverware and he had mostly butter knives and a few of them stuck in the wall. Shawn said, "You need to chill out." That's when he brought the gun out.

Mangus tied the man up and forced him to pay for the acid, which the man did with a check. Then he told Church, "We're going to ride somewhere and I'm going to kill him, throw him off a bridge." Church claimed he wanted no part of that. He had a pocketknife he had picked up in the man's apartment, along with the man's cigarettes. He said he used the knife to cut the man loose and told him to run. The man took the gun away from Mangus. Someone called the police, who arrested Mangus and Church and charged them both with robbery.

When Church was pulled out of his cell to tell what he knew about the Lawless murder, he didn't, as he put it, "fully ride" with the plan to implicate Josh "because I didn't feel comfortable and I knew I was getting out anyway, because Shawn did all the stuff and the dude said I didn't do nothing." He said the investigators asked him, "do you know of any violentness" of Josh because it would help them, "indicating that there was this girl died from Benton." He told them about three threats Josh supposedly made: some people who were screwing with his mother, the man he described as Amanda Drury's father who confronted Josh when he went looking for Amanda in January 1993, and the girl from Benton he met on Broadway in Cape Girardeau who "fucked him over." The girl from Benton Josh met on Broadway was supposed to be Mischelle Lawless, but Church explained he was careful to say that Josh only made threats about this girl.

Church made it clear in the deposition that he didn't believe Josh was a violent person. He said the only gun he ever saw Josh hold was a pellet gun. He acknowledged that Josh told everyone he joined the Latin Kings and had a tattoo to prove it. "[Josh] said he met some people or something like that and he got a tattoo or something like that, but we would always mess with him, you ain't in no gang."

18

THE HABEAS CORPUS HEARING

Bill Ferrell still had considerable influence in county Democratic politics, and he backed Bobby Sullivan, a detective with the Sikeston Department of Public Safety, against Rick Walter in the Democratic primary. Walter's decision to reopen the investigation of the Lawless murder wasn't overtly an issue in the campaign. Bridget DiCosmo reported the day before the vote that both Sullivan and Walter had said as much. Sullivan was quoted in the *Southeast Missourian* as telling her, "An experienced investigator would know that no case is ever closed. Anything that could be considered new evidence should be considered." But many of Sullivan's supporters weren't so sure about the new investigation. In particular, Walter said, his decision to reopen the case had upset some law enforcement officials. "If this hurts my election, then so be it. It's still the right thing to do." He had made similar statements privately to me that "I may end up being a one-term sheriff because I reopened the investigation, but it was something I had to do."

We needed the sheriff's support in the habeas hearing in December. We planned to have him testify, along with Branden Caid and perhaps one or two other deputies, and we hoped he wouldn't be a lame-duck sheriff when he took the stand. On August 4, Walter defeated Sullivan by 2,894 votes to 1,752. The voters of Scott County were more influenced by financial issues, or maybe the majority of voters agreed with Walter that reopening the investigation was the right thing to do.

In the November election, Sheriff Walter would face opposition from a Republican candidate, Wes Drury, the jailer on duty the night Mischelle was murdered who now was an investigator for the county prosecutor's office. Normally, the person who won the Democratic primary would win the election. A Republican candidate, if there was one, would mount only token opposition. But the minority that supported Sullivan in the Democratic primary and resented Walter's challenge to one of Bill Ferrell's crowning achievements might shift their support to Wes Drury. Those who were perceived as helping Josh had been the victims of threatening incidents, which may or may not have been connected to Josh's case. Jim Sullins found his dog shot. Bridget DiCosmo had the tires on her car slashed. November 4 came and went. Rick Walter was reelected by a wide margin, and he could breathe easier about his support for Josh.

The other race with implications for the hearing was the governor's race. In early 2008, Kenny Hulshof's old boss, Jay Nixon, was still Missouri Attorney General, but Nixon had kicked off a campaign to become the Democratic nominee for governor in 2005 and was considered the front-runner for the nomination. On January 29, 2008, Kenny Hulshof announced he was seeking the Republican nomination.

Jay Nixon won the primary easily with 85 percent of the vote. Kenny Hulshof was one of five candidates, but only State Treasurer Sarah Steelman gave him much opposition. Steelman said Hulshof's prosecutions revealed "a very disturbing pattern of behavior," which along with Steelman's criticism of Hulshof's record of spending in Congress, raised issues of "his overall competency and ability to do the job it takes to be governor." Hulshof won the primary with 194,556 votes to Steelman's 176,750.

Nixon didn't criticize Hulshof's record as a prosecutor. Nixon would be attacking the performance of his own office if he criticized his star prosecutor. We didn't want Josh's case to be an election issue anyway. The more publicity the case received, especially in coverage like Alan Zaiger's, the more Hulshof would feel compelled to defend Josh's guilty verdict. And it would not be good for Josh's mental well-being to see himself attacked in the media again as a vicious murderer. Fortunately, the Hulshof campaign seemed to largely ignore Zaiger's criticism, and the story of how Josh was wronged by the congressman faded from view as summer slipped into fall. Kenny Hulshof carried Scott County, but he was badly beaten statewide. Jay Nixon received more than 58 percent of the votes for governor on the same Democratic ticket as Barack Obama, who lost to John McCain by just 3,632 votes statewide, in a race so close that Missouri was the last state to be called.

★ ★ ★

In the last weeks before the habeas hearing was to begin in Jefferson City, we scrambled to pull together our exhibits, designate the deposition testimony we wanted the judge to read, schedule and prepare our live

witnesses, and write a prehearing brief that summarized the deposition testimony and the expected live testimony. We were happy with the results
of the depositions and believed we had put together a compelling case for
Josh's innocence that the judge could absorb before the public part of the
litigation began.

On two Saturdays in the last month before the hearing, Charlie Weiss
and I met with Josh in prison to prepare him to testify. He would have the
opportunity for the first time to deny the charges against him. That would
be easy for him to do, but we also wanted him to be prepared for the hard
questions Mike Spillane was likely to ask him regarding, for example, the
comments he supposedly made about guns and gangs on the long drive
back from Kankakee with Don Windham.

DAY ONE

The hearing on Josh's habeas corpus petition began on December 2. Josh
had been transported to the courthouse from the Jefferson City Correctional Center early that morning, and he was brought into the courtroom
in handcuffs and leg shackles, wearing an orange jumpsuit, just before the
hearing began. He was heavier and more muscular than when he first entered prison, and his brown hair was starting to turn gray. His guards from
the Cole County Jail removed the restraints and seated him next to me at
the counsel table. His parents and maternal grandparents were there, along
with two aunts and a small group of supporters. Marvin Lawless and his
wife were there too. They sat on the other side of the courtroom, wearing
circular pins containing a picture of Mischelle, in silent opposition to the
proceedings.

★ ★ ★

Our first witness was Rick Walter. He walked to the stand in his
sheriff's dress uniform, white shirt and dark pants, carrying his Smokey the
Bear–style hat in his hand. He recounted the discovery of Mischelle Lawless's body and said, "The driver's-side window was only partway down,
less than halfway down." He described subsequent events at the crime
scene, including Roy Moore's conversation with the Hispanic man looking
for gas and with Matt Abbott when he returned to the interstate exit after-
eporting the murder in Benton. Then the sheriff described the reopened
investigation. "About eight months after I took office in 2005, I started
looking at the old files from the Kezer case. Various people over the years,

some in law enforcement and some who were informants, seemed to think Kezer was innocent."

Walter explained why he hired Branden Caid. "I wanted somebody who didn't have notions about the case already and who wasn't involved; I wanted somebody who could take a fresh look at the evidence." He said, "I saw Bobby Wooten's report of his interview with Mark Abbott when I first looked at the files. I knew that his report seriously undermined Mark Abbott's credibility, but I didn't know the defense lawyers hadn't seen the report. I didn't understand how important it was legally."

Then he summarized some of the key points of what the investigation had found in the three years he and Branden Caid had been working on the case. Most importantly, he said, "We are looking at a few suspects, but we haven't found any credible evidence that Kezer was involved."

★ ★ ★

Our next witness was Branden Caid, dressed as a detective in a sport coat and tie. He told how he discovered, during a conversation with a Cape Girardeau detective, that Mark Abbott "told Detective Bill Bohnert in late 1996 or early 1997 that he saw Kevin Williams kill Mischelle."

Detective Caid authenticated originals of key documents from the Lawless murder case that he found in the Scott County Sheriff's files, including Brenda Schiwitz's notebooks and Bobby Wooten's interview report. "Bobby Wooten's report was attached to one of Brenda's note-books with a paper clip." He knew Ray Ring and testified that Ring had one white and one African American parent. "That clearly was inconsistent with Abbott's claim that he saw Kezer." He authenticated the photo lineup from which Abbott had picked Josh as the man at the Cut-Mart and the photo lineup from which Doug Brantley picked Josh as the man who threatened him with a gun on Halloween night a week before Mischelle was murdered. He noted, "The picture with Kezer in both lineups was the only one that obviously was a mug shot." He authenticated the eight Polaroids of small white cars of various makes from which Mark Abbott picked Christy Naile's little Plymouth. While doing that he observed, "Three of the eight photos have louvers on the back window but none of them have the spoiler or fin Abbott described to investigators."

We had depositions from three of the snitches—Weissinger, Church, and Rogers—denying that Josh had ever confessed to murdering Mischelle, but Branden Caid was the best source of information we had about the others. He testified about his two telephone interviews with Steve Grah. "I left my card at Grah's house when no one answered the door. Grah called me later, twice. The first time, he said he didn't remember anything about the case. I could hear his mother yelling something in the background. Then he called back a little later and recited what was essentially his testimony at the Kezer trial. It was like he just reread the transcript."

The most useful information Caid got from Grah was that someone from the attorney general's office came by his house while he was out on bond awaiting sentencing and offered him a deal. "We're having trouble locating Shawn Mangus," the man said. "How would he like to get 2 years instead of 10?"

Caid described his prison interview with Wade Howard. "I interviewed him in prison. He had long hair and bad teeth and a cross tattoo between his eyes. He claimed that Jeff Rogers gave him the story about Kezer confessing that he had told Sheriff Ferrell. Then he claimed Kezer actually did confess to him at a later date. It was like he realized he was admitting perjury."

Caid also testified that when he tried to locate Shawn Mangus, a relative told him that Mangus had died of a heroin overdose. He identified the signed statement Mangus gave to the prosecutor's investigator, which we obtained from the attorney general's files, as a document that wasn't in the sheriff's files and that he had only seen a week before when we sent him a copy.

Detective Caid surprised the lawyers on both sides when he said the highway patrol lab had found a DNA match with Leon Lamb when it retested the scrapings from under Mischelle's fingernails. That result was inconsistent with the results of the early forensics done right after the murder. On cross-examination, Mike Spillane challenged this statement. He was the one who had requested the analysis, but the lab hadn't informed him of this result. Caid said, "I didn't receive a written report, but I was told the result over the telephone by one of the lab employees. I think it was within the last 60 days." The judge told Spillane he expected him to check with the lab and get a definitive answer.

★ ★ ★

The State wanted to call Terri Williams as a live witness, not just file her deposition, because she wasn't going to be available on December 3. She wore one of the pins with Mischelle's picture, which Marvin Lawless apparently gave her, and sat with Mr. Lawless and his wife during the testimony of the first two witnesses. She testified out of order as the third witness on December 2.

On the stand, Terri Williams gave the same account of the night of the murder she had given in her deposition. "I was with my husband the whole night. We went to the party at Mr. Howell's house early. . . . I drove him home around midnight, and we went to bed. . . . Kevin didn't leave with Mark when he showed up at the party and asked him to go out. I wouldn't let him. . . . He couldn't of had anything to do with the murder." We could live with that. We didn't have to prove that Kevin Williams and Mark Abbott killed Mischelle to prove that Josh didn't kill her. More importantly, on cross-examination, Terri also told how Mark Abbott had shown up at their house the next morning and talked about finding Mischelle's body and seeing the white car at the Cut-Mart. She remembered Abbott saying, "I couldn't see who was in the car; I could only make out shapes and outlines."

★ ★ ★

Deputy Moore recounted driving out to the interstate with Rick Walter to check on the Householders' report of Mischelle's car sitting with the lights on and the motor running. He testified that "the driver's-side window was down about five to seven inches." In answer to a question whether that was far enough down to reach in and lift Mischelle, he said, "Not in my estimation it isn't." He described his encounter with the Hispanic man in a small white car who stopped at the crime scene and asked for help. "I could barely understand him. It was like broken English. I had to keep asking him to repeat." Then he testified about Mark Abbott (or maybe his brother Matt) showing up at the crime scene soon after the Hispanic man left. "I found out later what I remembered about his clothes and the vehicle he was driving was different from what Deputy Drury wrote down in the log."

Deputy Beardslee was the first investigator to interview Mark Abbott—early the next afternoon, after failing twice to find him at home. He had lots of reasons to conclude Abbott was lying. "[H]e said he reached through the window, and that was an impossibility. . . . He said that she was cold, but it would have been within minutes after it occurred. . . . He said he saw rings on her fingers, and I knew from the inventory of the vehicle that the rings weren't on her fingers." He continued:

> I teach interviewing and interrogation, so I know something about body language, and he had a very difficult time maintaining eye contact with me. I might ask him a question, he'd look around the room, fidget, sit down and cross his legs and cross his arms, all indications to me that he was being defensive and possibly lying to me. I told the sheriff and the

rest of them at the [November 4] meeting that I felt like we needed to look at him closer.

Of course, Beardslee's suspicion of Abbott wasn't known to the defense at Josh's trial because Brenda Schiwitz's notes of the meeting at which he asserted them were withheld and she had testified that Abbott was never a suspect. In addition, as Bill Ferrell's chief deputy, Beardslee had not mentioned anything about body language in his trial testimony.

★ ★ ★

Al Lowes, who was 76 at the time and still practicing law, described how Kenny Hulshof, whom he called "Cool Breeze," prevented David Rosener from contradicting the claims of Shawn Mangus and Wade Howard by moving to disqualify his whole firm from representing Josh a week before the trial was to begin. Hulshof's move forced Lowes to avoid disqualification by promising that Rosener would not testify.

Most importantly, Lowes identified key pieces of our *Brady* evidence as documents he hadn't seen before but wished he'd had for use in Josh's trial. He mentioned the written recantation that Shawn Mangus had given to the prosecutor's investigator six months after he had recanted to Rosener and the account in Brenda Schiwitz's notebook of the interview with Joseph Flores. "Those notebooks were particularly significant because I specifically asked Brenda in a deposition whether she had any interview notes. I even told her I was interested in notes because sometimes they aren't consistent with the typed-up official reports."

Finally, Lowes commented on the importance of Mark Abbott and Kevin Williams accusing each other as being the real killer. "In my opinion, these confessions were significant impeachment material. I'm confident Josh's trial would have ended differently if the jury had heard such testimony."[1]

★ ★ ★

Lacey Warren Hall and Dawn Worley Pierce finally got a chance to tell someone who would take them seriously what really happened at their Halloween party. They made a good impression, starting with the fact that they had driven four hours to testify for a man they didn't know. Both were 33 now and married, in Dawn's case, to the young man she was living with in 1992. Lacey had worked as a real estate appraiser but currently was staying at home with her two young children. In June 1994, both were following the news of the trial on television and in the local newspapers. Dawn said, "We saw Mr. Kezer's picture, so we were shocked to read that

Chantelle Crider said he was at the party." According to Lacey, "I knew Mischelle but not Chantelle and the other girl. We knew all the boys who were there, and I'm sure that Mr. Kezer was not there." Dawn said, "I saw Mischelle making out with Todd Mayberry. Then I saw them having a little altercation after Mischelle told him to stop."

Chantelle Crider's testimony at the hearing was a lot like our previous interviews. She admitted she was mistaken when she testified it was Josh who had harassed her and Mischelle at the 1992 Halloween party. It was those other things she had told us and repeated on the stand that caused us concern. Her thinking about the boy she had seen at the Halloween party was confused and difficult to follow. "Mark Abbott and Kevin Williams were at the Halloween party; they were wearing face paint." She told the story she had told us about going for a ride in the country with Todd Mayberry and Dwight Buckner and her saving her life by grabbing the wheel and causing an accident. "I realized then that it was Todd who harassed me and Mischelle on Halloween." Finally, she told how she had gotten to know Mark Abbott through her then husband's drug dealing and of overhearing Abbott say "I'm going to shut her up like I shut up her friend." Still, she testified through tears, on direct and again on cross-examination, that "I was horribly mistaken when I identified Mr. Kezer at his trial."

DAY TWO

Mike Spillane was waiting for us when we arrived early at the courthouse the next morning. He had checked with the highway patrol lab and discovered that there was a written report of a reanalysis of the scrapings from Mischelle's fingernails and that Leon Lamb's DNA was indeed mixed in with Mischelle's. He wanted to tell the judge before the hearing resumed, so we waited in chambers for him to arrive. As the judge came through the door, he looked at the assembled group of lawyers standing in front of him and said, "Well, one thing we know for sure; he wasn't at that Halloween party." Our concern about Chantelle was unfounded. One of the three pillars of the case against him was toppled, and only Mark Abbott and the snitches remained.

Then the conversation turned to Leon Lamb's DNA. Spillane provided everyone with copies of the report. He would enter the report in evidence and make a record of the findings.

After the judge was seated on the bench, he announced, "Our sound system isn't working, and it's going to be difficult to hear the testimony. If any family members want to come up and sit in the jury box, that would be alright with me." Some of Josh's family took him up on the offer. His father struggled forward. His kidneys were failing, and he was on dialysis. He seemed to go in and out of consciousness, his head lolling forward from time to time onto a pillow he held in his arms.

★ ★ ★

Bill Bohnert was the first witness. He's a large man who on that day was dressed like a detective, in a sport coat and tie. He started in police work as an MP in the Marines. When he got out in 1983, he went to work for the Cape Girardeau Police Department, first in the Patrol Division, and then, in 1996, he transferred to the Narcotics Unit and worked with the DEA in the regional task force. "I've known the Abbott twins since they were 12 years old. They went with their family to the church I attend in Cape Girardeau." Now, he was testifying about arresting them, and their friends, including Kevin Williams, on drug and weapons charges.

At the beginning of 1997, Mark Abbott was facing the possibility of a long prison sentence and hoped that Bohnert could help him get a deal. Bohnert went to see Abbott in the county jail. "He provided me with information on other drug operations, and he claimed he knew who really killed Mischelle Lawless." He told me, "Mischelle was having an affair with Kevin Williams. She came to see Williams the night she was killed, and they argued. She told Williams she was pregnant with his child and was going to find his wife and tell her." According to Abbott, Mischelle drove off in her car, and Williams and Abbott followed her, going northbound on the interstate flashing their lights. She pulled over on the ramp at the Benton exit. "[Abbott] said he stayed in the vehicle. Kevin Williams got out, they went up, talked a little bit, argued some more. And he said he heard some gunshots, and then he said Kevin Williams ran off towards the east, towards the Ferrell mobile homes business, and it was at that time he went to report the shooting to the sheriff's department." Abbott said Williams called him later for a ride from where he had been hiding and told him he would kill him if he told anyone what had happened.

Bohnert had never encountered anything quite like this before, so he went to see Morley Swingle and ask his advice. Swingle told Bohnert to call Don Windham and tell him what Abbott was claiming because Windham had been the lead investigator in the Lawless murder. Bohnert called Windham, and Windham wasn't at all receptive. Bohnert went back to Abbott and told him, "No one wants to listen to you."

★ ★ ★

Cathy Marie Fowler made a nice impression. She was the manager of a country club and was dressed in business attire. She, too, had driven hundreds of miles to testify for Josh. She had a similar story, only in her version, Kevin Williams was claiming that Mark Abbott killed Mischelle.

Cathy first met Kevin in March 1992. She was celebrating her second anniversary with her husband, Jim Fowler, at the Purple Crackle. Jim went to the bar to get a drink, and Kevin came over and "sucker punched" him. Despite that incident, a year later, Jim and Kevin were friends. "My husband ran into Kevin at a party at the home of a mutual friend, and they ended up hanging out all night together." The next thing Cathy knew, Kevin was coming to their house all the time. He had recruited Jim to help him deal methamphetamine. "He kept the meth at home and got hooked on it himself. He kept a pistol belonging to Kevin there too. Eventually, I think it was in the fall of 1994, I told him he had to quit the drug business and get rid of the drugs or I would leave. He agreed and told Kevin to come by and pick up his pistol too." When Williams arrived, Cathy, Jim, and their five-year-old son were sitting in the living room of their mobile home visiting with another couple. Suddenly, Kevin said, "Well, you know, the little girl that got killed up here . . . at 55 and 77 . . . they have got the wrong person in prison for that." According to Cathy, when she asked Kevin how he knew, he said, "Because I was there. . . . I was there with Mark Abbott. . . . It started out at one of the trailers at Ferrell trailer court. Things got rough that night. They hurt her, they had to move her, and Mark Abbott killed her." She said they all sat there in silence, stunned.

After that, Jim Fowler gave Kevin the gun, and Kevin left. When Cathy asked her husband about what Kevin had said, he told her to put it out of her head, and she didn't bring it up with him again. In December 1996, Jim Fowler was in the backyard working on his truck when the jack slipped and dropped the truck on him.

Over the years, the memory of her strange conversation with Kevin Williams haunted Cathy. She discussed it with her parents but didn't report it to authorities. She said she didn't know if Kevin was telling the truth. Then, in 2001, she ran into Matt Moore at her dead husband's brother's house. Matt Moore told her that Mark Abbott had bragged to him that he shot Mischelle Lawless.

> That seemed to confirm what Kevin Williams told me, so I decided to do something about it. I talked to one of my son's friends who worked in the attorney general's office, and he told me to contact Al Lowes. When Bill Ferrell didn't respond to Al Lowes's letter about my story,

I called him myself and offered to come in to talk to him about what I heard. He said, "There's no need. I have my conviction, and the case is closed."

★ ★ ★

Jim Sullins found a witness who said Mark Abbott told him he killed Mischelle Lawless. Ronnie Burton was 56 and lived in Marble Hill, about 20 miles west of Cape Girardeau. He was born in Gillstrap, and later lived in Benton, where he became friends with Marvin Lawless. They earned their black belts in karate together. He had a small construction business at one time and used to do a lot of work for Larry Abbott, who introduced him to his twin sons.

Burton testified in serious, measured tones with that same Southeast Missouri drawl. He was visibly emotional as he told how Mark Abbott claimed he had killed Mischelle. Sammy Johnson was a friend who had a fishing lake with a rough cabin in the hills outside of Commerce. Burton, not sure of the year but thinking it was shortly after Josh's trial in 1994, went to the lake with Sammy when Mark Abbott arrived. "I knew all about Mischelle's murder and Mark Abbott's role in Kezer's trial from the news coverage and the talk around the area, so we struck up a conversation about the case. In that conversation, Mark kind of snickered a little bit and said, well they got the wrong guy. And I asked him what he meant, and he—excuse me—but he said, I took care of that bitch." Burton was shocked. "Here's a man standing in front of me that said this, with me being friends of Mischelle and her father; I just couldn't believe it." Burton was so disturbed that he went home.

At first, Burton didn't know what to do. He remembered talking it over with someone close to him, his brother he thought, but otherwise said nothing. Then, two or three weeks later, he went to see Bill Ferrell.

> [I]t was a very, very brief meeting. I told him—I went into the office and told him that I had some information about the Mischelle Lawless murder that was important. And I basically was telling him about what Mark had said, and he pretty abruptly cut me off and said, we have got the right man. Case closed. And that's exactly what he said, so I just put my hands up and walked off.

With that, he decided to not pursue the issue further and spoke little about it for years.

★ ★ ★

The testimony of these first three witnesses on the morning of December 3 didn't prove that Mark Abbott or Kevin Williams killed Mischelle Lawless. The three accounts of conversations implicating them in the murder contradicted each other and couldn't all be true unless they killed Mischelle together, for different reasons. And there was no evidence at the time that Abbott or Williams knew Mischelle, let alone was having an affair with her or had involved her in their drug dealing. It seemed to me at the time more likely that their comments to law enforcement were meant as a means to get leniency, to those in the White Trash Mafia as intimidation, and to others like Ron Burton as a cruel and twisted joke meant to shock. In any event, these witnesses showed that Abbott and Williams said repeatedly that Josh was innocent and had been unjustly convicted on the basis of Abbott's false testimony.

★ ★ ★

We asked the judge if Josh's family could visit with him over the lunch break. Charles Kezer had diabetes and hadn't seen his son in years, and that morning he looked like he might not live long enough to see him again. There was a small holding cell in a waiting room at the end of the hall near the judge's chambers. The judge arranged for Josh to meet with his family in a secure area outside of his holding cell. Every relative who came to the hearing—father, mother, maternal grandparents, and two maternal aunts—crowded into the locked room. It was a joyful reunion, full of hope that the proceeding would end with Josh's release. The mood got even better when the judge knocked on the door and joined them. He stayed only long enough to meet Josh's family. Then, as he was about to leave, he looked at Josh and said with a smile, "This would not be a good time to try to escape."

★ ★ ★

Josh was our last witness on December 3. David Rosener had to have surgery right before the hearing began and wasn't released to travel in time to testify on December 2 or 3, so we scheduled a few hours the following week to finish putting on our case and called Josh to the stand.

Josh spoke without hesitation, showing his emotion with every word. He started by telling about his family and childhood—his birth in Kankakee and his parents' divorce, his problems adjusting when he moved to Southeast Missouri, getting kicked out of junior high for not living in the district, moving to Kankakee in early 1991 to live with his father, and back to Cape Girardeau in early 1992. That was when he started hanging out on the street.

Josh described how he met Amanda Drury and Christy Naile, that the two girls ran into him and Kelly Church on Broadway and gave them a ride. It became a regular thing that summer, cruising with the two girls around Cape Girardeau. Josh said, "A few times, when she got tired, Christy let me drive her car, but I never drove it without the two girls." They went to the REO Speedwagon concert in early August, and as Josh remembered it, Amanda broke up with him shortly after. He said, "I hung around Cape Girardeau for a while, but I moved back to Kankakee around the end of August or early in September." His voice rose a bit as he insisted, "I didn't return to Southeast Missouri until after Christmas."

There were a few interview summaries generated during the investigation in 1993 in which Josh was reported to have bragged about his membership in the Latin Kings. Some of these stories came from interviews of street punks like Steve Grah who weren't particularly credible. Don Windham's account of the conversations he and Deputy Hinton had had with Josh during the long drive back from Kankakee to Benton was different. At the time, I could see how Windham might have misinterpreted what Josh said, but I didn't think he would just make it up. In preparing Josh to testify, we knew he would admit that he said a lot of what Windham claimed he said. But we also knew there were a few things he would not admit.

Josh said he joined the Latin Kings shortly after he returned to Kankakee in 1992 and that he was in the gang during the rest of 1992. "And primarily the only reason I was even in the gang, in all honesty, was because my cousin Michael was in it and I wanted to be next to him, wanted to be close to him." He said, "I didn't sell drugs while I was a member of the gang," but he volunteered that gang members did that from time to time. He was only a sort of probationary member of the gang in the short time he belonged, without full access to all of its secrets or full participation in all of its activities. He admitted he got a gang tattoo but said, "I plan to have it removed or covered up when I get out of prison." He said, "All I did as a member of the Latin Kings was take part in occasional fights with members of rival gangs over territory. I didn't own a gun. I never shot anybody or shot at anybody. I've never even fired a handgun."

When it came to Windham's report that on the trip back from Kankakee, Josh claimed he was a good shot, I initially hoped that Josh could say he didn't remember the remark or that he might have said it but was scared and was just trying to act tough. I would have preferred that Josh not directly contradict Windham. But Josh was sure he hadn't said it, and that was how he was going to testify at the hearing. On cross-examination, Spillane asked Josh about his statements alleged in Windham's report:

Q. So if you haven't handled [a gun], how could you be a good shot, or was [Windham] lying?

A. I'm not a good shot. I wouldn't know what a good shot is, sir. I never fired a gun.

Q. So Trooper Windham's testimony was inaccurate, then. You never told him that?

A. I didn't say that. I didn't tell him that.

I didn't know Josh's story about shooting a rifle in the Boy Scouts until years later. Josh told me recently:

I told the truth. I didn't lie when I testified. I wasn't asked about the Boy Scouts. I wasn't asked about a rifle. I was asked about a handgun. I was accused of firing a handgun. I had never fired a handgun. I was fighting for my life. Spillane's question contextually asked me about a handgun. Windham tricked me in 1993 and misrepresented me in his report. It was used against me, and as a 19-year-old boy, I was wrongly convicted. I was 33 by the time of the 2008 hearing and Spillane's cross-examination. I wasn't going to be tricked again. I won't apologize for telling the truth when asked about a handgun.

Josh's mother came to Kankakee for Christmas in 1992. Josh identified a picture of himself taken then, with his mother in front of a Christmas tree. He made a point of the fact that he wasn't "dark complected" in the picture. He said he decided to surprise his mother by coming to Southeast Missouri shortly after Christmas to visit her but had to find his own place to stay because of her living arrangement with her boyfriend. "Kelly Church told me about Stacy Reed's apartment in Cape. But I didn't spend the nights there. I stayed with David Pengiel."

Josh remembered seeing Shawn Mangus and Chuck Weissinger in Stacy Reed's apartment. "Steve Grah wasn't there while I was. I didn't tell Shawn I killed Mischelle Lawless and wanted to get it off my chest." He denied that he confessed to Wade Howard or Jeff Rogers while he was locked up with them in the Scott County Jail. "No. Like I said, I never said that to anybody at any point ever. I'm 33 years old today, and it never came out of my mouth. And never will. I only told my cellies I was innocent. I was terrified, but I always thought I'd be acquitted."

Josh testified that he was in Kankakee the night Mischelle was murdered. He described his visit to Brenda Garduno's house to check on his cousin's condition after the car wreck.

> I arrived between 11:00 and midnight. Almost all of the lights were off and I saw a glimmer of a light and I assumed it was the TV so I went and I knocked on the door. Brenda heard the commotion at the door and came to see what was happening. She could tell from the look on my face that I heard about the accident and came to make sure Michael was alright. She told me Michael only got a bump on the head and Christina and the baby were fine.

Josh denied he was in Southeast Missouri on Halloween, the Saturday night a week before Mischelle's murder, where Doug Brantley claimed he threatened him with a gun. "I wasn't wearing face paint and hanging out at the Billiards Center in Cape Girardeau." He said he didn't know John Pierce or Dawn Worley. "I wasn't at that party behind their trailer." He thought his trial was going well until Chantelle testified on the final day. "And out of the blue, here comes this girl who'd been sitting in the courtroom the whole time, hearing everybody—what everybody had to say, and now she's trying to create something that's not there. I was stunned."

Josh described the scene when the jury came back with a verdict of guilty—how he passed out and woke up with his knees on the floor and his head in his Aunt Kathy's lap and how through all the confusion, his lawyers and his family kept assuring him everything was going to be alright. Josh talked about the appeal of his conviction. Al Lowes represented him on the motion for a new trial, but his grandparents had no more money to pay lawyers for an appeal. "I was represented by an appellate public defender I never met or even talked to on the telephone."[2]

Josh described his life in prison. "For my entire adult life, I've had shackles, cuffs, I've been in cells, I've had cellies. I haven't been able to go to the bathroom without somebody being in the cell, most of the time at least. I'm not allowed to really have an opinion outside of my spirituality in prison. It's very nerve wracking. It's been very difficult during that time because I'll acknowledge that probably 90, 95 percent of the men in prison, if not higher than that, are guilty and the prison I've been in is a level 5 institution. I'm in there with child molesters and murderers and serial killers and all kinds of different people."

Josh described how he adjusted to that reality, knowing he was innocent but with no hope of getting out much short of his sentence of 60 years.

I had made a decision when I first went to prison that I was going to do everything in my power to not become like prison. It was very difficult when I got locked up. Prison is still violent today, but back then it was extremely violent. And I wanted to surround myself with decent people. So I was raised in the church by my grandparents, Hadley and Jane James. I had gotten away from that for a while, but I knew that was probably where I needed to be. So I started attending chapel.

That was how Josh met Jane Williams, who he noted, was sitting there in the courtroom in the first row. He said he was at a Monday night service and apparently was the only inmate praying on his knees. He found out years later that seeing him like that led Jane to inquire about him and to begin a correspondence. "Eventually, I told her I was innocent, and I gave her a copy of a report Jim Sullins did for my mother." He said Jane met his grandparents, reviewed what they had of his file, and started the process of finding a lawyer to represent him, which eventually led them to Bryan Cave. Then came the news that the new sheriff of Scott County had reopened the investigation. "I went within a short period [from] being a man who was trying to accept hopelessness, it was very difficult, to a man who has a lot of hope now."

★ ★ ★

Mike Spillane introduced the new highway patrol lab report that identified the DNA under Mischelle's fingernails as consistent with Leon Lamb's but not with Josh's or Kevin Williams's and read that portion of the report into the record.

Then the State completed its case with testimony from Chris Pickering, the investigator from the attorney general's office who had interviewed Bobby Wooten. Over objections that the testimony was hearsay and contradicted Wooten's sworn testimony in his deposition, Pickering said that in the interview with him, Wooten didn't remember the contents of the interview with Mark Abbott that is recounted in his report and didn't think the signature on the report looked like his when compared to the signature on his affidavit provided in support of the habeas corpus petition. Pickering acknowledged, however, that the State's handwriting expert had concluded, in a comparison with other 1992 Wooten reports, that the signature was genuine.

In the midst of cross-examination, the judge intervened, saying a bit testily, "It doesn't matter. I accept that—and maybe Mr. Spillane can convince me otherwise, but I think the report reflects that the interview had occurred. And the fact that Mr. Wooten doesn't remember it, when he talked to this gentleman, doesn't strike me as a big issue. I don't remember some things sometimes." That put an end to Pickering's testimony. The judge scheduled additional time for David Rosener the following Thursday and asked both sides to start preparing their proposed judgments. He wanted them available as soon as possible in Word format for him to use in writing his opinion.

★ ★ ★

As he was leaving the bench, the judge announced that he wanted to see counsel in chambers in five minutes. When we went in to see the judge, he came right to the point, telling the two sets of lawyers that "the case is not just a matter of withheld evidence, but Kezer clearly is innocent." Spillane objected, claiming again that we hadn't satisfied the "minimum gateway requirement," but the judge dismissed his argument. He reiterated that "I want proposed judgments from each side, and I want them as quickly as possible." He told Spillane, "You can use your submission to try to persuade me otherwise, but I doubt you can. We can let the Court of Appeals decide who's right, but I intend to write something that will make it hard for the State to prevail." Hearing what the judge said, I had to struggle a bit to suppress a huge grin.

Josh had gotten his own signal that he was going to be released, and he was starting to think he might be out by Christmas. We didn't want him to take anything for granted. At first, we told him only that we thought the hearing had gone very well and we were sure the judge was on our side from comments he had made.

★ ★ ★

I started work on proposed findings of fact and conclusions of law the next morning and soon realized that the document would be lengthy and detailed. We wanted to make sure that it covered every bit of evidence we had introduced and every constitutional issue we had raised. The judge's comments had made us confident of victory, but we didn't want to take anything for granted.

The parties reconvened before Judge Callahan at 2:30 p.m. the following Thursday. Knowing what we knew, but the public didn't know, about the judge's tentative decision, Rosener's testimony was anticlimactic, but it was dramatic nonetheless. Rosener was middle aged by then, slightly pudgy in the face and slightly overweight. He finally was able to respond under oath to the charges Shawn Mangus and Wade Howard had leveled against him. "I didn't threaten Mangus with an attack in prison by the Latin Kings, and I didn't put anything in Wade Howard's affidavit that he didn't say." He got especially emotional when it came to the charge of coaching witnesses to commit perjury. "I didn't coach the alibi witnesses from Kankakee to give false testimony."

Rosener directed genuine anger at Kenny Hulshof's closing argument. "I was allowed to sit and get pointed out by Mr. Hulshof repeatedly. He accused me of threatening witnesses with gang violence within the penitentiary system. He accused me of putting words in other witnesses' mouths. In short, he tried to divert [the] jury's attention clearly away from the facts of the case and tried to make me look like a scoundrel." Rosener said he confronted Hulshof about using the claims of these felons and using the conflict of interest argument to keep him from testifying.

> He told me that it was just a case and I put myself in a bad situation by not having a witness with me when I interviewed these jailhouse snitches. He told me that by interviewing these witnesses that I left our defense with their pants down, so to speak, and gave him an opportunity to run through a hole and fabricate testimony through Shawn Mangus. He didn't say fabricate. He implied, though.

Rosener also said Hulshof told him that he sent Windham and Godsey to Louisiana to talk to Mangus and that they told Mangus that "if he didn't get his story straight he could be bumped up to a felony." He said Hulshof also told him his investigators reminded Mangus he was a prior and persistent felon who would get an enhanced sentence if he was convicted of that felony.

Rosener said that Josh's case, his first out of law school, has worn on him over the years. "But more than anything, I'm ashamed that I didn't go see Josh in prison. I wasn't a big enough man to do that. This has had a tremendous impact on my career. I don't trust the police. I don't trust prosecutors." He said, "I haven't seen prosecutors engage in misconduct as bad at any time in my career since."

19

FREEDOM

We submitted our proposed findings of fact and conclusions of law on December 12, one day after Rosener testified. It was much longer than the State's, which Spillane submitted one day earlier, but I wanted to cover everything important in what we considered to be an extremely strong case. I put a heavy emphasis on how Hulshof's closing statement had poisoned the minds of the jury against Josh and his defense team. We thought, and hoped for Josh's sake, that we might receive an official judgment if not by Christmas, then by the end of the holiday season. Then, having heard nothing from the judge well into January 2009, we started to get a little nervous. Josh, of course, was more anxious than we were, and in our regular telephone conversations, I tried to keep him upbeat and to persuade him not to jump to any negative conclusions. Like us, he believed we'd proven his innocence. He wasn't concerned with the outcome but rather, with the time it was taking. Understandably, he wanted out of prison. With the holiday season past us, he turned his attention to February 16, his 34th birthday.

On January 20, counsel received an email from the judge apologizing for taking so long and explaining that he had been sidetracked by decisions that were due in several other cases. Then, at 11:31 on the morning of February 17, we received the judge's written opinion by email. It was 47 pages long, but we could tell by reading the first few paragraphs that we had won. The judge wrote that Josh hadn't gotten a fair trial because of the withholding of material exculpatory evidence under *Brady*. He also concluded that Josh was actually innocent under the standard of *Amrine*. "Thus, there is no remaining evidence that Josh Kezer had ever met or known of Mischelle Lawless or had any motive for Josh Kezer to have killed her."

The judge's opinion was critical of law enforcement, the prosecution, and the courts for the way Josh's case was handled. "There is little about this case which recommends our criminal justice system. The system failed in the investigative and charging stage, it failed at trial, it failed at the post trial review, and it failed during the appellate process. The only bright note is the Scott County Sheriff Rick Walter who, after being elected sheriff, re-opened the investigation." Josh took particular notice of Judge Callahan's mention of the investigative and charging stage. "The Judge essentially entered into record that I shouldn't have been considered a suspect from day one."

Some of the harshest criticism was aimed at the prosecution, and the opinion singled out Hulshof for the excesses of his closing argument. Hulshof said Christy Naile's car "lit up like a Christmas tree" when sprayed with luminol, even though there were only a few specks invisible to the naked eye. And Hulshof sided with the snitches against Rosener to paint Rosener as a crooked lawyer promoting their perjury. The judge quoted Hulshof's summary at the end of his closing.

> You aren't just 12 individuals; you represent those people and you represent the small community down the interstate, in Benton, Missouri, and those people are looking to you for justice, ladies and gentlemen. You are our only hope. We put him at the scene, we put a gun in his hand, we put the victim with him, we have got blood on his clothes. Ladies and gentlemen, based on all of this evidence, I urge you to find this defendant guilty of murder and armed criminal action.

The judge commented on this summary with the following summary of his own.

> We now know that none of what Mr. Hulshof said in that final summary was true. Abbott's testimony putting him at the scene is totally discredited. No gun was ever found, and there is no credible evidence that he ever had a gun (other than a realistic-looking BB gun). There is now uncontroverted evidence that he was not at the Halloween party, which was the only evidence presented that he was ever in the presence of the victim. New testing indicates there was no blood on his jacket (or in Christy Naile's car).

Finally, the judge ordered the warden to release Josh if the Scott County prosecutor didn't decide to recharge him within 10 days.

We tried to contact Josh to give him the good news even before we finished reading the opinion. An inmate can use a communal telephone to call out of the prison during any free time either collect or using pre-paid minutes purchased from the telephone service, but even the inmate's lawyer can't just pick up the telephone and call a prison inmate. The usual procedure is to call the corrections officer responsible for the inmate in the inmate's housing unit, schedule a time for the call, and send a fax or email on firm letterhead proving you are who you say you are. We called the Jefferson City Correctional Center to make the appropriate arrangements and were told that a call couldn't be scheduled until the following day. By then, we were late for a scheduled lunch meeting upstairs in a Bryan Cave conference room.

In the course of working on Josh's case, the Bryan Cave legal team agreed to help with a fundraiser for the Midwest Innocence Project to be held in St. Louis later in 2009. The Midwest Innocence Project started in Kansas City and was based at the University of Missouri–Kansas City Law School, but the bulk of its potential cases in recent years had arisen in the St. Louis area and the eastern half of the state. For several months, we had provided a Bryan Cave conference room for periodic meetings of an ad hoc committee of lawyers and nonlawyers planning the fundraising event, which we eventually decided would be a banquet featuring John Grisham as speaker. One of those on this committee was Darryl Burton, an inmate convicted of murder whom Judge Callahan had ordered released from the Jefferson City Correctional Center the previous summer. Josh knew Burton; they had been incarcerated together. We apologized for being late and told the group we had just gotten Judge Callahan's decision exonerating Josh. We also mentioned we were having trouble getting the news to Josh because of prison red tape. Darryl Burton said, "I'll take care of it." He pulled out his cell phone and called a guard who had befriended him while he was incarcerated. He asked the guard to get word to Josh to call his lawyers, and we left the meeting early to wait for the call.

Josh had trouble getting through at first because we were on the speakerphone in Charlie Weiss's office with Rick Walter discussing the option the judge had left Scott County of recharging Josh. I left to take the call in my office next door. When Josh heard the news, there was a gasp on the other end, then silence for a moment, like all the air had been sucked out of his lungs and he was unable to breathe. By the time we were all on the call, Josh had recovered and was saying, "Thank the Lord," over and over again. We cautioned him that it was up to the Scott County prosecutor to decide whether he would be charged with murder again and retried.

We couldn't imagine the Scott County prosecutor, Paul Boyd, would want to retry Josh. Still, there were political pressures that could affect his decision, and nothing was certain until the decision was announced.

Josh was playing pinochle with some friends when he was told to call his attorneys. He quickly got up to get to the nearest phone. When he left the table, he heard a friend ask him, "Is this it? Are you going home?" Josh responded as he left the area, "I don't know! I think so! I hope so!" He remembers shouting, "I got it! I won actual innocence! I'm going home!" When he saw his cellie coming in the unit he lived in, he tried to get his attention but was unsuccessful. Josh thought it would be a good idea to prank his cellie. When he got back to his cell, Josh composed himself, sunk his shoulders, and walked in crushed. He sat down; put his face in his hands; and when his cellie asked him if he was OK, Josh told him, "No. I lost. They denied my appeal. I can't believe it." His cellie didn't know what to say. When he attempted to console him, Josh removed his hands from his face, looked up, started laughing, and said, "I won! I got actual innocence! I'm going home! I'm finally going home!"

Hulshof reacted quickly. He issued a statement to the press through his law firm shortly after the court released the decision to the public. Ben Poston, who had joined the staff of the *Milwaukee Journal Sentinel*, received a copy of the statement and forwarded it to us.

> In November 1992, Mischelle Lawless was brutally murdered alongside Missouri Interstate 55. I remain convinced that Joshua Kezer, a member of the violent Latin Kings gang, is guilty of this crime. Today's opinion goes to great lengths to cast doubt on the credibility of the state's witnesses. But twelve jurors looked these witnesses in the eye, dispassionately listened to their testimony, and found them to be credible. The jury came to a unanimous decision that Mr. Kezer's alibi witnesses were not credible and that the state had proven beyond a reasonable doubt that Joshua Kezer was the murderer. I remain confident in the jury's verdict. My biggest regret is that the family of Mischelle Lawless is experiencing a travesty of justice. —Kenny Hulshof, former special prosecutor for the Office of the Missouri Attorney General.

Later, as a guest on KMOX radio in St. Louis, Hulshof repeated this rationale and added that Josh had failed a polygraph test.

That afternoon, we talked more with Rick Walter about the reaction to the decision in Scott County. Walter told us that when Paul Boyd asked his opinion on what he should do, "I told him I wouldn't support a decision to recharge Josh because there was no credible evidence against him."

Chris Hayes, a reporter with the local Fox News affiliate, had been covering the case. After the hearing ended in December, he asked us to give him an interview, but we told him to wait until the judge had decided the case. He asked again on February 17, and we scheduled an interview at our office the next morning at 10:00. While he was there, we got word that Paul Boyd had issued a press release stating that he wasn't going to charge Josh because he didn't have the evidence to do so. Late in the morning, we heard from Jane Williams that Josh was going to be released at 3:00 p.m. She had gathered some clothes for him to wear and arranged for him to stay with her and her husband. We told her we would see her at the prison. Jim Wyrsch left for Jefferson City on his own right after lunch. Weiss and I rode together later, timing our departure to arrive a little before 3:00.

Josh was released earlier than expected. When he emerged into the lobby, escorted by a lieutenant and a captain and wearing the clothes Jane Williams had brought earlier in the day, Jim Wyrsch was already there, along with Josh's mother, Jane and her husband, and a group of print and television reporters from Jefferson City and Columbia. Josh greeted everyone with handshakes and hugs and spoke briefly in an impromptu press conference about other men he believed were innocent and his feelings upon being released. Suddenly, he realized that he could walk out the door if he wanted, and that is what he did, without a coat, into the February cold in the upper teens.

Rick Walter and Branden Caid arrived from Benton as Josh was coming out the door. Charlie Weiss and I were still racing down No More Victims Road toward the prison parking lot, right behind Chris Hayes and his camera man in the Fox 2 News van. We arrived as Josh was resuming his press conference outside. He was oblivious to the cold, but his supporters stood shivering in a semicircle behind him. After dealing with the usual questions about how it felt to be free, he switched the conversation away from himself and told the crowd, "Don't forget that there are other inmates inside who are innocent like me, like Ryan Ferguson."[1]

Later that evening, Chris Hayes reported Josh saying, "This is not gonna settle in on me probably for weeks, and I have no doubt that at some point, I'm gonna fall down on my knees, and I'm just gonna, gonna cry out and I'm gonna thank God and I'm gonna weep like a little baby, and I'm gonna be OK with that."

After 5 or 10 minutes of this, Josh finally realized how cold it was, and everyone hurried back inside. Walter approached Josh with an outstretched hand and asked him, "Do you remember what you told me when I visited you in prison?" Josh remembered. "I said I would decide whether to shake your hand after I saw what you did in your investigation." Recognizing that he was free in large part because of what Walter had done, he said, "Of course, I'll shake your hand." Josh eagerly shook Walter's hand, and the handshake quickly turned into a hug. Josh and Rick have since developed a relationship of immense respect.

PART V

THE AFTERMATH

"Talking about forgiveness is easy; actually forgiving is not."

—Josh Kezer

"I won't stop until Mischelle gets the justice she deserves."

—Josh Kezer

20

JOSH KEZER

Jane Williams and her husband planned to have Josh come live with them in Columbia, home of the main campus of the University of Missouri, until he got on his feet. Josh's mother lived in Columbia, too, but she was in poor health and was beginning to have problems managing her own life. The Williamses were going to take Josh and his mother out to dinner to celebrate with some other supporters from their church. After visiting for a while, the group going to dinner got into a Cadillac Escalade borrowed by the Williamses to pick up Josh. The lawyers headed back to St. Louis to have dinner at home. Rick Walter and Branden Caid began their much longer drive back to Scott County.

When Josh, his mother, and the Williamses drove away from the newer Jefferson City prison down No More Victims Road, someone asked him, "How do you feel?" Josh remembers his first thought and only answer: "I feel like I belong free and never belonged in prison." Josh wanted to visit the old Walls. Most of the prison had been torn down, but a few buildings were preserved as a museum, including one containing Josh's last cell before his move to the new prison just outside of town. Seeing the place stirred up bad memories, but it was part of a necessary catharsis.

I used to daydream about walking out of the old prison. When we pulled into the parking lot situated on the old prison yard, it was surreal. I walked around and picked up rocks. I remember thinking to myself, "These rocks used to hold me. Now I hold them." If I could have, I would have walked out of Crossroads as well. I lived through the valley of the shadow of death in that prison.

Then, Josh asked to go to the courthouse to try to see Judge Callahan and thank him. The judge was in chambers and invited Josh in. Josh went in alone. Judge Callahan said, "You need to think about what you want to do with your life. You should consider going to college." Josh remembers Judge Callahan telling him, "I apologize for taking as long as I did to write the decision. I wanted to make sure the State didn't appeal." Josh understood. As he put it, "If the State had appealed, it would have opened Pandora's box." Josh thanked the judge for his part in restoring his good name. The two men shook hands, and Josh walked away, this time without an orange jumpsuit, shackles, and guards escorting him. Judge Callahan and Josh have maintained contact over the years.[1]

After the courthouse, Jane and her husband took Josh and his mother out to dinner; he ordered steak, steak soup, and key lime pie. Josh had been suffering from car sickness recently, like when he was taken to and from the courthouse for the habeas hearing. He thought it was because he hadn't ridden in a car while in prison. In any event, after driving for a while and before dinner, Josh had to get out of the Escalade to throw up.

A few days later, Jane took Josh to lunch, this time with Ben Poston. Lunch at a nice restaurant, among families of ordinary nice people, was another experience Josh hadn't had in a long time. A woman at the next table, who had a baby boy dressed in full camo, overheard Josh saying he'd like to have one someday. She asked if he'd like to hold him. He said yes and cradled the baby in his arms. He told me, "I thought the baby was so cute."

The *St. Louis Post-Dispatch* represented Hulshof in an editorial cartoon showing him standing in a prison cell with his hands over his ears, a ball and chain locked to his ankle with "JOSHUA CHARLES KEZER" written on it, Judge Callahan's scathing rebuke above him, and in bold lettering beneath him "PRISONER OF HIS OWN CONSCIENCE."

The "real world" had changed in the nearly 16 years Josh had been locked away from it. He marveled at the tiny pocket cell phone that I used during breaks in the hearing. Urinals that didn't need to be manually flushed confused him. He was about to be introduced to the new world of the internet. But it wasn't just the outside world that had changed; it was Josh himself. He entered prison as a directionless teenager who didn't fit in and was young enough that he didn't need to, but he came back to the real world as a 34-year-old adult with an urgent need to find out where he belonged.

Josh started his new life living in Columbia with Jane Williams and her husband. For nearly 16 years, someone else had made every decision for him—what he could wear, when he could shower or shave, when he could eat. Then, suddenly, he could do what he wanted when he wanted. "I slept late because I could; no guard came to roust me out of bed. I could wander into the kitchen and make myself a sandwich when I wanted to or into the bathroom to shave or shower when I felt like it." But there was a darker side to his new status. "I couldn't live with Jane forever. Eventually, I'd have to find my own way in the world. Before prison, I lived with my dad or my mom or with families that took me in. When I did live on my own, it wasn't in a stable or healthy environment. I didn't really have a steady job." Then, as unpleasant as the experience was, the Missouri Department of Corrections clothed him and provided his room and board. Now, he would have to do all of that for himself.

Josh also had to adjust to dealing with people outside of prison. Prison culture is all about respect. There is a complicated set of unwritten rules on how you have to deal with other inmates. "You might look the wrong guy straight in the eye and get a knife between your ribs." At the same time, Josh had developed a reputation. "I gave respect, and I expected respect from other inmates in return." On one occasion, when he was reduced to tears, Jane asked Josh what was wrong.

> No one knows the rules. People, today, interact and speak with each other any way they want without fear of consequence. They think the worst thing that anyone can do to them for their actions and words is to not talk to them or walk away. It's disrespectful. It doesn't take into account that there are other consequences men and women are choosing not to inflict on each other every day, consciously and subconsciously. I'm a good man. I walk away because I choose to, not because I have to or because society's social rules say I have to. I'm capable of putting my hands on other people. Every time I choose to not do so is a victory. I've made that choice every time I've been confronted with disrespect, but it's still a choice. It isn't compulsory. I choose not to knock the teeth out of their mouths and break their kneecaps. I choose not to inflict physical violence. I choose to be peaceful, and they, the world, takes it for granted. Where I come from, not just from prison, but from Kankakee, men and women knew there were other consequences and appreciated when those weren't chosen. The world today is ignorant of those options and is never thankful or appreciative when those options aren't taken.

Josh later added in a conversation with me:

> I've been out for over 13 years now, and bullying, essentially what I was discussing with Jane when I was in tears following my release, is an

increasingly problematic issue and nearly always committed by people unaware of the potential for elevated consequences. Our nation's school shootings are one example. Where there's a school shooting, there's nearly always a kid that at least believes he was bullied.

How does a man go through what Josh went through and come out with that perspective? Maybe it's precisely what he went through that taught it to him.

Outside prison, he struggled to shake those rules, which weren't automatically applicable. "I had a tendency to be suspicious of the motives of strangers and to see a slight in ordinary conversations where none was intended. Gradually, and with some difficulty, I managed to overcome those tendencies."

Josh was self-conscious about being the man on the nightly news who had just been released from prison. It didn't help that Kenny Hulshof issued a press release calling the decision to free him a travesty of justice and, as a guest on KMOX radio in St. Louis, described him as a member of a violent street gang who failed a polygraph test. He felt compelled to tell people he met who he was—almost apologetically. Years later, he told me, "It took about two years before I was able to forget about what people thought of me." It helped that most people he encountered were firmly on his side.

Two months after his release, he spoke during Sunday services at Centenary United Methodist Church in Cape Girardeau. "I told the congregation of the importance of forgiveness and my struggle to forgive those who had wronged me." He also acknowledged that his prison experience had molded him in ways that were positive. "I wouldn't be the man I have become if it hadn't been for all the bad things that happened to me." The congregation was so moved that they raised more than $2,000 to help him get on his feet. On another occasion, he ate with a couple of friends at Lambert's Cafe in Springfield, Missouri. When they tried to pay, the waiter said, "It's on the house. The manager has been following your case in the news and recognized you."

Perhaps most significantly, Josh ran into Mike Spillane at a park in Columbia. He was with a girlfriend he had at the time. Spillane was there with his children. He came over and reminded Josh that he was the lawyer from the attorney general's office at his habeas hearing, the one who had tried to keep him in prison. Then he told Josh, "Your case is one of the few in my career that I didn't mind losing."

The Midwest Innocence Project held its benefit at a hotel in downtown St. Louis on April 22, 2009. John Grisham spoke. Chris Koster, the new Missouri Attorney General, served as auctioneer. Josh was one of several Missouri exonerees featured at the event. After the proceedings ended, we noticed that Josh had vanished. Someone said, "I think he went looking for John Grisham." Josh's entourage of lawyers and their family members went looking for him. We found him in the lounge of the hotel bar with Grisham, who was waiting for his plane to take him home and was patiently and graciously listening as Josh told him about his case. Grisham was noticeably astonished, and his mouth fell open several times as he listened to Josh's story. Josh ran into Grisham years later, and he remembered his name and what had happened to him.

Josh was invited to tell his story to college journalism students and at churches, sometimes for a small stipend. One of the first groups he addressed were employees at Bryan Cave's St. Louis office. He has a natural talent for public speaking, pouring forth his story without notes in cadences like a revival preacher. When a representative with CBS interested in pitching his story to *48 Hours Mystery* accompanied him to a presentation at the University of Missouri School of Journalism, she told him, "I've been in rooms with politicians, presidents, and Hollywood actors, and I've never seen anyone command a room like that." Everyone in the Bryan Cave audience was spellbound. Josh also has spoken to various legal organizations over the years for continuing legal education credit, usually with one or the other of his lawyers and several times with Judge Callahan. His presentation is rarely the same. Much of what I have learned about Josh that appears in this book I have heard during one of these presentations.

Josh joined the Williamses' church and got involved in its services and ministry. After four months, the Williamses arranged for him to take a job with Patrick McMurry, a painting and drywall contractor who was a friend. He earned enough to get his own apartment. Bryan Cave employees donated used furniture, clothes, appliances, a television, and a computer. He struggled with occasional bouts of depression brought on by a form of PTSD, the result of living under the stress of a false conviction and years of living in a violent environment. He persevered at the job until it appeared he would obtain some measure of financial independence from a federal civil rights suit.

We believed Josh had good grounds for such a suit against Scott County based on the sheriff's violation of his civil rights. We already had established in the habeas case that the sheriff's department withheld key exculpatory evidence, but there were a few other legal requirements to be met before Josh could collect any money.

Law enforcement satisfies its obligations of disclosure by providing exculpatory documents to prosecutors, who are responsible for disclosing to the defendant's counsel. If the sheriff's department gave the documents to Kenny Hulshof or Cristy Baker-Neel, Scott County couldn't be held liable for the prosecution's failure to disclose the documents to the defense, and prosecutors, along with the agency they represent, have absolute immunity from civil damages for failing to disclose exculpatory documents. We were confident we would be able to satisfy this requirement. The withheld documents were found in the sheriff's department files, but they weren't in the prosecution files produced in the habeas case by the attorney general's office.

Another prerequisite is that the withholding of documents had to be the act of the sheriff's department rather than the act of a renegade lower-level employee of the department. Because the sheriff led the investigation and Deputy Schiwitz was the lead deputy, the decision to withhold the documents was in effect the decision of the sheriff's department.

Finally, there had to be some level of malice underlying the defendants' actions. At a minimum, a reckless disregard for the rights of the plaintiff would suffice, but simple negligence would not. Intent is rarely easy to prove and must be inferred from the circumstances, but the circumstances in Josh's case strongly suggested reckless disregard at a minimum. It seemed unlikely that Bill Ferrell had forgotten about Lieutenant Wooten's interview report, which was clearly visible in the case file. And Mark Abbott's identification of Ray Ring as the man in the small white car at the Cut-Mart had made Ring a prime suspect. He was one of the few individuals interviewed in the case who were read a Miranda warning, and Ferrell participated in the Ring interview. The same is true of Brenda Schiwitz's notebooks. When Al Lowes asked her about interview notes in her deposition before Josh's trial, she claimed she had discarded them after they were typed on official department forms. The discrepancies between the notes and the official typed version were significant, suggesting the changes were deliberate. Ferrell and Schiwitz insisted they hadn't deliberately withheld these documents, but there was a good chance a jury hearing the facts would conclude otherwise.

Josh was reluctant to sue Scott County. He didn't think the citizens of the county—including Mischelle's family, Sheriff Walter, Branden Caid, and the other deputies who had testified for him at his habeas hearing—should have to pay for the actions of Bill Ferrell and Brenda Schiwitz. He didn't mind the possibility that Ferrell and Schiwitz would have to pay out of their own pockets. Ferrell was rumored to have plenty of money from his years as sheriff, in particular from his years of supplementing his income as the state auditor had noted. In addition, he and Brenda Schiwitz had gone into business together as Ferrell Court Services, a company that served all kinds of legal processes. But Josh didn't want the county to have to pay out of tax revenue. We asked Rick Walter if the county had insurance covering such things. "I don't know, but I can ask one of the county commissioners." The commissioner asked Walter, "Do you think Kezer's going to sue?" Walter answered, "Wouldn't you if it was your kid?" The commissioner answered, "I guess so." Then he told Walter, "We have two policies that might apply." That solved Josh's dilemma and frankly, a dilemma we had at Bryan Cave. We reviewed the policies, decided they did apply, and filed suit on Josh's behalf against Bill Ferrell, Brenda Schiwitz, and Scott County in August 2009.

There wasn't much need for discovery in the case. We had the documents we needed before we filed. The same was true of depositions of the key players except for the two prosecutors. We were ready for trial when Hulshof and Baker-Neel both testified in depositions that they hadn't seen the Wooten report and the Schiwitz notebooks and would have produced them to the defense if they had. Whether it was true or not, we had that one missing fact pinned down.

In the summer of 2010, all of the parties participated in mediation. One of the lawyers I knew representing one of the insurance companies for Scott County told me privately, "My client has low policy limits and a small part of the potential liability, but I hope Josh gets lots of money." Both of the individual defendants wanted the case to settle, and the only issue was how much Scott County's insurance companies would be willing to pay. We were still far apart at the end of the day, and the case didn't settle at the mediation. During the mediation, Schiwitz had become visibly upset and tearfully asked for Josh's forgiveness. After some thought, he agreed to speak with her. As Josh was politely speaking with Schiwitz and allowing her the opportunity to apologize, I saw Bill Ferrell approaching Josh and put my hand on Josh's shoulder, not sure how he would react. Josh had been shaking Schiwitz's hand when Ferrell approached. Before Josh could retract his hand, Ferrell extended his hand into Josh's and said something like, "I'm sorry this happened to you. Had I known the things we know now, I would have done things differently. I'm not the devil. I just want you to know that." I could feel the tension in Josh's shoulder. But Josh mumbled something and shook hands, and I let go of his shoulder, glad that Josh hadn't done anything rash. Josh told me later, "I wanted to break his hand and his jaw, but thought better of it.

For a second, I thought I had 16 years of credit and the state owed me as much, but I knew better."

Josh continues to blame Ferrell for what happened to him. He is convinced that even after Ferrell knew that he was innocent, Ferrell did everything in his power to send him to prison. That is not an unreasonable belief. When the snitches started recanting, he found two more. He hid exculpatory evidence (the Wooten report and the account of his interview with the inmate who said Josh always maintained his innocence). He may have coached Chantelle Crider to lie about Josh's presence at the Halloween party. She testified that the Abbott twins were at the party, too, but what if he had coached Chantelle not to mention that?

Eventually, the insurance company agreed to pay $4,000,000, which left Josh with a little more than $2,700,000 after deducting Bryan Cave's one-third share. After interviewing more than 20 candidates, Josh invested the money from the settlement with a broker and advisor, Jane Williams's nephew David Richmond, of Heritage Investments. Soon after the settlement, he paid cash for a house in a Columbia subdivision and a car. Otherwise, he lives simply, benefiting from the rising stock markets but being careful to stay within a budget his financial adviser says he can afford.[2]

Since his release, Josh has lived in Columbia, Missouri. Kenny Hulshof lives in Columbia too. Josh has said to me, "I've had people offer to show me where he lives. I haven't taken them up on their offer." In 2013, a friend of Josh, a Marine, invited him to attend Midnight Mass on Christmas Eve with his family and friends. Josh isn't Catholic; he's an evangelical Christian. He tried to politely decline, but his friend persisted until Josh finally accepted. When the two men walked into the church, Josh noticed Kenny Hulshof. His friend said, "Is that going to be a problem?" Josh responded, "I don't know. I haven't seen the man in person since my 1994 trial."

The friend's family were seated in the row of seats directly behind Kenny Hulshof's family and friends. Josh sat five feet away from Hulshof at his trial and could have attacked him then because he wasn't handcuffed or shackled during his trial. "There was nothing between us but air and opportunity." Now, Josh and Hulshof were no more than five feet apart again, this time in a church, with nearly two decades of history between them. "I had no idea he would be at the same midnight Christmas celebration or that the friend I was going with had planned our seats in the area directly behind Kenny Hulshof and his family." Josh's friend had crossed a boundary, but Josh didn't react.

I introduced myself to my friend's family and friends. Then I sat next to my friend, and prayed. I don't believe Kenny knew I was there at the time. When the service started, we sang Christmas music and familiar hymns. I found myself singing familiar words of faith I had sung before but never before with my prosecutor playing the drums in the group accompanying the singing. Then the priest asked everyone to stand and turn and greet each other, and Hulshof and his family turned around and extended a hand to my friend's family and friends. I was ignored as if I wasn't there. But in fairness, I didn't extend my hand either. When the service resumed, I watched Kenny interact with his daughter. I wanted God to show me my enemy's humanity and to show me someone he had sent his son to die and resurrect for as much as myself. In prison, I'd seen vile men saved and forgiven. I needed to see Kenny and his family as saved and forgiven. I needed God's eyes to see in Kenny what I hadn't seen before. I was raised in the church to never take communion with bitterness or rage in my heart, to wrestle with whatever I had to wrestle with, to essentially let go and to lay everything at the foot of the cross of Christ before I took part in the remembrance of the body and blood of our Lord and Savior Jesus Christ. Or to at least take what I was aware of to the foot of the cross. I eventually bowed my head, clasped my hands together, and asked God to take the anger from my heart. I prayed for Kenny and his family. I laid myself bare before God as led to in James 4:10.

While Josh prayed, his friend saw him shaking and asked if he was alright.

I told him to mind his own business. He told me to quit shaking, and again, I told him to mind his own business. I was literally in physical pain, and it hurt to be that close. I was shaking in inner turmoil, but I worked through some things and ultimately it was good. I didn't talk to him. I just worked through my own anger. I hadn't realized I was still angry at Kenny. I thought I had given it up in prison, but I discovered that I hadn't let it all go. I wrestled with God until my anger and hurt were disjointed and let the rage I had left in me go. We went on to take communion. Following communion, when I walked back to my seat, I walked directly past Kenny. I briefly thought about offering him my hand, but thought better of it. I was less than one foot from him at this point. He was with his family, and I didn't want to make a scene.

After his release, Josh reconnected with his father. Josh visited him in Kankakee when he could manage it. On his father's 60th birthday, Josh visited Kankakee. "I got to see my dad with his sisters, one of which was recovering from cancer treatment. For the first time, I met his older brother Lee. We went to see *Grown Ups* at the theater and laughed. We shot pool and ate steaks. We went on the Kankakee River on my dad's boat. We got a rope and tube and acted like idiots together. God heard my cry to let my father live in 2005." Josh remembers Charlie saying, "It's like everything is brand new." It was on one of those trips that the mention of his Vietnam service brought his father to tears. Having overcome his alcoholism, he was a different person. "I'm sorry. I know I wasn't a perfect father. I'm proud of the man you've become." Josh responded, "That's the past, Dad. We can focus on the present. I love you." Charles Edward Kezer died on March 5, 2012, with Josh at his bedside.

Josh's mother was diagnosed with a combination of PTSD, clinical depression, and mild alcoholic dementia and had become physically disabled. Josh found a nursing home for her near his house. He frequently brought her home for the day, often for as long as a week. "She loved spending time with my adopted pit bull Titan, her 'grand dog' as she called him."[2] She was still as feisty as ever, but the two of them had a relationship far different from the one they had when he was a teenager. He was the one taking care of her.

Josh has explained to me what his mother went through as a result of his wrongful conviction. He gets emotional when discussing it.

> She was alone in the world for the years I was in prison. She couldn't talk to counselors and therapists. No one wanted to hear her side. They told her to accept that her son was a killer, which she couldn't do. She knew better. So they medicated her with pills, and she medicated herself with alcohol. On more than one occasion, she attempted suicide. Once, she was discovered in her apartment after having ingested significant amounts of Drano and was rushed to the hospital to get her stomach pumped.

One night, she parked her car and drank vodka until she passed out. She was awakened by a police officer knocking on her car window. The officer told her to move her car. She had backed up only five feet, and the officer immediately put his lights on to stop her and give her a DWI. Josh believes the officer deliberately got her to move because DWI is a moving violation and sitting in a car passed out is not. "She was sent to the Women's Eastern Reception, Diagnostic and Correctional Center in Vandalia, Missouri, for the DWI. We corresponded while she was in prison. Eventually, she got out, joined a church in Cape Girardeau that accepted her side of the story, and stayed out."

Jane Williams moved her to Columbia to be near Josh after she was released from prison and introduced her to Joe Lemaster, a doctor who had often visited Josh in prison. He promptly took her off most of her meds, but it was too late to help his mother's mental condition. As Josh explained:

> By the time of my release, the emotional damage Ferrell and Hulshof had done had changed her beyond recognition. At first, we tried home care, but it wasn't long before I had to put her in a nursing home. She hated it at first but eventually understood why it was necessary. I did my best to make her comfortable. I got her nice furniture, a padded rocking chair, a big screen television, whatever clothes she wanted, and what seemed like thousands of books. Every Christmas, birthday, and Mother's Day, we went to Barnes & Noble, and I bought her hundreds of dollars in books. She would read one or two a week. She loved crossword puzzles and true crime. Her favorite television show was *Law & Order*. She loved silly things and coffee, so I once got her a coffee cup shaped like a gun that said Bitch Better Have My Coffee. She had a great sense of humor. I used to open her door at the nursing home and yell "HEY MOM" and watch her jump. I snuck up on her regularly when we were at Barnes & Noble shopping and would scare her while she was reading the inside jacket of some new creepy true crime book. The number of times I got a "DAAAHHH!" followed by an "I love you, son, but sometimes, I fucking hate you!" is priceless. That always made both of us laugh. I often called her crusty, and she called me buddy. "Why I got to be crusty?" "I don't know, Mom. Take it up with God." We laughed a lot.

During the coronavirus pandemic, Josh couldn't visit his mother, but they talked through the glass door of one of the entrances. In one of those visits, his mother pretended to be panicking about being held in quarantine. Her sense of humor was infectious. His mother had a series of medical problems toward the end of her life. Sadly, on October 22, 2020, Bessie Joan Kezer died from COVID-19, with Josh at her bedside. Given the severity of COVID, the doctors and nurses wanted Josh to move aside when they removed her breathing tube. When breathing tubes are pulled from COVID patients on life support, excessive amounts of spores are known to release in the air. He refused. "She was my mother. COVID wasn't my first concern. My mother was. She deserved having her son by her side when she passed. I held her hand. I felt the moment she passed. It was surreal. I remember looking at her one moment and recognizing my mother and the next not recognizing her. Her corpse wasn't her."

I attended a funeral service for her at a Pentecostal Chapel in a tiny village in Southeast Missouri, not far from Benton. Rick Walter was there. Josh's prison pastor, James Jackson, someone he is still very close to, was there and officiated the funeral with his wife.

A year to the day after Joni Kezer's COVID-19 death, Kenny Hulshof addressed a political science class on governance in America at Oklahoma City University. Josh was offended that it happened on that date. As he put it, "In his presentation, he lauded his service in Congress between 1997 and 2009, his political affiliation as a Republican, and his career as a prosecutor. He went on to brag about prosecuting three dozen murder cases. Finally, he quoted Ronald Reagan, 'We have to listen to one another.'"

Kenny Hulshof is currently listed as partner and chairman of Kit Bond Strategies Group. To quote his bio on the KBS website:

Kenny serves on the board of directors of the Congressional Sports for Charity, the group which organizes the annual Congressional Baseball Game for Charity at Nationals Park in Washington, D.C. He is a member of Missouri Main Street Connection, an organization which enhances historic downtown business districts in Missouri. And, he is a founding member of the Historic Downtown Charleston (MO) Board of Directors. Kenny has been awarded The Golden Plow Award, from American Farm Bureau Foundation, the Geyer Public Service Award from the MU Alumni Association, and the Lon O. Hocker Award for Trial Advocacy from the Missouri Bar. Kenny splits his time between Washington, D.C., and Columbia, Missouri. He owns and operates his family farm in southeast Missouri, and is also an avid cyclist, musician, and historic preservationist.

Having discovered this bio recently, Josh said to me:

Notice that his bio leaves out how he attempted to put me on death row for a murder he knew I didn't commit, endorsed obvious lies, and hasn't apologized. I wonder how Hulshof's current colleagues and clients would feel about him if they discovered the truth about the man they trust. I don't harbor anger for Hulshof, but I don't believe he should be "eulogized." Given the number of cases Hulshof has had overturned and the number of times he's been reprimanded for prosecutorial misconduct, I don't believe he should be allowed to possess a law license or serve in government.

Josh believes that:

Hulshof has betrayed victims and decimated innocent lives for political and personal gain and should face "real world consequences." Hulshof can't be prosecuted for his actions. He can't be sued. Where is his justice? Shouldn't it at least be in his career and reputation? Shouldn't he at least be reprimanded instead of rewarded? He shouldn't be paraded about in our nation's capital, states, or schools as an example of the American way or a beacon of justice. He should serve as an exemplar of what an ethical practice of law in America shouldn't resemble, and as a warning to prospective prosecutors, attorneys, and elected officials looking to serve our communities and country. I've forgiven him, but under threat of repetition, we as a nation cannot afford to whitewash and forget his inhumane misconduct.[3]

CBS's *48 Hours Mystery* did a segment presented by Erin Moriarty on Mischelle's murder and Josh's exoneration. First aired in March 2010, it was titled "The Girl Who Knew Too Much." The theme suggested by the title was that Mischelle knew something about some illegal activity. There was a lot of speculation among drug users and dealers in Southeast Missouri that Mischelle was somehow making things difficult for someone in the drug business. But there was no evidence in the episode to back up any of that speculation or to tie Mischelle to anyone in the drug trade. Whatever the title was meant to convey, it didn't make the cut.

Branden Caid's testimony at Josh's hearing that Leon Lamb's DNA was on Mischelle's fingernail clippings resulted in a lot of internet speculation that Lamb was the murderer. In an interview included in the episode of *48 Hours Mystery*, he addressed the issue, saying he and Mischelle were "passionate people" and guessed that she had "scratched him during sex" when she stopped at his house the night she was murdered. Lamb assumed his DNA was transferred by scratching, but there is another possible explanation. DNA in fluids such as semen and saliva can be deposited under a sexual partner's fingernails during sex, and sexually active couples frequently have each other's DNA under their fingernails. Josh doesn't believe Lamb murdered Mischelle. Later, these facts would play an important part in another innocence case that Josh brought to Bryan Cave.

On the Case with Paula Zahn, a true crime series on cable TV, was the second national program to cover Josh's case. That segment, titled "The Long Road Home," was shown a few months after the *48 Hours Mystery* segment. The producers invited Josh to travel to New York for a taping of his interview and surprised him with the news that Chantelle Crider was there too. "I was angry and felt manipulated. In the heat of the moment, I agreed to go ahead with the plan, but I'm glad I did. Zahn and the *On the Case* production crew proved respectful and pleasant to work with." Chantelle entered the set and tearfully apologized. Josh was gracious but noncommittal. "I still suspected that her identification of me at my trial was more than just a mistake."

This national publicity led to interest in Josh's story in Hollywood. He turned down a serious offer to have a movie made of his experience that Charlie Weiss and I helped negotiate. The movie would have had a Christian theme, but Josh was concerned about the way his parents and other family members might be portrayed if he gave up creative control, as the movie deal would have required. Josh is protective of his parents. He didn't believe the money and potential fame he may have amassed by making a film were worth, as he described it, "potentially throwing Charlie and Joni under anyone's bus."

Josh became involved with various innocence groups, attending conventions and supporting individuals he believed to be innocent. He has tried to use his fame as an exoneree to publicize selected innocence cases in Missouri. At the same time, he isn't naive and recognizes that many inmates who protest their innocence are lying. "Some men I knew personally in prison have disappointed me. When I dug deeper into the facts of their cases, I decided they probably were guilty."

Among those Josh tried to help was Ryan Ferguson—one of the inmates he told reporters was innocent as he stood outside the prison entrance, without a coat in the February cold. Ferguson was convicted, along with a friend, Charles Erickson, of the November 1, 2001, murder of Kent Heitholt, the sports editor of the *Columbia Daily Tribune*. Josh became involved in the effort to free Ferguson, attending court hearings and speaking to media outlets and journalists whenever he could. He brought him up in every speaking engagement in the hope of generating more attention. The Cole County Circuit Court granted a hearing but denied the petition in October 2012. The Court of Appeals in Kansas City disagreed with the trial court and granted Ferguson's habeas petition on November 5, 2013. It found that Ferguson hadn't received a fair trial because the prosecution failed to disclose that an eyewitness to the murder had seen a newspaper clipping with Ferguson's picture. The county prosecutor decided not to retry Ferguson.

In December 2011, Josh received an email from Diane Kelly, the daughter of Donald Nash, another Missouri inmate who consistently insisted he was innocent. She found him while she was researching innocence cases and asked for his help in finding a lawyer to take her father's case. Josh contacted his lawyers at Bryan Cave. We looked at the evidence against Nash and decided to represent him. Nash was convicted in 2009 of the 1982 murder of his live-in girlfriend, Judy Spencer. She had been strangled with her own shoelace and shot in the neck postmortem with a shotgun. Her partially nude body was discovered in an old outhouse foundation behind an abandoned one-room schoolhouse. As the boyfriend, Nash was automatically a suspect from the beginning, but he was never the leading suspect. He wasn't charged until 2008, when his DNA was discovered on clippings of Spencer's fingernails. As with Mischelle Lawless and Leon Lamb, the presence of a sexual partner's DNA under a murder victim's fingernails is essentially meaningless. But the State's DNA expert testified at Nash's trial that the victim's act of washing her hair before going out drinking alone the night she was murdered would have had a "great effect" on Nash's DNA present from cohabitation. The assistant attorney general trying the case told the jury in the closing argument that all of Nash's DNA would have been removed. When Nash's lawyer objected to the misstatement, the judge overruled it. The jury convicted Nash of first-degree murder at the age of 66, and he was sentenced to life without parole for 60 years.

During the State's habeas corpus proceedings, I took the deposition of the State's trial expert and interrogated her again at the habeas hearing. In the deposition, she changed her trial opinion from "great effect" to "some effect" and admitted at the hearing that both opinions were just speculation. Despite this new evidence, the trial court denied Nash's petition. Eventually, we reached the Missouri Supreme Court, which appointed a retired judge, Richard Zerr, as a special master to review the evidence and recommend how it should decide. The special master held a hearing in early March 2020. Josh spoke to a number of sheriff's deputies and jail guards who had heard the three days of testimony. He told me all of them were convinced that Nash was innocent.

Judge Zerr issued a lengthy report in early June concluding that Nash was actually innocent and that his trial was unfair because, among other things, his conviction was based on scientific speculation that should have been excluded. On July 3, 2020, the Missouri Supreme Court adopted Judge Zerr's findings and entered an order that Nash was actually innocent. Considering the COVID-19 outbreak at the prison where Nash was being held and his age and poor health, the Supreme Court ordered Nash to be immediately released on bond and gave the local prosecutor 30 days to decide whether to retry him. He was released with some restrictions but on his own recognizance on July 4.

Still, the local prosecutor decided to retry Nash. Ironically, the Missouri Supreme Court appointed retired judge Richard Callahan for the retrial. The attorney general's office decided to have the victim's shoelace that was used to strangle her tested again for male DNA because DNA testing techniques had advanced considerably since Nash's trial. There were two partial male DNA profiles on the shoelace, but neither one matched Nash's DNA. The local prosecutor dismissed the case on October 9, 2020.[4]

A number of key people in Josh's case have contacted him on social media. One of these is Amanda Drury, his old girlfriend. Amanda and Amanda's mother, Linda Proctor, have told Josh that Amanda was threatened by Brenda Schiwitz, Bill Ferrell, and Amanda's grandfather, Glenn Proctor, and forced to falsify statements and testify against Josh or face being charged with complicity in Mischelle's murder and that after she testified, she suffered a mental breakdown. Josh has compassion for Amanda. "She was a kid. She was victimized."

Melissa Elliot and her mother were among those mentioned in investigative files as having claimed seeing Josh at Mischelle's funeral. Both told Josh in 2019 that they hadn't claimed they saw Josh. This new information calls into question all the documented reports of these sightings. Even Mark Abbott contacted Josh by email from federal prison. He told Josh he had nothing to do with Mischelle's murder. When Josh made it clear that he didn't believe him, Abbott said of Mischelle, "She could of been a horror [*sic*], she could of stole money from old people, she could of been a crack horror, but I don't know and I care less more and more every day." Abbott also said, "The sad part is this. i couldn't tell you what that girl looked like a week later." Was that an admission he did know Mischelle? Was that an admission of perjury in Josh's 1994 trial?

Josh also got involved in the effort to save Ricky Clay, the death-row inmate who testified that Mark Abbott had told him the man he identified as Josh was Mexican. Clay was convicted as the result of another Kenny Hulshof prosecution. Early in 2011, Josh attempting to appear at a rally in Jefferson City the week before the date scheduled for Clay's execution and spoke on Clay's behalf. He also donated $10,000 to Clay's defense fund. Kevin Williams was there too. He approached Josh, attempting to appear friendly and sympathetic about what Josh had gone through, and told him, "I wasn't involved in the Lawless girl's murder. Those witnesses at your hearing who said that were wrong." Josh wasn't convinced. He told Kevin he believes Kevin and Mark Abbott killed Mischelle.

After the rally, Josh asked me to do something to help Clay. Clay was scheduled to be executed early the following week. The only thing that could be done on such short notice was to fax a letter to the governor, Hulshof's former boss, Jay Nixon, whose office had prosecuted Josh when he was attorney general. I wrote Nixon a letter asking him to commute Clay's sentence to life without parole. I mentioned that Clay had been instrumental in obtaining Josh's exoneration. I explained that I didn't know if Clay was guilty or innocent but understood there were indications he might not have been the killer. "Most importantly, however, it bothers me that the victim's wife, who testified that she hired Clay to kill her husband, received a 15-year sentence in exchange for her testimony against Clay, while Clay was sentenced to death." Nixon had a reputation as a law-and-order Democrat in a law-and-order state who hadn't previously granted a clemency petition for any condemned inmate, so I had little hope of changing his mind.

The following Tuesday, January 11, 2011, Nixon commuted Clay's sentence to life without parole. The decision surprised and puzzled the media, which referred to it as "out of character" for Nixon and said it "was not adequately explained." In his official announcement, Nixon said that Clay's "involvement in this crime is clear" and "the evidence clearly supports the jury's verdict of murder in the first degree." He continued by saying, "Having looked at this matter in its entirety and after significant thought and counsel, I have concluded, however, to exercise my constitutional authority and commute Richard Clay's sentence to life without the possibility of parole." He said several considerations went into the decision, including "the involvement of other people in the murder" and what he called "some issues" in the case against Clay.

Josh has been traveling regularly to Thailand to study Muay Thai, a form of martial arts that originated there. On one of these trips, he agreed to a match even though he wasn't feeling well and suffered a broken nose, which required surgery when he returned home. He recovered and went back to Thailand. He has been spending as much as five months at a time in a relatively remote part of Thailand. "I find the Thai people to be more welcoming and less complicated than Americans," he says. "The Buddhist majority live side by side with minority Muslims and Christians, and for the most part, everyone gets along."

Josh lives simply in Thailand. The cost of food and lodging is a fraction of what it is at home in Columbia. "I eat Thai food and exercise regularly. I lost almost 30 pounds during my first stay." He had the Latin King tattoo on his back covered over during a couple of trips to Thailand, choosing their traditional bamboo hand-poking technique. His fondness for Thailand doesn't necessarily extend to every aspect. He is horrified by the sex trafficking of children. "It's not unusual in certain resort areas to see middle-aged and older men walking arm in arm with underage Thai girls." Seeing this in Thailand (and the Philippines), Josh became an advocate for anti-trafficking.

On a 2019 trip to Thailand, Josh traveled to nearby Vietnam. He wanted to see Cu Chi, one of the places where his father had been stationed during the Vietnam War. One of the key features of the region is the tunnels in which Viet Cong and North Vietnamese soldiers hid from US troops.

> I wasn't prepared for what I saw or what I felt. For the first time in my life I understood his drug use, alcoholism, violent outbursts when I was young, and his trauma. I understood his reluctance to talk about it with me. I saw the weapons of guerilla warfare. I stood where he served, took in the landscape and reality, and imagined what he witnessed and survived. It was worse than what I had seen in movies. And then I thought about what he gave of himself in Cu Chi for his country.

Josh still sees Jane Williams from time to time even though he attends a different church. "The parishioners at the new church force me to engage with them." Jane's eyesight has always been a problem, and now she is totally blind. Despite that, in September 2018 she rappelled 140 feet down the face of the Tiger Hotel in Columbia as part of a fundraising event for Love, Inc. The title of the event was "Over the Edge," and each of a hundred plus "edgers" had to raise at least $1,000 from friends and relatives to participate. In a radio interview before the event, Jane showed a spark of wry humor when she said she has always been afraid of heights if she looked down but figured she wouldn't have that problem anymore.

Personal relationships with women have not worked out well for Josh so far. Despite his exoneration, a Google search reveals he was once convicted in the murder of a woman. Unfortunately, something like that isn't easy to shake off or live with even after an exhaustive innocence ruling.

As he told *Vox* magazine in an April 16, 2016, interview, "Relationships are very difficult for me. . . . I don't understand the world around me anymore." He observed that with texting on smartphones and emails over the internet, "People don't speak to each other anymore, and it's much easier for them to be rude to each other." In early 2019, Josh told the hosts of a podcast on *Crime Junkie* that his religious faith had prevented him from letting his anger about the injustice he had suffered overcome him while he was still in prison. He said he hates to think about the "monster I could have become" if he hadn't curbed that anger, "a monster like the violent criminals who surrounded me." He went on to say, "Talking about forgiveness is easy; actually forgiving is not."

So far, Josh hasn't taken Judge Callahan's advice about going to college. All the same, his personal collection of books is eclectic and extensive. I know that because he has recommended books to me. He's explained his reason for forgoing attending college at the moment. "I have living to do. I want to experience life beyond the cells and compounds I've lived in. I'll get to that when that's done. Until then, I'll read, live, and love. And I imagine I'll continue those when I finally decide to spend my days cooped up in a classroom." He occasionally takes online courses, which allow him to live life on his terms. Otherwise, Josh has kept busy with his activism on behalf of prisoners he believes are innocent and women and young girls abused and exploited by sex traffickers. I became close to Josh and consider him a friend. I treat him like a son, taking him along to dinners with my children and grandchildren. He has told me he is especially appreciative of being treated like one of the family.

Josh still struggles occasionally with the post-traumatic effects of his false imprisonment, but he has loosened up over the years. He bought a new truck and is looking into buying a motorcycle. He's been skydiving, white-water rafting, and diving with sharks. He's surfed in Hawaii; island hopped and served as a youth pastor in the Philippines; and studied martial arts in Thailand, the Philippines, and Vietnam. He attends Chicago Cubs and Bears games when he can. He enjoys playing pool. One of his prized possessions is his Brunswick billiards table. He's gotten into art and has become particularly interested in Vincent van Gogh, Michelangelo's *Pietà*, and John Martin's *Sadak in Search of the Waters of Oblivion*. Some of his favorite books have been authored by C. S. Lewis, Mary Shelley, Alexander Dumas, and Tolstoy.

Lately, Josh has been giving fairly extensive interviews to Bob Miller on *The Lawless Files* podcast and has assisted with this book. The podcast is available on Spotify. There are occasional contradictions in the podcast with this book but nothing significant. The more Josh thinks about his past, the more he remembers. It's painful for him. He doesn't enjoy talking about his past and his case but finds it difficult to stop until, as he's put it, "Mischelle gets the justice she deserves."

21

RICK WALTER

For Rick Walter and Branden Caid, the exoneration of Josh Kezer didn't mean the end of the search for Mischelle's killer. It was the beginning of an extraordinary effort, especially for a sheriff's department in a small, rural county with limited financial resources.

Walter heard about the "Crime Farm" from a *48 Hours Mystery* episode involving exoneration of a convicted murderer by touch DNA. It was a television show he rarely had time to watch. Recognizing the similarities to Mischelle's murder, he called Branden Caid and said, "I just saw this TV program that gave me a great idea about the Lawless case." Caid happened to be watching the same program and had the same thought. The next week, Walter contacted Richard and Selma Eikelenboom. They are the founders of Independent Forensic Services, originally located on the couple's rural property in the Netherlands but since 2011, headquartered in a Denver, Colorado, suburb. Richard Eikelenboom has been credited with developing a method of obtaining "touch DNA" from items such as articles of clothing. This method broadens the sources of forensic DNA evidence beyond that left by acts of sexual assault or deposited under fingernails by defensive scratching. Walter contacted Independent Forensic Services and asked the Eikelenbooms to look into the Lawless case.

Mischelle's friends and family held fundraisers to help pay for the analysis, starting with a car wash and a bake sale in August 2009. By October of that year, they had turned over almost $7,000 to the Scott County treasury. Later in 2009, Walter and Caid hand carried Mischelle's clothing to the Crime Farm.

Samples were taken from areas on the sweatshirt where the killer might have grabbed Mischelle. The analysis yielded a mixture of three DNA profiles and Mischelle's. One of those profiles was a match with that of Mark Abbott and his identical twin on all but one allele. Using three comparisons, Eikelenboom calculated the probability of the profile's nearly matching one of the Abbott twin's: (1) with all four donors; (2) with Mischelle, the Abbott twins, and one unknown donor; and (3) with just Mischelle and the Abbott twins. The probabilities in these comparisons ranged between roughly 12 million and 12 trillion times more likely that the person was an Abbott twin than that the person wasn't.[1]

The touch DNA on Mischelle's sweatshirt that matched the Abbotts' seemed consistent with Mark Abbott's story that he lifted Mischelle up from the seat of her car when he found her. But Mark Abbott said he had lifted Mischelle by the left shoulder, and the Abbott touch DNA was on her right side. More significantly, the Abbott DNA was on the inside of Mischelle's right arm. That location was more consistent with someone grabbing her roughly around the arm than lifting her by the shoulders.

Walter hired two reconstruction experts to test the credibility of Mark Abbott's claim that he had reached through the partially open driver's-side window of Mischelle's car and lifted her body. James Kent concluded from the data that he had gathered that it would have been impossible for Abbott to have done what he claimed. Walter also questioned whether Mischelle's body had been moved at all after it had fallen onto the seat with the third shot. The other expert, Scott Liscio, used young women approximately Mischelle's height and weight to test Walter's theory, and Walter believes the results tended to confirm his suspicion.

★ ★ ★

In 2010, Sheriff Walter contacted John Bond, PhD, a forensic scientist in the UK who had developed a technique for finding otherwise invisible fingerprints on metal surfaces, such as shell casings. Eventually, Walter obtained funding for the project and asked Bond to test the shell casings found in Mischelle's car. Bond's technique is based on the fact that fingerprint sweat changes the surface properties of the metal casing and is then fused onto the surface by the heat of the explosion that occurs when the gun is fired. The curved image that appears on the shell is then photographed with a digital camera and flattened using special software. Because the surface of the shell casing is round, the print may be only partial. Depending on how much detail appears, a law enforcement agency can either comparehe print manually to prints of known suspects or submit the print to a law enforcement database.

Of course, a good result would identify the person who had loaded the gun but not necessarily the person who had fired the gun, for example, if the gun had been stolen in a burglary. On the other hand, finding a print of someone connected with an existing suspect could be highly significant. The result wasn't detailed enough for submission to a database, but it was good enough for manual comparison. The sheriff's department has manually compared the print from the shell casing with prints on file of possible suspects, so far without results.

Walter won the Democratic primary in August 2012 with nearly 80 percent of the vote and was re-elected as a Democrat easily in the November general election. His opponent in the general election, as in 2008, was Wes Drury. It was rumored again that Drury had the backing of former Sheriff Ferrell.

In October 2013, Walter had Mischelle's body exhumed, after obtaining permission from her family and a court order, to test her body for DNA left by the killer. He had noticed references in the autopsy report to non-lethal wounds on Mischelle's arms. Nothing had been done at the time to preserve evidence from those wounds. The chances of finding DNA nearly 21 years after the murder would depend on the condition of the body. A scientist from Independent Forensic Services attended the exhumation and under the supervision of the county coroner, took 45 samples from various parts of the body. The body was in good condition, which was cause for optimism, but the county coroner happened to mention that he cleaned the wound and filled it with a waxy substance when he embalmed the body. The analysis took several months, but it yielded no usable results.

★ ★ ★

The investigation into Mischelle's murder continued in spite of occasionally disappointing outcomes, slowly making progress. Branden Caid felt the investigation would benefit from a new set of eyes. Walter agreed and hired Darren Sides as a deputy to continue the effort to find Mischelle's killer. As Sides dug into the case, new evidence began to emerge.

At the time of Josh's murder trial in 1994 and even in 2008 at the time of Josh's habeas proceedings, Kevin Williams had an alibi for the night of the murder. His wife, Terri, said he was with her at his boss's holiday party until early the next morning. The two divorced not long after Josh was exonerated, and Terri's support for that alibi began to unravel. At first, she said Kevin wasn't with her the whole time and may have left for a while at some point in the evening. That account evolved over additional interviews, and by the latter part of 2016, she told Sides, "Kevin and his girlfriend and Mark left the party right after Mark arrived, and Kevin didn't come back. Kevin's mother drove me and my son home, and I don't know when Kevin got home." Williams coached her to lie in her deposition in Josh's habeas case to give him an alibi for the entire night. "I did what I was told because I'm afraid of him." In her opinion, "Kevin knows who killed Mischelle if he didn't kill her himself."

In 2018, Terri reached out to Josh to apologize and ask for his forgiveness. "She didn't equivocate or offer excuses. She just wanted to apologize, explain herself, and be forgiven. The more I spoke with her, the more I understood her." Terri sent Josh this 2022 message:

> I'm so sorry that I let Kevin Williams manipulate me into believing that he never left the party. I was 13 when he groomed and raped me. Kevin was 19. He knew what to say and how to say it to draw me in. He took me in his truck to a dirt road and raped me. It was my first time being with anyone. Kevin Williams is a predator and knows how to groom underage girls. He's a monster.

After Kevin and Terri separated, Kevin left an angry message for Terri on an answering machine at Terri's mother's house. First, he ranted about Terri. Then, he started yelling about Walter, threatening to "shoot him between the eyes as he walks out his front door." Terri's mother gave the recording to Walter. When Williams was arrested in March 2010 for beating his 17-year-old son, Walter played the recording for him. At first, Williams said he didn't really mean it. Walter goaded him, saying, "You know you would kill me if you got the chance." That angered Williams, and he leaned forward, clenched his fist, and yelled, "You're goddamn right." Walter responded, "See, don't you feel better now that you admitted it?"

When Williams grew calmer, Walter asked him why former Sheriff Ferrell would be meeting with a convicted drug dealer. Williams admitted he met with Ferrell and accused Walter of knowing what they discussed by listening to their phone conversations, which wasn't true. Eventually, Williams calmed down and said he would like to talk some more and maybe give Walter some information. Later, Walter called Williams and tried to arrange another meeting, but Williams had changed his mind. Terri Williams was at the funeral service for Josh's mother.

In 2015, Dallas Butler was an employee at the state prison in Charleston. On the morning of November 8, 1992, he left a bar on Broadway in Cape Girardeau at about 12:40 a.m. and rode his motorcycle down I-55 to the southbound Benton exit. He crossed over the interstate on Missouri 77 and stopped at the northbound exit when he saw a car sitting at the top of the exit ramp. In 2015, he estimated he would have arrived there about

1:00 or 1:15, and that is consistent with the distance from downtown Cape Girardeau to Benton. In the headlights of his motorcycle, he could clearly see that the car was red and that a small female was sitting in the driver's seat with her head on the steering wheel. Her hands also were on the wheel but weren't gripping it. She didn't speak or move from that position while he was there. A man was standing next to her outside the car. Butler described him in 2015 as white, in his late 20s or early 30s, about 5 feet 11 inches tall and 200 pounds, with red or reddish brown hair that was short around the ears and long in the back. He was wearing light blue jeans, a red ball cap, and possibly a sleeveless shirt. There was a blue pickup, possibly a Ford F-150, parked across the exit ramp with its lights shining toward the red car. Butler asked, "Do you need any help?" Neither the man nor the girl responded, so he asked again. The man said, "No, I've got this," and waved him away. The man obviously didn't want him there, and Butler rode away down state highway 77 toward home.

The next day Butler saw news reports of the murder and told his mother he may have seen the victim. He went to the sheriff's department and told a woman at the "window" that he may have seen a suspect in the Lawless murder. The woman took his name and number and said someone would call him, but no one ever did. After Josh was arrested, Butler called the sheriff's department and asked to speak to someone about the murder, to give information he had seen someone else who didn't look like Josh. He gave his name and number, but again no one called him. Finally, Deputy Sides interviewed him in 2015. Sides showed him two three-picture photo lineups. The first contained a picture of Mark Abbott, and Butler said he didn't see anyone in that lineup who looked like the man he saw in 1992. The second photo lineup contained a picture of Kevin Williams, and he picked that photo almost immediately. Later, Walter had another police agency repeat the process with a younger photo of Williams, and that photo lineup produced the same result.

After his interview with Sides, Butler talked to a probation and parole officer he knew about his experience the night of the murder. Shortly after that conversation, a coworker at the prison who was a cousin of Kevin Williams approached him and asked what he had seen. Then a woman named Gayla Mooney showed Butler a picture of Kevin Williams and asked him if it looked like the man he had seen at the Benton exit. He said it did. Gayla Mooney was one of Kevin Williams's ex-girlfriends. These questions from people he didn't know well were unnerving.

Deputy Sides interviewed Gayla Mooney. She said she lived with Williams for a few years, ending in 2011. When the murder case was reopened, Williams "freaked out." He told her, "I may need to leave the country. I think I'll move to Belize." Mooney said she knew Kevin had a passport. Her interest in the evidence against Williams was not an attempt to help him. She told Sides, "Kevin beat me a few times during our relationship, and I was afraid of him." During a recent 2022 conversation about Kevin Williams with Josh, Mooney messaged him:

> I can tell you I am a survivor. Things were fine until either I or someone else pissed him off and he would fly into a rage and I would always get the blunt end of it. He is a poisonous evil master manipulator, and no one will ever convince me that he doesn't have a demon in him. I think about the women he is with now and I feel for them because I know what is happening to them. They are trapped. People say just leave. It doesn't work that way with Kevin.

Mooney also told Sides about a meeting in 2011 between Williams and Bill Ferrell on the Montgomery Bank parking lot in Sikeston. The meeting came about as a by-product of a Facebook exchange between Josh and Williams's sister in January 2011 following Josh's confrontation with Williams at the Ricky Clay rally. Josh told Kevin's sister there was a lot more evidence of his involvement in Mischelle's murder than was being made public, and Kevin's sister forwarded the message to Mooney so Kevin could read it. Mooney told Sides, "When Kevin saw the message, he telephoned Ferrell right away to set up a meeting. I went with Kevin to the meeting. Kevin got in the front seat of Ferrell's pickup, and I got in the back seat with Ferrell's dogs. Kevin showed Ferrell Josh's Facebook message, and Ferrell said Kevin had nothing to worry about because "there wasn't anything there." Was Ferrell trying to protect Williams or his own legacy? In an interview with the *Southeast Missourian*, Ferrell denied the meeting took place, but Mooney stuck to her story, arguing she has no reason to lie. She said she doesn't know if Williams killed Mischelle and added that Williams told her he didn't know Mischelle.

For years, there was no evidence that Mischelle knew Mark Abbott or Kevin Williams independent of their own finger-pointing. There were the references to someone named Mark in Mischelle's journal but no indication it was Abbott. It could have been the Mark who drove Mischelle and her two friends when they left the 1992 Halloween party for a short time. As Darren Sides's investigation progressed, two witnesses emerged who filled in that missing information.

Melissa Elliot was one of the people who, according to investigative reports, told investigators she saw someone who looked like Josh at

Mischelle's funeral (which she denied to Josh). She had known Mischelle from high school but was pregnant during much of 1992 and didn't go out a lot. She told Sides, "Mischelle came to the place where I was working on my birthday the summer before she was murdered to give me flowers. She told me she met Mark Abbott and thought he was cute, and she said she gave Mark the same kind of flowers she gave me. I told her to stay away from the Abbott twins because they were trouble."

Elliot's mother, Luann Schaeffer, corroborated her daughter's account. "I remember once in 1992 when Mischelle was visiting Melissa, I heard them talking about Mark Abbott, and I had to say something. I told Mischelle to stay away from the Abbott twins and their friends, especially Kevin Williams. I worked at the M & M Diner in Benton, one of the places they hung out. The twins liked to pick fights, and I was convinced they were on drugs."

★ ★ ★

For a time after Josh was released, the following still appeared in the results of Google searches of the name Mark Abbott.

> Hi, My name is Mark Abbott and I'm looking for nice female pen pals. I'm 5'11" tall, I weigh about 190 pounds and I'm also 40 years old. I was born in the State of Missouri, which will be the state that I will be returning to in about 36 months. I've been locked up since 1996 so it has been a very long time for me. I received a 20 year sentence for the sale of meth so I can't really claim to be a smart person. Drugs are out of my life and that is all that matters. I will never ask for money. I have my own. I also have email. So feel free to try me out. You probably won't be sorry.

In early 2017, the Abbott twins paid for polygraph tests they hoped to use to clear their names. Matt Abbott told the *Southeast Missourian* he was "tired of all the bullshit." He was referring to the persistent rumors that he or his brother or both of them were involved in the Lawless murder, rumors his brother Mark spread about himself and his friend Kevin Williams. Lee Boyd, a certified polygraph tester, performed the interviews, which lasted for two and a half to three hours, on January 17, 2017, at the office of private detective John Mackey in Cape Girardeau. Boyd and Mackey said they would release the results to the *Southeast Missourian* when they were ready. Those results have never been released. What are they hiding?

In August 2017, Mark Abbott's probation was revoked for possession of crystal meth and other violations, and he was sent to the federal prison in Greenville, Illinois. According to the Federal Bureau of Prisons Inmate Locator, he was released on October 15, 2018.

At age 52, Mark Abbott has been posting pictures on Facebook that show him posing with young children and saying he is "in a relationship." Then, on May 3, 2022, he was indicted by a federal grand jury sitting in Cape Girardeau as a felon in possession of a firearm. In a motion for pretrial detention, the government alleged that there is a serious risk that Abbott will flee or will threaten or injure a prospective witness or juror. The federal judge ruled that Abbott cannot be released.

★ ★ ★

The four-year election cycle rolled around again in 2016, and Rick Walter ran as a Democrat for a fourth term. He defeated Ron Meredith in the August Democratic primary with 63.52 percent of the vote, and Wes Drury was the Republican nominee again in November. By the fall of 2016, Walter believed he had enough evidence to seek an indictment. He approached Paul Boyd, still the Scott County prosecutor, with the evidence. Boyd suggested they wait until after the November general election. The election campaign wasn't contentious, at least not as reported in the local media. Drury's criticism of the incumbent was relatively mild; he told the press he could run the sheriff's department more efficiently. He didn't criticize Walter publicly for helping to exonerate Josh or failing to solve Mischelle's murder.

Drury won the election on November 8 with 55.21 percent of the vote. He was the only Republican to win a Scott County office, but Republicans swept all statewide offices by wide margins not reflected in the results of pre-election polling. Donald Trump led the Republican ticket in Scott County with nearly 76 percent of the vote. The sheriff's election, the only county office for which law-and-order issues are relevant, may have followed the statewide trend in favor of Republicans. But as he was preparing to leave office at the end of the year, Rick Walter told the press, "I intend to continue to look for Mischelle's killer."

After the election, Kevin Williams posted on Facebook that because Wes Drury was sheriff, it was "open season" on Rick Walter "and I can whip his ass." Williams and Walter have not seen each other since then, and the threat has not turned into action.

★ ★ ★

Walter believed he had enough evidence to go to the grand jury before the 2016 election and charge Mark Abbott and Kevin Williams. He was urging Paul Boyd to charge them during that year. After Walter's loss, Boyd decided to wait for Wes Drury to weigh in on the issue of indictments. When the prosecutor's office seemed slow in presenting the case to a grand jury, Walter submitted probable cause affidavits to the circuit court, which didn't act on them. After Walter left office, both Boyd and Drury referred to the investigation as ongoing, but rumors were circulating that Bill Ferrell was seen with Kevin Williams and was advising Drury on the matter, which raised doubts in some quarters about how serious Drury's investigation would be. According to a five-part series of articles that appeared in the *Southeast Missourian* in April 2018, Boyd did present the case to the grand jury over several months in 2017 but didn't get an indictment. The newspaper reported, however, that Boyd didn't call certain witnesses who were considered to be critical. Richard Eikelenboom, Scott Liscio, Terri Williams, and Dallas Butler all told the reporters they hadn't been asked to testify.

The articles reported Drury's and Boyd's responses to Walter's concerns about the investigation. "My job is to find facts and seek justice," Drury said, and he continued by saying that those who are investigating the case want to make sure "justice is done," which includes ensuring that "injustice is not done." In a letter to the *Southeast Missourian*, Boyd said, "The difference between knowing someone committed a crime and proving a person committed a crime are opposite poles that are misunderstood by the public at large and some peace officers."

Running as a Democrat in the November 2018 election, Paul Boyd lost his bid for re-election as county prosecutor to the Republican candidate, Amanda Oesch, who received almost 60 percent of the vote.

★ ★ ★

After leaving the sheriff's department, Rick Walter had some temporary work here and there in law enforcement. His wife has a good job as a consultant for an education company, and he accompanies her on consulting trips when he can get away. In the spring of 2020, considering his job as sheriff unfinished, he decided to run again for sheriff of Scott County, this time as a Republican, but he lost in the primary to Wes Drury. He told me he thought he lost because he marched in a Black Lives Matter parade in Sikeston.

Josh has spoken with Amanda Oesch about the Lawless murder. She didn't immediately reject his theories regarding the true murderers. Rick Walter had similar conversations at first, but then, he told me, "In October 2020, I called her office twice and left messages, but she didn't return my calls." Then, in a letter dated January 24, 2022, Oesch revealed that both the cold case unit within the attorney general's office and the highway patrol's cold case unit had agreed to assist. Oesch also has stated publicly that there is a lot of DNA evidence in the case.

In early 2022, Rick Walter came back into law enforcement as the Chief of Police in Scott City. In a telephone conversation, Rick told me that Amanda Oesch lost the August Republican primary to Don Cobb by only three votes. Cobb was someone Rick had worked with when he was Scott County Sheriff and Cobb was Chief of Police in Scott City. Cobb subsequently graduated from law school and went on to defeat Oesch in the primary. Cobb has no opposition in the November general election. Rick is confident that Cobb will continue Oesch's work on the investigation of the Lawless murder.

Cobb will take office on January 1, 2023. Josh is cautiously optimistic. In October 2022, Josh sent this message to Cobb: "There is a history of corrupt prosecution in the Mischelle Lawless murder investigation and the attached (murder for hire and perjury) cases [referring to the apparent attempt by Sheriff Ferrell to have Josh murdered in prison]. Oesch did some good things to break the cycle. I hope you completely shatter the cycle."

22

THE LAWLESS FAMILY

As he recounted in his podcast, Bob Miller went to see Marvin Lawless at his place of business, hoping Lawless might give him an interview. He knew that Lawless was disappointed with law enforcement and that he had pretty much given up hope that his daughter's murder would ever be solved. He also discovered that Lawless was outright hostile to "the media." As Miller reported in his podcast, while they visited, Lawless googled Mischelle's name to show Miller what people were saying about her. Try it yourself. Some of the hits are hurtful: false speculation about her involvement in drugs or her pregnancy by key characters involved in drug trafficking. Most of the hits are podcasts, trying to make money in some way off his daughter's murder. Lawless responded after the visit with an email that said in part "my prayer is that justice will be done." That was the end of their communication.

Josh recently has become friends with Mischelle's sister, Valerie. Their relationship has been cathartic for both. When Valerie and Josh met in February 2022, Valerie immediately thanked him for fighting for the justice her sister and family deserve. She thanked him for keeping the case relevant. She's told him she recognizes what it has cost him. When Josh attempted to tell her he understood that he wasn't the primary victim, Valerie told him there wasn't a need to say that. She went on to say some things to him and share some things with him meant to remain between them. Josh told me, "I couldn't breathe without choking up. It took everything I had to hold the tears back. Others have said as much to me but no one as close to the case as Mischelle's sister. It was the first time I truly heard what she said. I hadn't realized how much I needed to hear it." Josh and Valerie have maintained contact and text often to encourage each other.

Josh arranged for me to meet Valerie and her mother in Cape Girardeau to get their blessing for this book. We arrived at the hotel where Josh was spending the night about the same time, and Josh told me he was nervous about meeting Esther for the first time.

When Valerie and Esther arrived, the hotel manager provided us with a conference room. I said I was taking a different approach to Mischelle's story. I told them I could find no evidence that Mischelle had "loved" with anyone other than Leon Lamb and toward the end of her life, Lyle Day, and then only in an attempt to forget Leon.

Esther told me she was angry at Bill Ferrell because she believed what Ferrell had told her about Josh. She trusted him because he went to the same church she attended. She had come to believe through Valerie that Josh was nothing like the version that Ferrell fed her and that Ferrell had helped to convict an innocent man.

Valerie told Josh something similar. She feels terrible that she believed what Ferrell told her about him. She also said she has become estranged from her father, that Mischelle's murder destroyed her family. Esther said Mischelle never missed her curfew until the night of her murder. She always knocked on the door to tell her parents she was home. As she told us that, she began to cry. At the end of the interview, Esther hugged Josh, and she told me she looked forward to reading my book.[1]

★ ★ ★

After the interviews, Josh and I had dinner at an Irish pub. You could see the river from the pub entrance. After dinner, as we walked back to the hotel, Josh reminisced about the "Strip," where Christy and Amanda had picked up Josh and Kelly Church. He mentioned the Billiards Center closer to the river, where he was falsely accused of pointing a gun at a group of people. He mentioned the places where he and Kelly had spent much of their time as homeless "lost boys." He pointed out the *Southeast Missourian*, whose reporters covered his trial and exoneration. We shook hands, and I got in my car for the long drive home.

NOTES

CHAPTER 7

1. Josh told me that neither Ferrell nor any of his subordinates gave him a Miranda warning.

CHAPTER 8

1. There is no record of an interview with Isaac Johnson in the Scott County or attorney general's files that were produced to the defense, and the prosecution didn't use him as a witness at Josh's trial. Josh believes that Johnson ultimately refused to say anything or would not support the story the others had agreed to tell.

CHAPTER 9

1. While exiting the judge's chambers, one juror tearfully apologized to Josh for not being able to fulfill her duties.

2. In fact, Bob Miller interviewed Cathryn Maya, a reporter, on his podcast, who told him that two weeks before the trial started, Sheriff Ferrell said he had a witness who placed Josh and Mischelle at a party together.

3. The appearance of this witness may not have been so sudden. The person obviously was Chantelle Crider from the Lawless files interview with Cathryn Maya. In addition, according to David Rosener, Ferrell was placed in a room alone with Chantelle while the judge was being briefed.

4. In fact, a police report, from which Windham could have read, is not hearsay. Lelicia O'Dell had previously testified she had never seen Josh prior to seeing him in the trial. Lowes could have recalled Lelicia O'Dell to rebut Chantelle's identification of Josh.

CHAPTER 11

1. When Josh met with a caseworker, he learned that his two 30-year consecutive sentences had been changed to 60 without the permission of the court. Years later, he was told the adjustment was made to simplify paperwork.

CHAPTER 15

1. In an interview summary, dated September 24, 2007, Jim Sullins wrote about an interview with Laura Conklin, which Josh believes provides an alternative explanation to which twin came into the sheriff's office the night of the murder. Laura said Missy Williams told her that Mark Abbott "came in with blood all over him." Laura also said Missy told her that she "had to help [Mark] into the trailer." Josh believes that because neither deputy reported seeing blood on the twin who did appear there, the twin who did appear was Matt. Josh also believes this is supported by Ron Burton's claim on The Lawless Files, after watching closed circuit video of the twin's walk, that he recognized Matt's "gait." Mark could have gone to Heather Pierce's after Missy helped him. Laura has denied that she told Sullins that. I'm not convinced but maybe.

2. This passage ends as follows: "Can wicked rulers be allied with thee, who frame mischief by statute? They band together against the life of the righteous, and condemn the innocent to death. But the Lord has become my stronghold, and my God the rock of my refuge will bring back on them their iniquity and wipe them out for their wickedness; the Lord our God will wipe them out."

CHAPTER 18

1. Al Lowes died on December 9, 2019, eight days after his 87th birthday, from complications after a fall. His obituary said he continued to practice law until 2015.

2. For an inmate to file a 29.15 motion, he must either file it himself or trust a law clerk in the prison law library, another convicted felon, to help him. Josh believed he wasn't qualified to file a Rule 29.25 and didn't believe he could trust a felon to do it for him. Brotherton restricted his help to telling Josh to do it and why he needed to do it. Sometime in 2008, Josh called Gary Brotherton to tell him he would soon be free. Josh told me, "He apologized to me for his past mistakes. I told him I'd forgiven him and didn't find it necessary to go over the past."

CHAPTER 19

1. During the course of his press conference, he also mentioned Jonathan Irons and James Scott. Scott is charged with causing a catastrophe: He is said to have caused the flood in West Quincy, Missouri, during the Great Flood of 1993. Scott garnered some attention following Josh's mention but unfortunately, not enough to restore his freedom. He remains incarcerated in JCCC. Josh continues to believe in Scott's innocence. Irons has since been exonerated. He married WNBA star Maya Moore and has become a father.

CHAPTER 20

1. President Obama appointed Judge Callahan US Attorney for the Eastern District of Missouri in 2009. He served in that position until early 2017, when President Trump ordered all of the Obama US Attorneys removed.

2. After he had his own house, Josh adopted a year-and-a-half-old dog, a brindle-colored pit bull and mastiff mix from the Columbia Humane Society and named him Titan. Titan turned 12 this past St. Patrick's Day.

3. Josh came across an ABC 17 online article written about Morley Swingle facing discipline from the Missouri Supreme Court's Office of Disciplinary Counsel for misconduct while he was an assistant prosecutor in Boone County. The article alleged Swingle had inappropriate relationships with defendants and crime victims. Swingle sent texts to defendants requesting check-ins that slowly evolved into asking for the woman's picture. Swingle also wrote reference letters for housing for the women. After Swingle was elected prosecutor in Cape Girardeau County in 1986, he hired Kenny Hulshof as his first chief assistant. Swingle said, "Hulshof was fearless about going to court." In 2008, when Josh's innocence case was before Callahan and Hulshof was attempting to become Missouri's 55th governor, Swingle would go on to say Hulshof "had a great courtroom presence." Swingle said, "Hulshof was articulate and handsome—just what you look for in a trial lawyer. He was very persuasive in getting the jury to see the case the same way he did." Hulshof began his career under Swingle. Josh told me, "The apple and tree as they say."

4. As a result of the Nash case, Charlie Weiss, Jonathan Potts, and I were named Missouri Lawyers of the Year.

CHAPTER 21

1. In December 2011, KFVS 12, the local CBS affiliate in Southeast Missouri, reported, "A new twist in the search for the real killers of Mischelle Lawless." Josh wrote a check for $10,000 to be used only to fund DNA testing in the Mischelle Lawless investigation.

CHAPTER 22

1. During the interview, I learned that Amanda Oesch had told Valerie that the only transcript she could find from the Boyd grand jury was for Dallas Butler but that Dallas hadn't come across well. That isn't consistent with the story in the *Southeast Missourian*.

INDEX

ABOUT THE AUTHORS

Stephen R. Snodgrass has an AB degree in English and history from Boston College and a JD from Washington University in St. Louis. Before law school, he earned a PhD in psychology from Johns Hopkins University and taught psychology for four years at the State University of New York in Brockport.

Josh was his first innocence case, but he, along with others from his firm, has since represented two more men wrongfully convicted of murder. One, David Robinson, a Black man framed by the police in Sikeston, a city on the southern border of Scott County, was exonerated and released in May 2018. Erin Moriarty told his story on *CBS Morning News* right after his release and did a follow-up feature a few weeks later. The third case, Donald Nash, involved a man referred to him by Josh. Nash was ordered released by the Missouri Supreme Court over the Fourth of July weekend in 2020 (although the case continued into October 2020 before the State dropped its plan to retry Nash and dismissed the case). Along with the other two lawyers in the case, Snodgrass received the 2021 Missouri Lawyer of the Year Award for work on the Nash case. His role in the case was getting the State's expert to admit the DNA evidence against Nash was nothing but speculation. This admission was critical to Nash's release, and the Missouri Supreme Court focused on it in its release order.

Joshua C. Kezer spent sixteen years in prison as an innocent man. In 2009, he became the first man in the history of the State of Missouri to be given an *Amrine actual innocence* ruling. Since his exoneration and release, he's successfully assisted in the exonerations of other innocent men. Seeing parallels between wrongful incarceration and sex-trafficking as modern forms of slavery, Josh has also become involved in the fight to end sex-trafficking. His story has been featured on *48 hours Mystery*, *On the Case with Paula Zahn*, *The 700 Club*, and on popular podcasts including The Lawless Files with Bob Miller and Crime Junky with Ashley Flowers. He currently resides in Columbia, Missouri, with his adopted pit bull, King Titan. He can be found on Twitter as @joshkezer, Instagram as @josh_kezer, and Facebook as Josh Kezer.